KU-176-217

WINNER OF THE LOUIS ROEDERER
INTERNATIONAL WINE BOOK OF
THE YEAR 2018

LONGLISTED FOR THE BIG BOOK
PRIZE 2018

'Rich and multi-layered, full of love and family, erudite and
dense with fascinating detail while being as deliciously gluggable
as a fine pinot noir. Intoxicating stuff.'
Marina O'Loughlin, restaurant critic for the *Sunday Times*

'Thank heavens for Nina Caplan, who brings a bit of hinterland
to this often dry subject … *The Wandering Vine*, her first book,
is about much more than wine. It's a heady blend of travel,
literature, memoir, history and what I can only describe as
psychogeography … *The Wandering Vine* has a depth and soul
lacking in most wine books'
Spectator

'*The Wandering Vine* is ultimately both a wine and a travel book.
Wine writing has descended to reams of indigestible tasting
notes and over-inflated scores and travel writing appears to be
mostly composed of gobbets about spa treatments in expensive
hotels, somebody needs to rescue both. Caplan is surely on
the right path.'
New Statesman

'A lively journey from the vineyards of antiquity to the modern
dining table. You'll savour every last drop.'
Daisy Dunn, author of *Catullus' Bedspread*

'A travel journal like no other I've ever read: evocative, intelligent,
beautifully written, a pilgrimage of the soul through a love of
wine and the vineyards that produce it.'
Elisabeth Luard, food writer and author of *Squirrel Pie*

'A wine travelogue of humour and delight – what more do you need to know?'
Emerald Street

'An enthralling account of her journey of research into the history of *vino*, reaching back to ancient Rome, her liquid capital'
Jewish Chronicle

'Caplan's knowledge always enhances and never obscures the flavours … reliably delicious'
Mail on Sunday

'Nina Caplan and I share a family tree; I had no idea, until I read this marvellous book, that it was a vine. I am drunk with her passionate knowledge.'
Maureen Lipman, actress

'This is by far my favourite of all the wine reads I sampled this year … Caplan meditates on human mortality as she contemplates the beauty of landscape and varietal, weaving in historical and literary references that add depth and charisma to the story of her quest. I was blown away.'
Mail Tribune (Oregon, USA)

'A journey through the wine world from the Roman Empire to the present day.'
Marie Claire Australia

'Richly detailed, often poetic, [a] sometimes disarmingly personal book, which repays careful, attentive reading'
Financial Review (Australia)

THE WANDERING VINE

THE
WANDERING VINE

Wine, the Romans and Me

Nina Caplan

BLOOMSBURY CONTINUUM
LONDON · NEW YORK · OXFORD · NEW DELHI · SYDNEY

Bloomsbury Continuum
Bloomsbury Publishing Plc
50 Bedford Square, London, WC1B 3DP, UK

BLOOMSBURY, BLOOMSBURY CONTINUUM and the Diana logo are trademarks
of Bloomsbury Publishing Plc

First published in Great Britain 2018
Paperback, 2019

© Nina Caplan, 2018
Photographs © William Craig Moyes, 2018
Map © Michele Tranquillini

Nina Caplan has asserted her right under the Copyright, Designs and Patents
Act, 1988, to be identified as Author of this work.

For legal purposes the acknowledgements on p.329 constitute an extension
of this copyright page. Every reasonable effort has been made to trace copyright
holders of material reproduced in this book, but if any have been inadvertently
overlooked the Publisher would be glad to hear from them.

All rights reserved. No part of this publication may be reproduced or
transmitted in any form or by any means, electronic or mechanical,
including photocopying, recording, or any information storage or
retrieval system, without prior permission in writing from the publishers.

A catalogue record for this book is available from the British Library.

Library of Congress Cataloguing-in-Publication data has been applied for

ISBN: HB: 978-1-4729-3844-2
        PB: 978-1-4729-3845-9
        EPDF: 978-1-4729-3841-1
        EPUB: 978-1-4729-3843-5

2 4 6 8 10 9 7 5 3 1

Typeset by Newgen KnowledgeWorks Pvt. Ltd., Chennai, India
Printed and bound in Great Britain by CPI Group (UK) Ltd, Croydon CR0 4YY

To find out more about our authors and books visit www.bloomsbury.com.
and sign up for our newsletters

For my father, Harold Caplan, and my partner, Craig Moyes, with profound sadness that this page is the only place they'll ever meet

Contents

IX
BARCELONA
(BARCINO)

X
TARRAGONA
(TARRACO)

XI
SEVILLE
(HISPALIS)

XII
GRANADA
(ILIBERRIS)

XIII
PALERMO
(PANORMUS)

XIV
SYRACUSE
(SYRACUSAE)

XV
NAPLES
(NEAPOLIS)

XVI
ROME
(ROMA)

List of Photographs

All photographs by William Craig Moyes

She sent out for one of those short, plump little cakes called 'petites madeleines', which look as though they had been moulded in the fluted scallop of a pilgrim's shell. And soon, mechanically, weary after a dull day with the prospect of a depressing morrow, I raised to my lips a spoonful of the tea in which I had soaked a morsel of the cake. No sooner had the warm liquid, and the crumbs with it, touched my palate than a shudder ran through my whole body, and I stopped, intent upon the extraordinary changes that were taking place. An exquisite pleasure had invaded my senses, but individual, detached, with no suggestion of its origin. And at once the vicissitudes of life had become indifferent to me, its disasters innocuous, its brevity illusory — this new sensation having had on me the effect which love has of filling me with a precious essence; or rather this essence was not in me, it was myself.

MARCEL PROUST, *Remembrance of Things Past*

(Trans. C. K. Scott Moncrieff)

I was born very far from where I'm supposed to be so I'm on my way home.

BOB DYLAN

Introduction

Come in, sit down at my table, this large circle of oak, and let me open a bottle of wine. There are many kinds of preparatory travel rituals; this is mine. We will drink together. With all five senses primed, we will be ready to depart.

First, we hear the abrupt exhalation of a cork, the melody of falling liquid, the chime of meeting glasses. (I use the Jewish toast *l'chaim*, which means 'to life'.) The thud as the bottle comes back to rest on this table my parents bought in the early 1970s, when they still loved one another. It is almost the only tangible relic of my childhood, and I like to think it bears the ghostly imprint of bottles they shared. I remember my father, that twinkly eyed wine-lover of excellent palate and obsessive bent, standing at its curved edge, pouring wine, commencing an instructive commentary on the bottle we were about to share. 'Now, this—' he would begin, and my adolescent self would immediately tune out. All that knowledge, falling on deaf ears and the table's indifferent surface! What a waste. Or was it?

My love of wine began where my father ended. So many marvellous wines he shared with me, down the lucky years. He taught me to drink, just as he taught me to read, and I have spent the years since his death recovering the knowledge he tried to pass on to me, and handing it on in turn. Through wine, I have found a way to continue a conversation that, when he was alive, had barely begun.

I am not alone in this. Wine is often a dialogue with the dead. There's nothing macabre about that. Who among us would not like to find our way to the Underworld, across the River Styx, guarded, say the ancients, by the three-headed dog Cerberus, to see our loved ones again? Provided, of course, we could return.

Wine is alive, ageing and changing, but it's also a triumph over death. These grapes should rot. Instead they ferment. What better magic potion could there be to convey us to the past? Only our senses can truly transport us, as Proust well knew. But they cannot do so alone. His vehicle was the madeleine, the cake shaped to imitate the scallop shell that is the symbol of the pilgrimage to Santiago de Compostela; mine, surely as potent, is wine. And my journey, too, is a pilgrimage, sensual rather than religious, in honour of the person who taught me, and who is now gone. While I was figuring out where, in all the wide world of wine, to go, it became clear to me that you can't go looking for roots without a careful look at the ground on which you yourself are planted. I would need to start in England, and to do so I would have to deal with two questions: how did I get here, and how did wine get here?

Our glasses burn soft gilt, like candlelight: they brim, briefly, with superannuated Champagne. Made by Alfred Gratien, it has no vintage on the label (the contents will be a blend of several years' base wines) but it is so old that its colour has mellowed almost to amber and I am surprised at the force of the bubbles – tiny pockets of 1990s air, finally freed from their golden bondage. It belonged to my father. He would have enjoyed how it has developed and evolved: it lives up to expectations. And he would have been delighted at my enjoyment of it. The love of wine crept up on me, a stealthy passion. These days I lay down wines for the future, drink in the present. Now I am asking wine to help me recover the past.

The wine, one of a case, arrived shortly after Dad's death in 2003. This was not in itself a surprise: my family home was being cleared for sale, and a few of the remaining fruits of his decades of infatuation were trickling fitfully into my possession. Champagne, the essence of celebration, seemed singularly inappropriate to the occasion, but that turned out to be wrong. For this most unpredictable of wines, exhaling restless bubbles, is the indispensable adornment to life's astonishments – the departures and arrivals we must all experience – and evidence of one of those was hiding in this box of bottles. Somehow, a green card folder had wound up atop the wired and foiled corks, and somehow – I will never know how – the birth certificate of my grandfather, Jack, was inside. He was born in Leeds in 1907; these facts I already knew. But there was no mention of Jack on the document I held. This baby's name was Isaac.

I can see how it happened. The parents survive one pogrom too many and flee Russian anti-Semitism for the English Midlands. (Later, they would move again, to Australia.) They call their son Yitzhak, a good Hebrew moniker – and when they realise that it will make life easier if people around them can pronounce their child's name, they anglicise it not to Isaac, which is the direct translation but sounds so very different, but to the unimpeachably English but more phonetically comforting Jack. His siblings ended up as Harry, Pearl, Belle and Ida. What, I wonder, were their real names?

Any story of wine is a story of displacement, as we shall see. So when I started planning this journey in search of wine's roots, my grandpa's birth certificate sprang to mind. Within this little story are encapsulated, after all, my family's displacements, both linguistic and physical – disruption and chaos aptly illustrated by the important document thrust, inexplicably, into an entirely inopportune place. A birth certificate is evidence not only of who you are (in this case, not quite who the certified would become), but of where you have the right to be. My Australian-born parents were able to move to England because of this piece of paper, this confirmation of an English beginning. Leave to remain: it's almost an oxymoron, but a poetic one – particularly to those who are forced to depart.

According to the Bible, Adam was the first exile. And if you believe, as some Jews do, that the Tree of Knowledge was not an apple tree but a giant vine, then he may have been the first drunkard, too, even if that honour is traditionally ascribed to Noah, who planted a vineyard in what must have been extremely waterlogged soil, and then got disastrously drunk – presumably out of grief for all that had been lost during the Flood. The confusion is thought to have arisen over the translation of the Latin *pomum*, which means fruit, but has come to mean apple (as in the French *pomme*). According to the fourth-century Jewish scholar Rav Chisda, God scolding Noah for his inebriation confirms this: 'Did you not learn from what happened to Adam? Wine was his undoing!' Certainly, the grape seems a far more logical locus for sin – unless the ancients were particularly fond of cider.

The bottle before us has been displaced via a benign and deliberate network of trade but its earliest ancestors arrived very differently. The Gauls fleeing Julius Caesar's conquest of their homeland came north to Britain, bringing the beverage they had become unable to do without: wine. There was no French wine, not yet. Theirs had come north from Italy, which meant that the Gauls brought their conquerors' beverage into exile as a paradoxical comfort for being conquered. It also means that, like me, wine came to England because somebody, somewhere, got thrown out of somewhere else.

Both kinds of immigrant, plant and human, proved tenacious, but one had the advantage. Wine was an essential part of the culture that was coming to dominate most of the Western world. 'For the Romans,' writes Roger Dion, the great French historian of wine, 'the gift of civilisation meant bringing order but also, simultaneously, propagating the vine … because for them, the notion of really savouring the pleasures of life in any place where … [it] did not grow would have seemed almost impossible.' This begs the question of whether chilly England ever counted, for them, as truly civilised. But in the event, the inhabitants of this island adopted the creed – and found a cunning way to savour life's pleasures without having to cultivate too many vines of their own.

Civilisation has its linguistic and philosophical roots in the Roman *civitas*, the community of citizens that constitutes the city. These exiled conquerors anchored themselves by building cities and by embedding their vines, bringing civilised life to the barbarians, while also looking backwards, to the civilisation they had left. Making wine was a way to reconcile two places, one longed-for but inaccessible, the other all too present. Long before Proust, this most sensual of foodstuffs was used to travel in time.

We lift our glasses, inhale our Champagne: fresh-cut apples and toasted almonds. Every bottle of wine contains the perfume of a particular past. The sun that warmed and thickened the grapeskins, the oak sliced and bent and toasted into barrels, and further back, the hopes of the man or woman who planted that vine. (Did you know that hope has a fragrance?) The allur-ing force of my expanding lungs draws these persis-tent droplets upwards, a short molecular journey from place of origin to foreign territory, bringing scents that pitch me back in time. This wine is transporting me to a lunch party in the house where I grew up, sunlight falling through curved French windows to join the golden wine in a row of flutes, opera flowing through the speakers, the blue-toned peace of a room used only for social occasions punctuated now by bubbles of pre-prandial chatter.

That is my Rome – my lost centre of civilisation. Or, if you like, my Jerusalem. Because wine performed the same magic for the Jews. It was already crucial to Jewish ritual, ushering the Sabbath in and out again, celebrating a *bris* (circumcision) or mourning a passing, long before the Romans destroyed the Temple of Jerusalem, in AD 70. When Emperor Hadrian threw the Jews out of their homeland and barred them from returning, 65 years later, home became a chimera, that vanished Temple gleaming perfect in the inaccessible distance. The first-century Jewish historian Josephus, who saw it, wrote of the giant sculpted golden vine above the door, 'a marvel of size and artistry', with grape clusters each the size of a man. (He may have exaggerated. Then again, he may not.) After its destruction Jews, wherever they were, would lift a cup of wine each year at Passover and drink to the hope of return to a place that no longer existed: 'Next year in Jerusalem.' And, just like the drinkers, the wine in that cup would hark back to the soil from which it had come. The distance between where they were and that other, mythical place they wished to be was bridged by wine.

Fortunately, given the variety of people thirsting for it, *vitis vinifera* is a resilient plant. This once-wild vine, now the very essence of civilisation, thrives in inhospitable soils, its depressing appearance during the cold season (a winter vineyard looks like a field of dead sticks) gloriously reversed when those sticks bud in spring. This miraculous resurrection makes an appearance in all sorts of myths. For the Romans, the wine god, Bacchus, was the son of a mortal woman who died before giving birth, and of Jupiter, king of the gods, who then sewed the child into his thigh to gestate. This dual spirit – human and divine, delightful and dangerous, and twice-born – was itself recreated in Christianity, which inherited a great deal from both

Rome and Judaism; more, often, than Christians have been willing to admit.

A person who leaves home involuntarily, thrown off the soil that nurtured them and forced to inhabit an alien elsewhere, is also, in a sense, twice-born. This new soil may be inhospitable (the Latin root, *hostis*, enemy, stranger, is connected to *hospes*, host or guest, a salutary reminder of the universal ambivalence to visitors). Or it may be welcoming. But life there will be different and probably difficult, and some version of home will gleam ever more perfect and unattainably far away.

My grandfather was, in a sense, born twice: as Yitzhak and as Jack. Many wine grapes have also changed their names as they travelled: Cot in southern France is Malbec in Argentina, northern Italy's Trebbiano is Gascony's Ugni Blanc, and so on. Those exasperated by what could be considered one of wine's many unnecessary confusions might want to spare a thought, instead, for the difficulties that come with moving culture: new soils, new customs, new language and, often, a new name.

Let's raise our glasses to the courage of those who journey, willingly or otherwise. And in doing so, let's savour the pleasures of something closer to hand. Smooth glass against my fingers, chill wine punctuated by the indignant prickle of roundels of captive air across my tongue: the fourth sense is touch, followed swiftly by taste. Acidity, warm toast, those almonds again. How else to reach back to what we can no longer hear, see, smell, touch or savour? I am going looking for Europe's collective past but also for my own, in places where wine seems particularly intertwined with the culture.

In all that is written of the importance of Rome to a modern Westerner's sense of self – the words we speak, the borders we cross, the *civitates* we inhabit – how often does anyone mention the wine we drink? Yet if I admit that what I drink, and where I drink it, is largely their doing, I must also acknowledge that they may, in their unending bellicosity, have done me something of a favour: their hunger for land has fed my thirst. I can blame them, but I also owe them, and this book, tracing their path back from England to France, Spain and Italy – those countries where Rome's gifts slide most insistently over the tongue, whether you are speaking or drinking – is an attempt to understand how they conquered the world through wine, and to look at some of the more unlikely consequences of that conquest. After all, I believe that the grapes the Romans ushered across the world may be their greatest legacy: the roots of our civilisation in the most literal sense.

I won't be travelling in a straight line; that's not how things happen in my family. My maternal grandparents yearned to go to Israel but ended up in Australia; my parents, in the 1960s, took six weeks to get to England by sea, my father hired as ship's doctor, paid, according to family lore, a shilling a week. My mother's last place of residence was a one-horse town in southern Turkey called Kayseri whose only claim to fame is as the birthplace of Mimar Sinan, an Ottoman architect whose apprentices helped design the Taj Mahal. I took my first trip, from England to

Australia, at six weeks old, and even that involved a detour. The Greek airline stopped in Athens, and since there was precious little airport security in the early 1970s, my parents grabbed my carrycot and dashed off for a quick look at the Parthenon: two young Antipodeans, carrying their future, desperate for a glimpse of the past.

Every generation of my family seems to grow up in a different place from the previous one. Only one of my four grandparents spoke English without a foreign accent. Home has become a complicated notion, as have roots, and my affinity with wine, while partly a personal inheritance, from my bibulous, gregarious, much-missed father, and partly a tradition, precious as myrrh to a deracinated Jew, is also a strange empathy with these grapes whose relation to their soil, native or otherwise, seems as convoluted as mine and in some of the same ways.

So here we are, the vine and me, given leave to remain on this damp but interesting island 3,200 miles from Jerusalem and 1,160 miles from Rome. The surprise of finding my grandfather's birth certificate in his son's case of Champagne is a strange illustration of an unlikely truth: wine can tell us something of who we are and where we come from. We are lucky to have this sensory route back into the past – and one so pleasing in the present, too. Trust our senses, and they can teach us a great deal, if we educate them. Educate, from the Latin, *educare* – to lead out. (Here, too, the road takes us to Rome.)

The bottle is finished, our glasses drained. Let's sit still for just a moment: *zetsn zich zuch*, another family tradition, or superstition. I don't know where it comes from, this brief reminder of stillness before we move. Run your hand across the smooth-grained oak, with its promise of permanence. It will wait for us. But now: let's go.

'A winter vineyard looks like a field of dead sticks' – Hush Heath, in Kent

I

ENGLAND:
Rootlessness

We are the last people on earth, and the last to be free: our very remoteness in a land known only to rumour has protected us up till this day. Today the furthest bounds of Britain lie open – and everything unknown is given an inflated worth. But now there is no people beyond us, nothing but tides and rocks and, more deadly than these, the Romans.

TACITUS, *AGRICOLA* (Trans. Anthony Birley)

How far was ancient Britain from sunny, sophisticated Rome, and in how many ways! Over 1,000 miles, or a march of at least 300 hours, and then, at the northern tip of France, where the last road stopped, there was the Channel – to us a paltry, even swimmable, strip of water, to the Romans a terrifying watery chasm that roiled with monsters, according to the poet Horace. Beyond, a grim land, unpaved, uncivilised, possessing neither cities nor tilled fields, and certainly no vineyards, inhabited by tent-dwelling barbarians who shared their women and confounded their enemies by retreating to the swamps, where they could comfortably exist, with only their heads above water, for days at a time. Or so wrote Cassius Dio in the early third century AD, in an account so imaginative it suggests that, even after 200 years of Roman Britain, this was still largely a 'land known only to rumour'. My journey begins where the civilised world once ended, in a damp land populated by beer-swilling savages.

It is only on arriving at my starting point, Richborough Fort, now reduced to a splendidly hotchpotch wall and a few strokes in stone on the green sward, that I discover that I have already begun. I follow C, my partner and travelling companion, towards the phantom exit, and beyond I see the faintest depression in the grass, as if permanently marked by a hundred thousand ancient boots. This was Watling Street, which became the highway north-west, up past the city of Londinium, and on, towards Britain's left haunch (now Wales) and Viroconium, or modern Wroxeter. They were very hard to obliterate, these Romans, once they decided to mark a territory. You can zoom blithely down the A2 from London to Dover, as we have done, without ever realising that this, too, is part of that ancient Roman road.

This country has only been successfully invaded twice, and both times the conquerors brought wine – they wouldn't have dreamed of making inroads into uncivilised territory without it. Wine was portable comfort and a taste of home, the juice of roots sunk in much-missed soil; it was forgetfulness, even oblivion (and a soldier's life was surely in need of that), and it was a guarantee that the drinker in barbarian lands was a civilised man – a liquid very different from the Channel waters, drawing a potent boundary between the uncouth native and his conqueror.

The first Roman to set foot in Britain with intent to make a permanent imprint was Julius Caesar, in 55 BC; he probably landed in Kent, somewhere near where I am now. He was Governor of Gaul at this point, not yet leader of the mighty Roman Republic that was founded, says the myth, either by the wolf-suckled twins Romulus and Remus or by Aeneas, the wandering Trojan, subject of the Roman poet Virgil's great work the *Aeneid*. Either way, it was established by exiles. As Professor Mary Beard puts it in her book *SPQR*: 'However far back you go, the inhabitants of Rome were always already from somewhere else.' Maybe this is the root of their compulsion to go forth and conquer. And few will do so as successfully as Julius Caesar, who in eight busy years added all of modern France and Belgium to the Empire.

Caesar, as everyone knows, will become a dictator whose assassination will end the Republic: his adopted son and successor, Octavian, will be crowned Emperor. But in 55 BC he is still glorious, a great leader who has yet to compromise his reputation. His arrival in Britain, something of a propaganda gesture, will be cut short by an uprising of the recalcitrant Gauls he has been busily conquering with an enthusiasm that has since been termed a genocide.

Britain, with a little help from rebellious Gauls and fictitious sea monsters, withstood Rome for another century: it was elderly, uncharismatic Claudius who in AD 43 took credit for the Roman sandal firmly planted on English soil at last, dashing in once his general, Aulus

Plautius, had done the dirty work to lead the victory parade and claim the glory his lacklustre reign so badly needed. Surprisingly, this more or less worked, although a less glittering prize than the intemperate home of swamp-dwelling barbarians is hard to imagine. In his history of his father-in-law Agricola, who would continue the conquest where Aulus Plautius left off, Tacitus, that old curmudgeon, sourly claimed that the English climate was wretched, the sky 'obscured by continual rain and cloud'.

That isn't the case today, and I'm fortunate that the weather is kind since Richborough Fort, once perched on a fine natural harbour at the mouth of the Wantsum Channel which separated the Isle of Thanet from the mainland, is now landlocked and mostly just a stone equivalent of an architect's drawing: you can see what went where, but traces of foundations are all that remain save that impressively large grassy wall, huge flints embedded in its mass. Provisions would have come through here, and soldiers, through 400 years of Roman occupation. The faint remains of a gigantic arch, built to celebrate the conquest of Britain, are visible, although I need telling that it was once 85 feet high and encased in Carrara marble imported from Italy. One of the Empire's largest triumphal arches, it could be seen from halfway across the Channel. Take that, monsters!

Until about AD 200, troops stationed here patrolled that long-vanished channel and the entrance to Rome's latest possession. It would have been an unpopular posting, and, given the distance, it can't have been a short one. Those soldiers would have been in dire and frequent need of their allocation of wine, downing that mild poison (as the root of the word intoxicant has it) to palliate the greater bitterness of a long farewell.

The waters receded towards France; the reliable rain grassed over the road. Two thousand years later and 140 miles west, another ship made land. This was no end to a mythic voyage, such as Caesar's first glimpse of Britain or the arrival, at long last, of Aeneas's fleet on Italian shores. No: this was Southampton, in 1967. My parents had crossed the globe for my father to complete a final year of medical training. Here were the barbarians, stepping off the ship and into a latter-day Rome that had not yet shed its arrogance, despite the Empire's collapse. This was the soil on which they would mature – by studying, but also by steeping themselves in European culture, growing older, having children. They were three years married but very young, still, when they reached England: my mother 22, my father 29. He would fall in love with wine (retaining, always, an affectionate attachment to the wines that, like him, came from roots transplanted to Australian soil). Here, he would become civilised.

The question of who was and wasn't civilised was problematic from the very beginning. The Romans imported their wine, lapping up sun, southern soil and a few ingredients less palatable to a modern tongue: resin, honey, herbs, pitch – and water, for only barbarians drank their wine undiluted. (And rebels, of course. 'Away with you, water, no friend to wine,' wrote the first-century BC poet and sophisticate Catullus, 'and take up abode with scrupulous folk: *the Bacchus here is neat.*') They brought other comforts, including baths, porticoes and banquets, to these barbarous shores. The English took to all of them enthusiastically, but that didn't make them civilised – in fact, according to Tacitus, it made them fools. Of the locals' enjoyment of these foreign luxuries he wrote, contemptuously: 'They called it, in their ignorance, "civilisation", but it was really part of their enslavement.'

At least some of that imported wine was no rotgut. Among the many amphorae that have been found here, one has a stamp believed by Joanne Gray, an English Heritage curator, to show that it contained wine from the slopes of Vesuvius in southern Italy, which would mean that the Romans weren't stinting their soldiers at the end of the world: until the volcano eruption in AD 79 buried the vineyards, and Pompeii, under an onslaught of ash, wine from Vesuvius was considered very good. Perhaps they felt they deserved the best, the juice of Italian sunshine, given Tacitus's unremittingly gloomy weather forecast. Still, even allowing for two millennia of weather fluctuations, his damning assessment feels a touch harsh. I visit Richborough and a couple of nearby wineries in early spring and while the vines are clearly not going thirsty, it doesn't rain once in four days. The wind is fresh, the sky palest blue, the sun a precious commodity as it never can be further south. It peeks out shyly at the vines that testify to its presence, a visible rebuke to centuries of badmouthing. 'This country is mostly fertile; its inhabitants are brave, active and enterprising, but all is in the grip of perpetual winter,' wrote al-Idrisi, Muslim geographer at the court of Roger of Sicily, a thousand years after Tacitus, but there never was a country whose fertility could withstand permanent cold, as this clever man should have known. Perhaps if you live in Palermo, as he did, winter means something different to you.

Amphorae, popular, disposable and conveniently – sometimes, as we shall see, extraordinarily – durable, turn up everywhere, but Gray's is very satisfying. It is sturdy and almost intact, its two handles tapering in slightly, like human arms gently touching their own thighs. The writing, indecipherable to an amateur, sends off faint, exciting vibrations just as the grass on Watling Street does. It is as though these inanimate relics retain something of the powerful desire that pushed their creators deep into an alien interior or led them to send Italian wine bouncing across the waves to a land that had none of its own.

As well as the wine's provenance, the inscription tells us the grape, Lympha, the quality, which was excellent, the time in amphora (three years) and the weight (196lb) of that container while full. The name of grower and shipper are both mentioned. This tells me two things. First, that the Romans wasted no time in setting up their imports: there were only 36 years between their arrival and the eruption that ended Vesuvian wine, along with Pompeii. And second, that a fair bit of muscle would have been involved: 196lb is the weight of a six-foot-plus man.

There is the faintest trace of a chapel at Richborough; it is Saxon, not Roman, and was dedicated to St Augustine, who helped embed in Christianity the belief in free will, and in suffering as a consequent punishment for misbehaviour. In every wine country we visit, we will hear that vines need to suffer – by which people mean that the best wines come from grapes grown on unpromising terrain, sloping, stony, or water-deprived. Chalk, in Champagne, in southern Spain and, yes, on England's South Downs, is worshipped because of its porosity – thirsty vine roots must grow down deep to reach the water the soil refuses to hold. Give a vine a fertile, well-watered patch and you will get an abundance of grapes and an excess of dull wine; even on difficult soil, vintners tend to reduce the number of bunches in order to get more concentrated grapes. This, to me, does not say that vines love to suffer, any more than humans do – and goodness knows we have thrived in some peculiar places. It suggests instead that they are good at overcoming suffering.

Pampered modern urbanite I may be, but I feel a certain affinity with the hardy folk whose architectural remains now dissect this moist, flat field, and not just because of our shared fondness for wine. They were footloose by profession: you don't conquer the world by sitting at home. Jews have been footloose by compulsion. Most of the historic insults levelled at us had to do with our rootlessness and consequent lack of loyalty to the country in which we lived – a self-fulfilling prophecy, of course, since the people you throw off your land may reasonably mistrust the landowners in the next place they attempt to settle, especially after the tenth or the hundredth displacement.

In a wintry Kentish field 40 miles south-west of Richborough, I am admiring the symmetry of bared vines. In fact, as Virgil noted long before me, they look a little like serried ranks of soldiers, drawn up in formidable formation in order to conquer the world. And I suppose that, in a sense, they are, although given his countrymen's tendency to find their way into all sorts of unlikely nooks and put down roots, perhaps the reverse – armies creeping like vines – is true, too.

Like many of England's vineyards, Gusbourne Estate grows the same trio of grapes that make the world-famous sparkling wine of Champagne: Pinot Noir, Pinot Meunier and Chardonnay. Despite very different soils – Champagne grows mostly on chalk, while 'we are Weald clay down to at least twenty-seven metres,' says vineyard manager Jon Pollard cheerfully, as we squelch back to the corrugated iron barn that serves as a winery – Gusbourne's sparkling wines are some of the best England is producing. Their success has led to a big injection of cash from the business world, a partnership still as rare in southern England as it is common in Champagne.

We turn our clay-coated shoes away from the quiet vineyard and trudge upstairs, past the tractors and the wine presses, to a tasting room. I last came here in 2010, before their windfall, and my assumption was that they would have spent visible money: a shop, maybe, or even the beginnings of a restaurant. In fact, when I visit it is still just a big shed, with a basic tasting room. There are wellies at the foot of the stairs and slippers above: it would be homely if it weren't so full of metal machinery. Since then, they have added a wood-lined tasting room and there are plans for food pairing events and maybe even dinners, but almost all the injected cash has gone on those vines we can see from the plate-glass window; the company has also bought others like them across the county border in Sussex. It's hard to believe that this field full of orderly sticks, bare as the trees surrounding them, will eventually give forth the elegant pale liquid in my glass. Since the distant past the vine has been a fertility symbol, and its ability to look astonishingly dead – and then regenerate, with leaf and bud – is surely one reason, although the effect of its fermented juice on the average libido is another: wine has served many purposes and Viagra for the pre-chemical generations was surely one of them.

Wine, made from fruit that springs from seemingly dead wood, juice of a process that thwarts rot, the blood of the grape spilled over and over, has symbolised regeneration since long before the Romans began worshipping Bacchus. Dionysus, the Greek god of wine, was torn limb from limb (like grape stems from their branch) and revived by his father, Zeus – that is to say, he was resurrected, like the Egyptian Osiris before him and Bacchus, the twice-born, afterwards. He is the god of fecundity and unbounded sexuality. He is also – are you listening, Tacitus? – the god of revival after winter.

So it seems appropriate that English wine is also regenerating. By the eighth century, 300 years before William the Conqueror's arrival, a monk known as the Venerable Bede could write that Britain 'is rich in grain and timber; it has good pasturage for cattle and draught animals, and vines are cultivated in various localities', although, irritatingly, he doesn't say which ones. Over 40 vineyards are mentioned in Domesday Book, and winemaking continued here at least until Henry VIII's despoliation of the monasteries in the sixteenth century and possibly beyond, by which time we didn't really need it, so good had we become at trading with places that were far better at making wine than we were. (Not that we always received the cream of their crop – far from it. One seventeenth-century English traveller through Spain, France and Italy kept hearing growers 'blesse themselves in wondering what Kinde of Creatures those be, which shall drincke those wynes'.) Which again begs the question: why grow wine in Britain at all? If we managed to avoid developing a thriving wine industry when religion and the inadvisability of drinking the local water made wine an essential, why on earth start now?

Perhaps because everyone, no matter how much territory they own and how much power they command in the international marketplace, longs for the taste of home. One of the most potent symbols in the Old Testament is an enormous bunch of grapes, brought back to Moses by the men sent to scout out Canaan, the land that God has promised the Jews. It comes from the Valley of Eshkol (which means cluster in Hebrew) and is so big that the two men must carry it on a pole between them. This extraordinary bunch is the assurance of plenty: the Promised Land is not, in fact (or not only) a land of milk and honey, but a land of grapes and wine. It is also the only direct contact with that land that Moses will ever have.

Driving through the hedgerow-lined lanes of Kent, I consider the opposing temptations of travelling and of staying still, finding a home where you can put down roots and perhaps even grow your own grapes. I am thinking of Gusbourne's founder, Andrew Weeber, a South African surgeon who bought the land next door to his married daughter in 2003 in order to plant a few vines, which he did the following year. A whim became an obsession: people get funny about wine. 'He used to sleep up here,' Jon had told me, gesturing around the tasting room, which bore no obvious resemblance to a crash pad, with the exception of a microwave. It seemed very … temporary.

Weeber's business arrangements mean he – and Jon and winemaker Charlie Holland – now have another 21ha in West Sussex, which is on the chalk. Why, when Gusbourne makes the best Kent wines I've tried on 40ha of land so claggy you could probably make pottery with it, do they need them? The weather, he says. In 2016, Sussex and Hampshire both suffered damaging frosts; Kent didn't. 'You'd be very unlucky to get the same bad weather in both places.' So: security, so often associated with a tie to one place, is here the ability to move between two locations. Also, Weeber admits, the opportunity to play mix 'n' match with base wines from very different soils was too good to pass up.

Weeber is clearly a man with a deep respect for northern France: his estate's still wines are Burgundian, in grape (Pinot Noir reds, Chardonnay whites), in their restrained style – and, alas, in price. But he's a transplant who knows there's little point in looking longingly south. You must work with what you have; world domination can come later, once the wine is in the bottle.

Richard Balfour-Lynn is another wealthy Kent landowner – he has a Tudor house, a third of a property developing company named after him, and he, too, is funny about wine. His estate, Hush Heath, near

Tunbridge Wells, resembles an old-fashioned fiefdom, with lots of people working busily in sight of the master's house on the hill. The estate is exceptionally beautiful but has no chalk either: it is sand underneath Wealden clay, yet nonetheless makes a good sparkling (the still wines are less interesting). Standing in the dense Tudor woods that fringe the scenic vineyards, beside a pond that is apparently home to a sparrowhawk as well as freshwater mussels, I find myself wondering what is so great about chalk anyway, apart from its value as a marketing tool. I peer at giant oak logs, re-earthed to keep the trellising wires stable when storms come, permanent as a monument in the waterlogged soil, because oak, rather marvellously, does not rot in water, and ask myself: how much, really, does soil matter?

Less than it once did, is one answer. Chalk, as we have seen, drains itself, but you can grow good grapes on clay, if you know what you are doing, and as long as you have a lot of money for drainage. Many other soil types that no Roman would have considered fit for vines now produce wine, although wines that are a pure expression of technological skill may not express much else. The right soil can be irrevocably harmed by pesticides or erosion or other man-made disaster, of course, but it can also be treated remarkably badly and still provide a home for great grapes: in Champagne, the greatest sparkling wine the world has so far seen is grown on chalk covered by some of the most fought-over topsoil in the world. 'They will beat their swords into ploughshares and their spears into pruning hooks [a type used, incidentally, specifically for pruning vines]', promises the Book of Isaiah. 'Nation will not take up sword against nation, nor will they train for war anymore.' Maybe. It hasn't happened yet.

I know that my imagination is drawn by the idea of a carpet of chalk, unrolling north from the tip of France beneath ghostly Roman footprints. I like the idea of those layers – modern wine atop the tracks of centurions carrying amphorae over the ancient submerged cretaceous rock, itself the impacted remains of millions of prehistoric creatures. I also know that this idea has been taken surprisingly literally by locals, winemakers and even planning officers who insist that the Romans didn't just import wine but made it here – that the surrounding hills were, 2,000 years ago, covered in vines. Myths are much more interesting than facts: they tell us what we long for. And while a worship of antiquity is far from new – the West is full of new-built columns and porticoes that signal in stone our great admiration for those long-vanished cultures – this dreamed-up winemaking past seems an odd myth for a culture that has been a great importer of other people's wines rather than a great producer. Faintly, I hear the echo of Tacitus's contempt, as people who have never heard of him insist that England, then and now, is a civilised land according to the Romans' definition – one that seems to have proved as durable as their roads.

How much does soil matter? More than it once did, is another answer. The wine world is obsessed with *terroir* – a word with no direct translation, which means both the land and something more mystical than just the land: the sense of place that finds expression in the wine. *Terroir* is the ultimate point of difference, the indefinable something that makes Pinot Noir from one slice of Burgundy taste so different from the same grape grown on the neighbouring segment. The extreme predominance, there, of that one red grape and one white (Chardonnay) leaves little margin for error. In Bordeaux, they blend their red wines – the Merlot that loves clay and the Cabernet Sauvignon happier on gravel – and yet you can still taste your way from one commune to another, and the wines will alter, gently but insistently, as you move. Blending is man's retort to nature, but nature still gets the last word.

A vine that remembers the warm Mediterranean climate could be forgiven for considering England too extreme a penance – even Kent, England's flower garden, her breadbasket. Whether it wound up in Wealden clay or on chalk or green sand, that poor exile might wonder what the point was in sending down roots to fight for water when so much of it fell from the skies.

Which brings me to the third answer to that question: does soil matter? Because it does if you're a newcomer. Those who are fully at home may never consider the soil that nourishes them. But immigrants can't afford such insouciance. Will this soil welcome me, can I stay here, can it sustain me and my progeny? Humans, too, change depending on where you plant them. I am not exactly the person I would have been had my parents stayed in Australia, or their parents been able to remain, unscathed, in Poland. Language or accent aside, there's no way to say what the difference would have been. But we are all a product of some kind of serendipity. History, too, is porous.

So, if we agree that soil matters, would the Romans not have begun, here, the process they brought to such fantastic fruition elsewhere: working out where *vitis vinifera* grows best for that particular climate, and giving

27

it the opportunity to do so? I ask because there is no evidence. There are traces in England of vines from the Hoxnian interglacial, a warm break between the Second and Third Ice ages, but that predates any evidence, anywhere, of winemaking by more than 390,000 years. A few possible Anglo-Roman vineyards have been unearthed – in Northamptonshire, Cambridgeshire, Lincolnshire and Buckinghamshire – but there is at present no way to know whether the inhabitants were vinifying their grapes or just eating them.

Kent is beautiful when the sun pokes coyly around the clouds, beaming gently on high hedgerows and oast houses, the odd, circular buildings, originally used for drying hops for beer. 'The most civilised of all these nations [i.e. the tribes of ancient Britons] are they who inhabit Kent … nor do they differ much from the Gallic customs,' wrote Julius Caesar – a kinder judge than Cassius Dio would be, if not necessarily a better informed one. Surely, if you were looking to grow grapes anywhere in England, it would be here, where the grass is lush and the sun, relatively speaking, bright and warm. You'd have to be an optimist to plant grapes so far north in Europe – but isn't every winemaker a kind of optimist? We have already seen the value the Britons placed on appearing civilised. Surely they would have looked thoughtfully at their muddy fields and lowering skies, at their supercilious overlords with their amphorae, and taken a bet on optimism – just as their distant descendants would do.

As I drive through the tawny February landscape, past tractors tearing into the black earth and clusters of leafless, patient trees dotted with blackbirds, towards the South Downs, I recall that there is one other sense in which soil can matter: it can offer protection. Of the three Sussex estates I'm visiting, only one is on the chalk, but two – Ridgeview and Stopham estates – are protected by those chalky Downs, which rear up as a barrier against the cold Channel winds. So, instead of Horace's fearsome monsters causing trouble, you get the fossilised remains of ancient creatures, performing a service. Protection, for vines as for humans, is important – a home must rest on solid earth. 'For what can be considered safe, if the earth itself shakes and reels and that which protects us totters? If the one thing that is supposed to be immovable and fixed, on which everything else relies, wavers; if the earth loses what is most particular to it: stability?' asked the writer, statesman and Stoic philosopher Seneca, on the occasion of the Campania earthquake that damaged Pompeii and Herculaneum 16 or so years before the eruption that destroyed them. The earth is supposed to offer certainty, continuity, not quake or erode or spit out lava and deathly ash. It is ironic that volcanic soil, given a few centuries to calm down, makes an excellent home for vines.

The Romans knew this, transplanting grapes from Etna on Sicily to the slopes of Vesuvius, but then the Romans knew a lot: we are still rediscovering some of the wine knowledge they accrued, but which sank into oblivion during the Dark Ages. The current fashion for making wine in amphorae is one example of this, as is a great deal of biodynamic practice, such as planning the farming calendar according to the phases of the moon. This kind of thing was mocked, until very recently, as primitive mysticism;

now there is a sheepish acknowledgement that the so-called mystics may have got it right. They knew that vines thrive in thin soils and on steep hillsides that face south or east, and that if you give a vine an easy life you will get boring wine. It is possible that the same is true of humans, and that our simultaneous enchantment with and unsuitability for that very life of ease is one of the factors that compels us to seek comfort in drink. Winemakers, hard at work creating the world's finest conduit to relaxation, are very well acquainted with this conundrum. They don't tend to understand the concept of an easy life: if they did, they'd be sitting around drinking, like the rest of us. Take Simon Woodhead of Stopham Vineyard. The French have spent two millennia figuring out that Chardonnay, Pinot Noir and Pinot Meunier are the best grapes for making sparkling wine on chalk soils under frequent rain, and most English winemakers have planted accordingly. Simon is not one of them. It's not that he doesn't have these grapes, or make sparkling wine from them; actually, he makes a Brut Prestige in his own name, plus the house fizz for a major department store. But unlike most of his colleagues, he is more interested in his still wines, his apricot-flavoured Pinot Gris and pineapple, citrus-fresh Pinot Blanc. (He also grows Bacchus, which is, despite its promising name, an early-ripening but not terribly interesting German variety.) 'Who says that Champagne-like soil must mean some variant of Champagne?', he wants to know. Even in Champagne there are a few still wines – a reminder of Champagne's quieter past, before sparkle became so desirable and before the land became so valuable that making anything else on it was a deliberate extravagance or a devotional gesture to the gods of history, akin to the ancient libations that were poured on the ground to propitiate pagan deities.

The serene beauty of the South Downs National Park is deceptive: this 100-mile curl of ancient chalk is a working area, as Simon points out. He'd know: his vineyard sits atop a slope of remarkable loveliness, the calm rows of trellised vines leading the eye, with all the compulsion of a pointing finger, down towards a tall tangle of trees, variously green, and a thick-wooded hill fringing the Channel beyond. Still, 'it's terrible soil,' says Simon, blasting my romantic vision of chalky vinous glory with three little words. He planted in 2007 but it took years for the vines to take – the sandy soil was too acidic, 'it lacked all kinds of important minerals', but then it somehow went alkaline and now the Stopham Vineyard vines thrive and the wines, those still whites in particular, are gorgeous. Even Simon doesn't really understand how this happened, and he is a former engineer who used to make automotive sensors for Formula One, so there's no hope for me. His approach is highly scientific – he manages to explain his process for measuring fermenting temperatures so I am nei-ther bored nor confused, although I'm not going to risk trying to repeat that feat – which makes it all the more surprising that his choice of *terroir* was nothing of the kind. He found his patch of land by coming to a party nearby and spotting 'a field no one wanted, with trees, ragwort and rabbits. The rabbits are a pain but I really like it here.' He has just under six hectares and a very unglamorous winery, although there's a vague plan for a café in the rather nice barn behind it. He and his colleague Tom do everything, from tying up the vines to leading the vineyard tour. 'I'm an engineer, so I love creating things,' he says, neatly reversing the usual correlation whereby artsy people create things while engineers construct them. Wine, he maintains, is something created from the land, and even if there is a scientific process to it, he is not wrong. A vineyard, even in a rainy country with soil that would rather house rabbits, is the ideal home for a dreamer with the soul of an engineer.

We drive away from the South Downs, which are not Down but Up. *Dun* is an ancient Celtic word for a hill or citadel, and so probably responsible for the second half of the name London, a place that already existed in some literal and etymological form when the Romans showed up and Latinised it to Londinium. An arc brings us back onto the same chalk swathe 25 miles east, where the late Mike Roberts started Ridgeview Estate in 1994, planting Champagne grapes in an effort to challenge the northern French winemakers who have made the world's greatest marketing success out of an accident: a climate cool enough to send the yeast to sleep in winter with its job half done, prompting a second fermentation when spring arrives.

Ridgeview is now run by Mike's two children and their spouses in a charmingly medieval set-up: both son and son-in-law are called Simon, and childcare and work must fit round each other, with everyone tumbled together in the same place. Mardi, who is son Simon's wife, shows me around: the day is moist as an unaired wine cellar but her enthusiasm remains undampened. There's going to be a barbecue and picnic area over there, she tells me, gesturing. In a month or two, I know, this lonely patch of forest dirt will be violet with blue-bells. It all feels very fledgling, very promising: a brave new world, perhaps. The Roberts love what they do so much that Mardi named her son Miller, after Pinot Meunier: the underside of the leaves have a flour-like dusting of white powder, and *meunier* means miller in French.

The South Downs protect Ridgeview as they do Stopham, but there the resemblance ends. Simon makes sparkling wine well but reluctantly. Ridgeview makes nothing else. The estate's small repertoire of wines, most of them cannily provided with evocatively posh London names (Grosvenor, Bloomsbury, Fitzrovia), have won all kinds of prizes and been served to world leaders and to royalty. (In fact, the Queen's wine, from grapes planted in Windsor Great Park in 2011, is made in the Roberts' winery.) They are at the forefront of England's phalanx of winemakers but, like many others, they also look back to an earlier style of winemaking, burning fires in the spring vineyards to ward off frost, just as the Romans did elsewhere, so long ago.

The Roberts' frost eliminators are enormous *bou-gies* – French for candle – and their methods are pretty primitive, too. 'If we think we're going to need to light *bougies*, everyone stays here and we get up at intervals during the night to tend them,' says Mardi. 'It's quite bonding but you don't want to have to do it too often ...' Mardi herself is an Australian, from Wangaratta, north of Melbourne. Winemaking country, too, I say, but she points out that it wasn't 30-odd years ago when she was growing up there: the Italian immigrants all planted tobacco, only switching to wine with the advent of the anti-smoking lobby. The grapes they planted then were those they had grown up with: Nebbiolo and Sangiovese and Prosecco (now known in Italy as Glera). So that is, I suppose, another wine region that owes its livelihood to the Romans – if even more tangentially than southern England does.

I love Mardi's Aussie twang – those particular bends of the English language are, after all, the first I ever heard. Fleetingly, those cadences bring my parents back to me. Which is an irony, since their accent was a signal, every time they spoke, of the place they had left: a flag waving from an abandoned shore. They never lost that distinctive, choppy inflection, nor did they entirely untangle their conflicting allegiances. My father never showed the slightest interest in the fledgling English wines, although a good Aussie sparkling – Green Point or Pirie – often graced his table, that large roundel of oak we have so recently forsaken. I still love those citrusy antipodean wines with their fierce bubbles. They are made, like so many English sparkling wines, from Chardonnay and Pinot Noir, the grapes of Champagne – in fact, Green Point is owned by Möet & Chandon. There's a lovely circularity to these grapes and flavours and longings circumnavigating the globe, just as the bottles once circulated at that table, while I learned the importance of good taste and good conversation, along with commonality and the expectation of laughter, in cadences that had also crossed the world. Tone and taste: sometimes, they do the same job of evoking the irrecoverable past.

Ridgeview's great rival for primacy in English wine's sparkling new present is Stopham's neighbour Nyetimber, 20-odd miles back west. (You could walk, Roman-style, from one to the other along the top of the Downs; it would, says Google, take 8 hours 13 minutes.) In the early 2000s, Andy and Nichola Hill used some of their record-business money (they had created Bucks Fizz, the group that won the 1981 Eurovision Song Contest) to buy a beautiful house that is mentioned in Domesday Book, although with no reference to vines. In the twentieth century, however, Nyetimber came with a vineyard, so they hired Dermot Sugrue to improve its output. Sugrue, a voluble Irishman with sharp blue eyes, a sharper mind and a fondness for flat caps and large dogs, was so successful that Nyetimber started beating Champagne in competitions. When the divorcing Hills sold up, Sugrue left Nyetimber for Wiston Estate; he also makes other people's wine on contract, with equally articulate enthusiasm – 'beautiful, radiant, gleaming fruit!' is his description of Meopham Estate – and has a couple of small vineyards of his own, under the name Sugrue Pierre, which he talks of with the fondness of a parent discussing a high-achieving child. His principal wine is called The Trouble With Dreams, although, after trying it, I fail to see where the trouble comes in.

Sugrue is a man who appears entirely comfortable with the past: his own, as a County Limerick boy with an environmental science degree who turned out to be England's finest winemaker, and his winery's, which was once, he gleefully informs me, a turkey factory, and then a commercial garage (he keeps the sign above the front door, if that isn't too grand a name for a hinged slice out of a corrugated iron shed: it says Crash Repairs). He may be an immigrant of sorts but he is a very grounded man, one who knows himself to be in the best possible place. 'Wine production is agriculture, full stop!' he exclaims as we stand among his barrels. 'It is tedious, laborious and fraught with risk.' As if to underline that this is, in fact, a string of compliments, he points to a barrel from Domaine Jacques Prieuré in Meursault, Burgundy. 'I had the religious experience of my life tasting wines at that domaine,' he tells me. This combination, of tedium, hard work, risk and revelation is the best description of winemaking that I have ever heard.

Sugrue dances between one barrel and another, offering me tastes of his base wines – that is, wines that have not yet gone into bottle for the second fermentation that will make them sparkle – and waxing lyrical about the best ones ('I just can't help but drink that,' he says of a Chardonnay, 'it's so fecking delicious'). At one point, he asks me to compare the contents of one barrel with those in an identical barrel that was, while empty, left out in the rain. There really is a difference. In fact, the rain-barrel wine is better. Sugrue breaks into a rendition of 'MacArthur Park' ('Someone left the cake out in the rain') and affectionately strokes a barrel. The dogs are upstairs in the office; I wonder if they get jealous.

It's all so makeshift. The wines are good and will get better, but the wine culture is so raw and untried that I feel as if I'm venturing beyond the borders of the known world in a way that Caesar might have recognised. Dermot in his turkey cooler, the Roberts at Ridgeview planning picnics. Simon at Stopham has plans for a tasting room, open weekends only in conjunction with another winery, as well as his hopes for a café but, at this stage, most English wineries have precious little on offer for tourists. So C and I retreat to Ockenden Manor, a quiet, plumply upholstered Elizabethan country house hotel in Cuckfield, on the Weald between the North and South Downs. Wine, for the original owners, would have meant claret and sherry, and I start to wonder if centuries of sending our countrymen out to Jerez in southern Spain and Porto in Portugal and Marsala in Sicily and Cognac in France, to make wine the homebodies wanted to drink, hasn't bred in us a mistrust of our own capacities. Just as the popular (although now badly outdated) conception of English cuisine is that it consists exclusively of overcooked vegetables, there seems to be a sublimated concern that our wine is viewed as the viticultural equivalent of soggy sprouts. Why else does everyone keep talking about Champagne, in the context of English sparkling, or Burgundy when it comes to the still wines?

Once, everyone planted vines in their back garden, regardless of *terroir* or final quality, in order to have wine to drink, and to worship with. Now there is so much great wine that we must justify our drive to create more. Which brings me back to the question: why bother? Is it a deep-seated attachment to our soil, the wish to let it speak? Is it our perfectibility, the persistent capacity to see opportunities and resolvable problems everywhere? Or is it the compulsion to expand, to have more, bigger, better, mindlessly and avidly, that is one of the least likeable human traits – and eventually leads, as the Romans demonstrated, to disaster?

Most European countries don't need to answer these questions. They have had wine since the Romans, or before. In England, meteorological weakness, later combined with political power, left us in a peculiar position: underendowed with home-grown wines but extraordinarily well supplied from elsewhere. While William the Conqueror may not have dreaded Horace's 'ocean teeming with monsters, that roars around the distant Britons', he did share other fears with his predecessors, not least among them thirst. The Bayeux Tapestry, created a decade after his glorious victory, has extraordinary images of soldiers wheeling a cart whose principal load is a giant wine vessel, so large it makes the spears and helmets look like the merest decoration. After Joanne Gray's amphora, it's another testament to the amount of effort invaders were prepared to expend on staying well-watered, and it's also an oddly prescient image: Norman culture, like Rome's a thousand years earlier, would change this northerly island far more than her weaponry could.

What's strange is that by the time the Roman Empire crumbled, Britain was Christian, and no Christian country could do without wine for the Eucharist – the sacrament in which the blood of the grape is transformed, by faith, into the blood of Christ. The Normans would have known their foes were Christian. Still, perhaps they were unsure of the quality of English wine, and like good, forward-thinking soldiers, were taking no chances.

That flow of wine from northern France to southern England became more regular when, a century later, we took control of a part of France that still makes the wine considered, by many, to be the peak of vinous perfection. In 1152, Eleanor of Aquitaine married the man who would shortly become England's King Henry II. For centuries after, clarets, as Bordeaux reds are known, were tailored to the English overlord's palate by his humble and avaricious subjects. ('We were very 'appy to be English', a wistful Bordeaux tour guide told me as she pointed out the civic splendours that England's craving for wine had bought.) Champagne's immense popularity would be partly our doing, too, as would sherry in Spain and port in Portugal. Even before her more conventional invasions, England initiated a longer-lasting suzerainty of thirst, sinking her roots so deep into those foreign soils that there are still English names in Jerez, where sherry is made, and in Douro, the home of port. I have met winemakers from both places, families ensconced for generations, who nonetheless consider themselves English.

And today, although the sun has long set on our Empire, all roads still lead to London – at least, if you love wine. Centuries of economic importance (and viticultural insignificance) mean that the world's finest offerings, from Bordeaux and Champagne to South African whites and Australian reds, find their way here. The last relic of Empire, apart from the worldwide prevalence of English, may be our power in relation to winemakers still in thrall to the English palate and wallet – and the stuffed and varied shelves of shops that had, until recently, no home product to tout.

How strange that so many countries are planting vines now – or is there a possibility for a different type of conquest, one based on the civilised impulses and their offshoots? Maybe I am more optimistic than the most stubborn winemaker, but I have hopes. C and I have neither nationality nor religious background in common: we meet, in every sense, at the dinner table. Belief in the importance of good food with fine wine, and genuine communication as sauce for both, is our common ground. Perhaps, even, our faith.

In Ockenden's mahogany-lined bar, where the cushion covers are tapestries of medieval peasants pressing grapes and a wine list the thickness of a novel has two whole pages on Sussex, I order a glass of Sugrue's Wiston Estate, which has a fine mousse and rapier-sharp acidity, its steely modernity a surprisingly good fit for these self-consciously retro surroundings: two sides of Englishness, and not an overcooked legume in sight. When we sit down for dinner, that acidity will cut beautifully through the oil of home-smoked mackerel with beetroot and horseradish, but every other wine the sommelier will recommend, over a lovely five-course meal, will come from beyond the Channel. Somehow, the effortlessness of rosé wine in Provence or Pinot Noir in Burgundy – 'you have come into my territory, and therefore naturally you will drink my *terroir*' – is almost entirely missing in England. Stopham, Ridgeview and Gusbourne have their ambitions; of the bigger estates, Bolney has an old-fashioned English café and Chapel Down a restaurant with AA rosettes and Michelin Bib Gourmand. Elsewhere, there seem to be a lot of people doing wonderful things in sheds and squabbling over whether Sussex wine should be a dedicated denomination, while Champagne buys land here and quietly makes plans to conquer. Two millennia after its arrival, wine is a frivolous essential and a welcome guest at most English tables – but it is not yet quite at home.

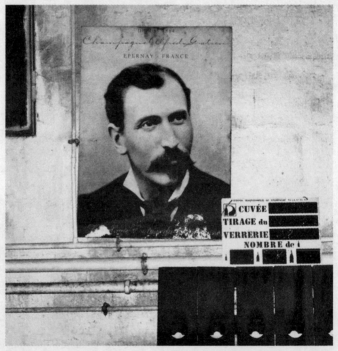
Alfred Gratien, founder of the Champagne house, who bears a remarkable resemblance to Marcel Proust

2

CHAMPAGNE:
Resilience

When wine goes in, secrets come out

THE TALMUD

When you cross the Channel – on Eurostar, in my case, speeding quietly beneath the water from one patch of ancient chalk to another – the weather doesn't change but the landscape does. From Calais to Paris is some of the flattest earth in this enormous country, and some of the most ruffled by soldiers' boots, scarred by trenches and excavated for cemeteries. The Romans were not the first warmongers to arrive here, and they certainly weren't the last. If there is a deep-dug irony in Champagne, it is surely that every grape that makes the world's most celebratory drink has been nourished by soil soaked, many times, in the blood of battles.

And yet Champagne, like its namesake wine, is irrepressible. The shells of ancient creatures pop out of the tropical sea that once, 45 million years ago, covered this land: the chalk that seems to give grapes such verve is their crushed remains, and the native Champenois

I spoke to could remember sifting shells from the crumbling white soil they played in as children.

At least one such native found that activity too absorbing to abandon. Patrice Legrand makes Legrand-Latour Champagne, although when he finds the time is hard to fathom: he has spent almost 20 years hollowing out the mountain at Fleury-la-Rivière, creating a tourist attraction that is unlike anything I've seen. 'Yes,' he says proudly as we climb the stairs behind the open-air bar, 'we're nothing like anywhere else here – we climb up to get to the cave!'

Well, that is one difference. Once you are inside the mountain, there are others, including 70-million-year-old fossils and a 60-million-year-old vine leaf. These were not found here – the leaf, which Legrand claims is the oldest so far discovered, is from nearby Sézanne – but everything else was, and it really is amazing, with huge shells jutting out of the walls or displayed atop ledges made of the soil they came from.

There are shark teeth and crab claws and around 300 kinds of shellfish, some of them enormous. Patrice will show you the painstaking excavation process if you like. We each follow the gods we choose: he looks at Champagne soil and sees ancient creatures, waiting to be unearthed; I look at his fossils and their habitat and see Champagne. This is the soil into which the vines burrow, questing for water, sucking it up through the porous remains of an ancient sea. There's plenty of rain from above, goodness knows, but it doesn't sit – it sinks, and the hard work of retrieving it is one of the trials that makes these grapes great.

Patrice's cave may be a tourist attraction but he is clearly more interested in revelation than in profit.

Here, wine is used in the service of a higher calling, although that calling is palaeontology and the loftier place is below the surface. He earnestly shows me all the brushes and other paraphernalia of his obsession, like a monk uncovering saintly relics. His shop, with its spiral staircase and wooden shelving, was excavated from a defunct pharmacy. It puts me so in mind of Cary Grant's palaeontologist in the screwball comedy *Bringing Up Baby*, battily pursuing his Brontosaurus bone, that I keep looking round for Katharine Hepburn.

There have been vines here since the Romans planted them and wine before that – enterprising Roman merchants turned the barbarians on to their wares and reaped the rewards. Caesar, no great wine-lover himself (Cato said that of all those who tried to overturn the Republic, only Julius Caesar was sober – and Cato hated Caesar, so it's probably true), justified his invasion of Gaul by the need to protect the Italian wine trade: an odd claim, given that the Italian wine trade was doing very nicely, thank you. By the time he came in on his bloody mission to claim the place for Rome, this abstemious general would have been greeted by cups as well as swords: from the canny tribes who chose to ally with Rome, and from those of his countrymen who were making a fat living insulating the natives from their rotten climate.

So enamoured were they of wine, according to Diodorus, a Greek historian from Sicily, that they 'partake of this drink without moderation … and when drunk fall into a stupor or a state of madness'. According to him, those Italian merchants weren't just doing nicely, they were making a fortune: in exchange for a jar of wine they received a slave, thus 'exchanging the cupbearer for the cup'. No wonder that, under the Romans, the locals began to plant, and if the early wine was thin red stuff, it turned out not to matter, once Clovis, King of the Franks, was baptised at Reims, probably in 498. The church became the coronation cathedral of France's kings: the place where the things rendered unto Caesar meet those rendered unto God, most famously when Joan of Arc led Charles VII in to be crowned, after raising the Siege of Orléans.

The five-hour ceremony included a Mass, reinforcing the status of the king as God's chosen representative with the offering of bread and wine. The wine would have been local – why not? (Only Philip VI, in 1328, tactlessly insisted on drinking his own Volnay.) And so began a tradition comparable, as well as connected, to the Eucharist: the passing of the crown of France to the next royal head celebrated with the same wine used to symbolise Christ's blood, a transformation of the crown of thorns into a rather more glittering – and earthly – symbol of dominion. Messiah means 'anointed one', so anointing one's kings may bring them closer to God … or, perhaps, give them ambitions to replace Him.

We are staying very close to the cathedral, in a lovely art deco *chambres d'hôtes* called La Demeure des Sacres: The Abode of Coronations. There's a great deal of art deco, that elegant, luxury-loving style from the interwar period, in this city, testament to the rebuilding required after 80 per cent of Reims was destroyed during the First World War. The cathedral was badly damaged – not for the first time in its eventful history. But it has been restored, and one night, as we leave our lodging, we see it truly returned to medieval splendour via

a *son et lumière* installation that uses light to paint the
ancient church as it might once have looked, every saint
and sinner individually lit, the great rose window out-
lined in violet, the Holy Family glowing, each delicate
peak of the extraordinarily intricate Gothic stonework
etched in multi-coloured illumination. It is a pretty
show for the tourists, to be sure, but there is yearning
there, too: the plaintive desire to see through our ancestors' eyes, to understand their world view – to colour in
the historical gaps.

Roman Reims – Durocortorum – is almost all
gaps. Of the four entrance gates, the Porte de Bazée,
or Bacchus Gate, lives on in minimal, vestigial form
on the rue de l'Université, but only the Mars Gate
remains impressive: three gargantuan arches, thick-
lined in stone, just north of the cathedral. It was preserved thanks to its incorporation into a medieval
archbishop's palace, the sanctity of the offspring protecting its heretic forebears. How grimly appropriate
that war (or revolution) should have destroyed these
monuments and left standing only the gate dedicated
to its own deity: Mars, god of war! Even the city's
modern name harks back to the Remi tribe, loyal to
Caesar, who arrived here first. The Romans would no
longer recognise their city. And they certainly wouldn't
recognise the area's wine.

Like Patrice's fossils, the vestiges of this region's oldest winemakers are buried, not quite invisible but easily
ignored. Shops and restaurants (including a good wine
bar with a terrible name: Le Wine Bar) surround the
remains of their Forum, at a lower level in a central
square still known as La Place du Forum; only part of
the *cryptoporticus* (covered walkway) remains, but that

part is very well preserved. And beneath the Houses of Taittinger, Ruinart and Pommery, miles of premium Champagne ferments quietly in caves carved out of the chalk to build the city above, 2,000 years ago.

The Champagnes in the case preserving my own vestiges were a mixture: an appropriately haphazard hotchpotch of excellent blends, including Bollinger, Taittinger and Alfred Gratien. When my father and stepmother first met, she was so intimidated by his wine expertise that at dinner she served him nothing but Veuve Clicquot – a nice example of Champagne's ability to transcend daunting complications, and of the munificence of blossoming love. (I don't think my father especially liked Veuve Clicquot.) The wine of kings that reassures plebians: there surely aren't many liquids that flow so smoothly across social boundaries.

Beneath a heavy grey sky, seeming almost to touch the vines, we drive out of Reims towards Ay, through the unlovely city fringes perched atop those romantic chalk caves where the wine ferments a second time in ideal, unchanging cool. As for the lees, the gunk of dead yeast cells produced by that fermentation, an ingenious system called riddling – tiny tips and turns to the bottles, over several months, until they are practically standing on their heads – ushers it gently towards the bottle neck. There, it can be frozen, mechanically removed, and replaced with a top-up liquid, the *liqueur d'expédition*, containing as much, or as little, sugar as the winemaker deems necessary for the level of sweetness he or she requires of the finished Champagne.

The doppelgänger of the *liqueur de tirage* – the sugary, yeasty liquid introduced into the still wine to ensure the second fermentation takes place as planned – the *liqueur d'expédition* is the winemaker's final flourish before the cork is introduced, and sends his (or her) bottle on its travels: the phrase translates as shipping liqueur.

The rain holds off as I arrive at Bollinger's pretty château in Aÿ to join a guided tour of their vineyards, which cheers me until our guide points out that the harvest is now a month or more earlier than when she was a child here, 30 years ago. For an Englishwoman, even one a little unsure of her bearings, it is hard to reconcile the delight in warm weather with the knowledge that climate change is a terrible danger, melting our icecaps, destroying our wildlife, upending our wine map and shortening the future of our destructive and unimaginative species. Like a grape, I thrive in sunshine; like a grape, I'm not always aware when a little less flourishing might be better in the long run. 'I am not looking to make Burgundy, but these days, what with climate change, you can do that in Champagne if you want,' Eric Rodez had told me the night before, over a splendid dinner matched with his wines at two Michelin-starred Les Crayères, a restaurant named for those ancient chalk caves that lace the *terroir*. Eric is a ninth-generation Champagne-maker in Ambonnay, as well as the village's mayor. He is bald and charismatic with blue-rimmed glasses and a stock of musical metaphors for wine because, he says, everyone understands music even if they don't understand what it is they understand. He had a hand in the successful application for UNESCO world heritage status for Champagne's vineyards and he has more than a hand in promoting biodynamism, the belief in natural, pesticide-free viticulture that includes various rites, such as burying a cow's horn packed with manure in the vineyard at a certain phase of the moon. It is, apparently, a form of inoculation for the vines, far healthier a prevention than chemicals are a cure, if rather more labour-intensive and time-consuming. Biodynamism, like most religions deprived of their context, sounds nuts. I have met a winemaker who plays Mozart to her vines, morning and evening, for exactly seven minutes, as part of her fanatical belief in biodynamic practice. Does it work? Her wines aren't nearly as good as Eric's, but, then, his are exceptional. And surely one needs faith of some sort to achieve the stoicism necessary to make wine in the least hospitable climate in France. When I meet Eric, the gargantuan quantity of recent rain has made his ground too soggy to work and put his vines at risk of mildew and rot, and, if he is able to retain his calm, it is surely thanks to his unwavering belief in the right-ness of his methods. It is a heavy responsibility, to care for land that has been handed down for so long. 'I am putting down bottles to age now that I won't bring up again; my son will,' he says. 'There's something magical about that.'

There is: people tied to their land, sure of their past, trying to care for their children's future. We are not a species with much talent for forward planning – part, perhaps, of our reluctance to acknowledge our own mortality. I think of the long-dead builders of Reims Cathedral. Did the masons chipping out scenes of the Apocalypse in limestone (for the cathedral is hewn from the same material as the Champagne caves) comfort themselves with the prospect of the life to come, when they would at least be able to look down from heaven on their completed handiwork? This incarnation of the ancient church, give or take a few fires and bombs, is over 800 years old; what are we making for the children we hope might still be able to occupy this planet in another eight centuries?

At Bollinger, there exists a great rarity: a field humped with rare and venerable plants that have survived devastation. The invasion of the dreaded, vine-killing phylloxera louse, in the late nineteenth century, was the wine world's Holocaust, a defining destructive event. American vines are immune to phylloxera but, when those vines were brought to Europe, the tiny insects they bore attacked the roots of native vines, causing terrible damage. In France alone, an annual harvest of between 40 and 70 million hectolitres had plunged, by 1879, to 25 million. The cure turned out to be something out of Greek legend. Telephus, son of Heracles, was wounded in battle by Achilles after Dionysus, god of wine, caused him to trip over a vine. The injury could only be cured by the weapon that had caused it, and Achilles had to be persuaded to sprinkle rust from his spear into the gash in his opponent's leg. The European vine, too, could only recover through the good graces of the New World interloper that had caused the trouble in the first place: the phylloxera blight was ended by the realisation that grafting European vines onto American roots rendered them immune, too.

If we were better at looking ahead, the first victims of that dreaded louse might have been the last. Instead, the pest wandered, via vines and soil-encrusted boots, from one region and one country to another, ruining livelihoods and altering geography as people were forced to leave tattered economies and look for jobs elsewhere.

In Rioja and Sicily, the destruction of France's vines was a boon to the wine industry, as they moved in to fill the enormous gaps … until those regions fell victim in their turn.

This must have been the strangest emigration of all: people actually forced into exile by wine. And, successful as Champagne now is, she has still not attained her pre-phylloxera glory, geographically, anyway. There are 35,000ha planted, as opposed to 50,000ha in the nineteenth century. That may be no bad thing, in terms of the quality of the wines, although whether you agree probably depends on where your ancestral vines were planted.

They say the Romans planted grapes in Ay because there was a wind to keep the grapes dry and the river to transport the wine. The nearby villages were named in relation to this important centre of production: Avennay, meaning before Ay, Épernay, after Ay. When Henry IV, King of France and Navarre and an upstart keen to display his equal status to a Spanish prince, decided to match his rival in the matter of titles, he presented himself as Sire of Ay and Gonesse, the latter representing good bread and the former fine wine.

Bollinger's château sits calm, pale and regal across the road from a small, enclosed field, where those precious pre-phylloxera vines are planted in an ancient style that leaves the trunk of the vine below ground; the result resembles regular molehills sprouting grapes. These are still used to make tiny quantities of a Vieilles Vignes cru. (Lots of wines are labelled Old Vines; these are on a different scale of venerability.) The winery also has a few neat rows of 'ancestor' grapes: ancient Gouais Blanc, mother of Chardonnay (among many others – it's known as the Casanova of grapes); Savagnin, parent of Blancs Sauvignon and Chenin; Arbane, its name probably from *albana*, Latin for 'white grape', its origins in southern Champagne, although it is now almost extinct. How enviable, to have your ancestors laid out in orderly rows, documented and protected and honoured! This is the other side of wine, the certainty, the roots grafted, maybe, but still lodged in familiar soil.

Bollinger wines are some of the best of the *grandes marques*: the big, international brands that everyone around the world associates with Champagne. They are beautiful, biscuity treasures, made principally from Pinot Noir. Their non-vintage Special Cuvée, the blend of different years that is every house's pride, is lovely but the vintage wines are something else: I drank my bottle of Grande Année 2002 about three years ago and it was rich and rounded and slightly tropical, and I wish I had another one to open now. That's the trouble and delight of wine: it lives and changes, and the game is to drain the cup of anticipation without waiting so long that your treasured bottle has died by the time you drink it. There are wines of my father's that I could not bear to open, and, when I eventually did, they were faded and sad, and I could almost see his spirit shaking its head in disappointment at such a failure of profligacy. Nothing is supposed to last forever – not empires, nor people, nor wines.

Like a surprising number of Champagne houses, Bollinger was made great by a young widow (*veuve*, in French) with the business sense and toughness of character to take on the job in a man's world. As with Nicole

Ponsardin, aka La Veuve Clicquot, Mathilde Laurent-Perrier, Camille Olry-Roederer and Louise Pommery, Elizabeth Bollinger's personal misfortune freed her up to burnish the region's renown – an irony you might not care to recall next time you raise a glass of bubbly at an engagement or wedding. When her husband died in 1941, from exhaustion at trying to manage the German occupation and a winery simultaneously (a fighter pilot in the First World War, he became mayor of Nazi-occupied Ay, and may well have found conciliating the enemy more stressful than trying to kill them had been), Madame took over, and a woman born Scottish helped ensure that her married name would become synonymous with the highest level of French gastronomic glamour. Zooming from vineyard to winery on her bicycle (there was no petrol), Lily worked to ensure that Bollinger produced wine despite war, occupation and deprivation: her only rebellion, apparently, was to seat the fat-bottomed Nazi officer in charge of requisitioning her precious product on the narrowest chair she owned.

When the Allied bombardment began in 1944, she slept in her cellars, emerging to help care for the wounded as well as to work. Many people hid out in Champagne's capacious cellars to escape the bombs, replacing the bottles more habitually sheltered there, and not for the first time: in the First World War these tunnels housed schools, offices – even hospitals.

There is nothing romantic about being forced out of home and underground, but there is, perhaps, a little comfort in the thought of lives saved by crumbled-up prehistoric shellfish, carved hollow by the Romans. And the story has, after all, a happy continuation: Bollinger now produces three million bottles a year, and Lily, if she is looking down from some great château in the sky, is surely pleased with both quantity and quality. I do not believe in an afterlife, to my great regret – how I would like to see my parents and grandparents again! – but Lily did. So Catholic was she that Bollinger did not make a rosé Champagne during her lifetime, rosé being, according to her, wine for *cocottes*: courtesans.

Champagne started producing rosés for many reasons, some of them creative and some cynical, but I can't help wondering if one of them wasn't aesthetic. This is such a dun, flat land. I imagine those long-ago Champenois giving up their *vin rouge* with great regret, only because they realised their onionskin, light-coloured wine was in fact *vin gris* (as such white wines from red grapes are called in France) – and, really, who needs more grey in this part of the world? 'A parcel [of land planted with vines] is like a colour,' the guide said: 'you keep each one separate so you can blend them carefully at the end and reproduce the Special Cuvée each year with more precision.' A recipe to defy time: always the same, only better. Different years and parcels of *terroir*, carefully assembled to offset all uncertainties, so that each year should precisely resemble the one before, in the glass if nowhere else, glowing gold like a vision of never-ending sunshine.

It's ironic that the man who invented this technique has almost vanished from the historical record. Archival information on Dom Pierre Pérignon went up in smoke, thanks to the revolutionaries who also chopped the heads off cathedral statues, mistaking saints for monarchs and, perhaps, venting their anger at a Church that had proven as durably exploitative as the Crown.

Really, it's a surprise if anything – gates, cathedrals, archives – has survived the procession of hostile visitors. The Romans, the Huns and the Visigoths, the Protestants fighting the Catholics, the peasants fighting the aristocrats: 'It was the Normans destroying the monastery in the ninth century, then the English burning it down in the fifteenth ... everyone came and had a go,' says Gillian Bouzy of Möet & Chandon, who, despite her name (Bouzy is a village in Champagne), is from Yorkshire.

His papers may have disappeared but his home remains. Within the Abbaye Saint-Pierre d'Hautvillers, Église Sendulphe, the church where Dom Pérignon lies buried, is peaceful despite its formerly turbulent location. Only the wooden pews, says Gillian, would be unfamiliar to him if he returned. At the world's crossroads that is this much-trampled patch of land, here is something unchanging, as reliable as blended Champagne. Leaving the pretty little church and walking past the monastery, its great size now reduced to just a gate, the Porte Sainte-Hélène, it is easy to see where the temptation would lie, to create something that defies time and fate, fizzing with unfaltering joy.

Möet, says Gillian, has 1,300ha, which is enormous but is only a quarter of what they need. They are part of the LVMH conglomerate, the world's biggest Champagne producers (they also own Krug, Ruinart, Veuve Clicquot and Mercier), but since 1936 they have created an annual homage to Champagne's first star, and the person currently responsible for that label is walking towards us across the grounds, sheltered by a

Dom Pérignon-branded umbrella. 'Rain – the secret of Champagne!' says Richard Geoffroy, winemaker, turning an ironic eye on the dark grey sky. 'Really, there's no such thing as smooth here, but we have been in business for three hundred years so it must be sustainable.' The problems require creative solutions – like training the vines very low, so they absorb reflected heat from the white chalk even when none is on offer from the skies. Geoffroy is an advocate of balance: 'Silence is as important as music,' he says, obliquely.

We go upstairs to an elegant long room with a refectory bench that looks as though it should still support the dinner of genuine monks. 'Last year [2015] was drier than the drought year of 1976,' he says. 'It was the hardest vintage I've made in twenty-six years.' But that's all right: 'You've got to have a challenge, otherwise it's like being on the motorway in sixth gear for too long: you fall asleep!' A former physician, he considers winemaking very similar to medicine. 'It's not an exact science; wine is living matter.' There is also a long history of wine *as* medicine, back at least to Hippocrates: the fifth-century BC Greek physician used it as a drug but also as an antiseptic for treating wounds. The Bible, parts of which were probably being written during Hippocrates' lifetime, is full of recommendations for wine to ease pain. It has always been a cure for what ails you, from gallstones to ennui.

Geoffroy only makes the Dom Pérignon cuvées, in their distinctive retro bottle, both pot-bellied and elegant, like a portly gentleman who dresses well. All his wines are blended, fittingly since they are named for the inventor of Champagne blends, and Geoffroy also brings older vintages back into circulation – the first time he does this, he calls it a P1, for Plénitude; the second is a P2. The P1 we try is a 1998 that was first released in 2005. Wines, like people, have moments when they show to best advantage; for the last 11 years he has waited for this to regain its beauty.

Even for those who can't afford such premium Champagne, this is a beautiful place to visit. The Dom's little church has paintings from the life of St Helena, mother of Rome's Emperor Constantine, and suppos-edly responsible for his conversion to Christianity – a vital step in the upstart religion's journey to dominance. She can take credit in another way for this church's glory: part of her corpse was stolen from her last rest-ing place in Rome by an enterprising ninth-century monk and brought back here – holy remains, no matter how you got hold of them, being the way to ensure a steady flow of pilgrims. It was this that enabled the monks to buy vineyards, which means that Champagne owes its existence, in part, to faith-driven body-snatch-ing. Helena was not noble and may even have been a barmaid before she married; she has certainly been responsible for a great many servings of wine. Beyond the seventeenth-century Porte Sainte-Hélène, which is named for her, the vines roll downhill in orderly rows, south towards Épernay.

Geoffroy is a man of very definite likes and dislikes, as you surely need to be with two million premium bottles under your control. He dislikes the worship of history for its own sake, and the advent of an English sparkling wine industry pleases him: 'It is a sting for the Champenois, a reminder that we can't take pre-eminence for granted, we need to keep challenging ourselves. All the greatest wines on earth were made by people who took risks.' There is no great wine without a winemaker's self-belief; wine requires human intervention, and even a hands-off approach is a decision. Wine, like its maker, is fallible. Some makers are more fallible than others, naturally enough, and my next stop is at a winery that was nearly destroyed by broken faith.

There is a glum American leaving the office of Champagne Pierre Peters, in the little chalk-coloured village of Le Mesnil-sur-Oger, as I arrive: he has just been informed that the wines are all allocated to long-term customers. Rodolphe Peters, a twinkly, loquacious man, is sorry, but philosophical. His time is limited, and he has a lot to say.

Like me, he is interested in the gaps in our knowledge of the past and in the stories we pour into those gaps, a narrative *liqueur d'expédition* that can range from hypothesis to pure fiction. In his family, the documentation starts four generations back, and so do the problems.

'Every other generation we get a winemaker; the same goes for a politician,' says Rodolphe. Such is the tortuous history of the region that neither has necessarily worked out well. There have been Peters in Le Mesnil since the 1850s, and Doués (the family that the first Mr Peters married into) since well before that. In 1912, Camille helped found the first Champagne cooperative, and in 1919 he started bottling his wine and selling it under his own name. Back then, the winemakers were simple grape-growers hit by bad harvests, pests such as phylloxera and brutal businessmen in control of grape prices; they banded together out of anger and desperation to fight for a living wage for their work. In 1930, Camille gave a ringing speech, during a time of national wine crisis, about the iniquities of capitalism – which meant, among other things, that the peasants who worked the Champagne vineyards could only afford to drink *coco* (a kind of liquorice tea) or cider, rather than the wine that every Frenchman loves. Which must be a rare instance of a politician insulting capitalism for its failure to provide the peasantry with Champagne.

Camille spoke a little German; he helped with administration under the Germans and 'was not much loved,' says Rodolphe – 'in fact he died after a banquet and there were rumours that he had been poisoned'. It is not known whether he was actually a collaborator but he certainly had unpleasant friends: his son Pierre's godfather was Marcel Déat, who became a minister in the Vichy government and fled to Italy after the war, sentenced to death *in absentia* for treason. And that is why Pierre renamed the brand his father had begun, a name change that was, like my grandpa's, intended to consign the unacceptable aspects of the family to oblivion. However, Pierre's absolute refusal to let his son François go into politics suggests that Camille's memory lingered. 'He would have loved to be a deputy [in the French government]', says Rodolphe, wistfully, of François, who was his father. Instead, he left school young to take over the family business, while one of his brothers, Jacques, went off to be winemaker at Veuve Clicquot and the other played the horses and frittered away his inheritance.

We are in Rodolphe's tasting room, trying his wines as he talks. Mesnil is known for very mineral wines – 'Mesnil wines have masses of personality but they are not generous and they don't have a great deal of fruit,' says Rodolphe, pointing out that their austerity and high acidity make them capable of long ageing. These wines, which are pure Chardonnay, or Blanc de Blancs, are fairly mature – the youngest, a Les Chétillons 2008, is eight years old, and even the non-vintage Blanc de Blancs Grand Cru is blended from base wines largely from the late 1990s – and they are lovely, austere but not unkind, with a touch of iodine that serves as a reminder of the ancient petrified seas on which these vines grow.

Rodolphe's uncle Jacques worked for Veuve for 20 years, but then Veuve sold up to LVMH. Jacques, worried for his career, wanted to sell his share of the family vineyard to the conglomerate; François bought him out and they didn't speak for 20 years. The big Champagne houses – the *grandes marques* – would seem to be Goliaths in comparison with small landholders but actually it's a little more complicated, since none of the giants owns enough land to make the millions of bottles their customers and balance sheets demand. Their purchase of others' grapes is becoming more difficult as 'grower Champagnes' – wines made from the maker's own grapes, like Eric Rodez's – become increasingly popular.

Rodolphe, perhaps unwittingly influenced by the soil he was born to, fell in love with the sea – 'I wanted to be Jacques Cousteau,' he says, naming France's, and probably the world's, most famous deep-sea diver – but went into business, until he realised that he actually wanted to be a winemaker. So he went back to school, staged a rapprochement with his father and together they went to see Jacques – who had, it turns out, been following Rodolphe's career and had even shown up, unseen, at his wine-school graduation.

It is a fascinating story, of a family thrown into chaos, forced into compromise and obfuscation, by war and human failings. And part of the solution is a change of name. I never expected to have so much in common with a family of French winemakers who have farmed the same land for centuries.

I accept a glass of Rosé de Albane, a pink blend of Pinot Meunier and Chardonnay tasting of bitter orange and pomelo that Rodolphe named for his daughter, and ask why all the stories are about the sons. He replies that until recently it was certainly harder to be a woman winemaker in Champagne but that that is changing, and he is trying to give Albane, as well as his son, the belief that this is her birthright, too (both are still teenagers). Women are hardly negligible here, though: not with all those important widows. And, after all, Clovis, inadvertent originator of Champagne's greatness, only converted, apparently, because his (Burgundian) wife insisted.

All along the moist green grassland, the vines sit low, seeking to tug the sun's heat from the chalk. This was once the monks' land, given them by sinners in need of redemption (it's no coincidence that Last Judgements are everywhere on churches). But it wasn't all church land. In Épernay, a large stone building has Hebrew writing carved on its outer walls; a synagogue, with another in Reims. By the time Rashi, an eleventh-century Jewish Bible commentator – one of the greatest who ever lived – was born in the region, many of the vineyards were in Jewish hands. Judaism has no direct equivalent of the Eucharist; in fact, to be kosher, meat must be drained of blood. Still, in the Old Testament (which has more than 800 mentions of wine and vines), there is that insistent likening of Israel to a vine, and that preeminence is reflected over and over in the importance of the 'blood of a grape' in Jewish ritual.

The Jews had come in with the Romans, as soldiers, tradesmen, merchants. They found tolerance, at first, anyway: Gaul took longer than many parts of the Empire to become fully Christianised, and it was the Christians, those people of the same Book, whose need to differentiate themselves from the Jews soon hardened into persecution. The Romans had generally treated these people, with their peculiar belief in a single God, gently, exempting them from the Emperor worship that would have run contrary to their faith, taxing them but leaving them be. Julius Caesar was considered such a friend to the Jews that they were the first to wail in grief when news of his assassination spread through Rome. For the Christians, however, Israel could not be the vine if Jesus was the true vine. (The New Testament is pretty clear. 'I am the true vine, and my Father is the gardener' – John 15.1.) If one was to flourish, the other must be pulled up, and from 1182 they were fitfully expelled and allowed back, until in the early fourteenth century they were banished for good. That Épernay building is a synagogue, but provides no evidence of an ancient presence: it is not much more than a century old.

The Romans planted vines; and the Jews, or some of them, became vintners, because observant Jews always need wine and that wine must be made by observant Jews to be kosher – and, besides, country-dwellers need a livelihood. Rashi himself was a vine-grower, near

Troyes, in between writing commentary on the Bible and on the Talmud, which is a kind of ancient Jewish handbook: a collection of laws, stories, arguments and counter-arguments, still used today. He planted words and ideas like vines and, like the Bible he studied so closely, probably saw all three as intertwined. Later rabbis have described his work as 'the wine of the Torah' because, like wine, 'it opens the heart and uncovers one's essential love and fear of God'.

Rashi, like his vines, was able to stay in one place; he died in Troyes, too, and his lost burial place was recently rediscovered via an ancient map that pinpointed what is now a town square. Today, a large black and white monument commemorates his resting place, and he lies beneath a minor conurbation, and between the wine areas of the Côte des Bar and the Côte de Sézanne. Which seems apt.

There is not much evidence left of those long-vanished Jews of Champagne, who once made so much wine they sold some on to the Christians for their Mass, unless you count the enormous figure of a blindfolded woman in the Palais du Tau in Reims. She is one of many statues from the cathedral frontage that have been replaced with copies better able to withstand the affronts of weather and time, while the originals are preserved in this former archbishop's palace next door. This gigantic lady represents the synagogue. She is paired with a more fortunate sister who can see. This is, of course, the Church.

In Épernay, we stop at Champagne Alfred Gratien, a 150-year-old company that has provided the Wine

Society's house Champagne for over a century. These bottles taste, to me, of tradition – and sentiment: my father was a long-standing member of the Wine Society, a commercial wine cooperative which began after the Great Exhibition of 1851, and bought me membership (which lasts a lifetime) for my eighteenth birthday. Nearly 15 years after his death, there are people working there who still remember him with affection, who invited me for a tasting of their wines relevant to this book and for lunch, where they opened a bottle of Château Ausone from 2003, the year he died. Ausone, which is a Bordeaux Premier Grand Cru Classé – that is, one of the most prestigious wines in existence – is named for Ausonius, third-century Roman poet and tutor to future Emperor Gratian, and winemaker, or at least owner of a vineyard. He was the first person we know of who wrote about the vines of Bordeaux, and I would like to trace a line from his efforts to excite the world's wine-drinkers to the Wine Society's, my father's and my own.

The wine was beautiful, concentrated, mineral, with a latticework of tannins you could climb. It tasted of my past: there is something distinct – not a flavour, exactly, more an echo – that I recognise in wines good enough to have been served by my father. The conversation was easy, interesting, and when my father's name came up, nostalgic. The Latin root of conviviality is *con vivere*, to live with, but a *convivium* was the Roman banquet, where food, wine, music and conversation flowed. 'The man with whom I do not dine is a barbarian to me', says the Pompeii graffito – only another way of saying that the dining table, solid while the wines flow and the conversation flutters, is the centre of civilisation, and dining together the epitome of civilised life. And what has changed? The French for a guest is still *un convive*.

I am not, it turns out, the only one with a paternal attachment to Gratien. The company's *chef de cave* (cellarmaster) Nicolas Jaeger is the fourth generation of his family to hold this post. Gratien has been owned since 2000 by the German firm Henckel but that has not changed their Champagne-making style, the oak barrels sitting patient above ground and the bottles in the cellars that stretch for a kilometre underneath. Nicolas ushers us in. 'Here, you are a little bit *chez moi*,' he says, almost jokingly, and I feel like replying: in a sense, you are a little bit *chez moi*, too.

Nicolas is young but well trained and knows his *terroir* and, perhaps because of the presence of Monsieur Le Conseiller Municipal, a local politician who has also dropped in for a tasting, he is opening some lovely wines. The Brut 2000, a blend with lots of very ripe Chardonnay grapes from an excellent year, opens up into cool liquorice and menthol; the Blanc de Blancs 2007 is austere but fresh. I'm delighted to see a Cuvée Paradis, and raise a glass of it to my dear departed dad; if there were such a place as heaven, surely it would contain Champagne.

It is a fact that would probably have irritated Camille Peters that the *grandes marques* are much more accessible to the thirsty traveller than the smaller, family-run grower Champagnes. Some of the latter are extremely profitable in their own right: 'Maison Jacques Selosse is just as much a brand as we are,' Richard Geoffroy of Dom Pérignon maintains, and given that the beautiful little boutique hotel with excellent restaurant opened by domaine owners Anselme and Corinne Selosse

features a sign warning that staying here will not necessarily grant the possibility to try, much less buy, their
sought-after and eye-wateringly pricey Champagnes,
he may have a point.

Corporates such as LVMH are the Romans of the
commercial world – expanding relentlessly until perhaps, with the logic of the bubble, they burst. The grower
Champagne-makers have a more personal relationship
with their wines and, inevitably, such intimacy has its
own difficulties. Raphael Bérêche, like Eric Rodez, is
the product of several generations of winemakers and
an advocate of biodynamism, which seems to come
with a certain fierceness. He will do things his way,
regardless – he and Rodolphe Peters have even invented
their own lighter bottles, for ecological reasons. 'There's
Champagne for everyone but we are not here to please
everyone: we make Champagnes for ourselves,' he says.
And not for many others: like Selosse, he just can't
make enough of his lovely wines to satisfy demand. In
a little tasting room attached to his family home, with
his business partner, who is also his brother, nipping in
and out, he gives me wonderful wines to try and talks
about holding on to his birthright. 'I prefer to make
100,000 bottles well than 160,000 with compromises,'
he tells me, and although to me there could be no bigger compromise than working with one's family, I close
my lips on my Champagne glass and keep the thought
to myself. This is, after all, the old way, just as working
without modern pesticides is, which may be why he
has chosen to call a wonderfully creamy, almondy cuvée
made purely from reserve (that is, older) wines Reflet
d'Antan: the name translates as Reflection of Yesteryear.
The running shoes propped outside the front door and

the concern with reflecting the vineyards, not 'creating a perfect assemblage, composed like a perfume to please', are testament to a healthy mistrust of perfection and a set of old-fashioned values, albeit allied to a pragmatic embrace of certain aspects of modernity ('Do you work with your wife?' I ask. 'No! You can treat your family, even your mother, like employees but with your wife that's really not a good idea …'). Raphael himself is like yeast in spring, fizzing and occasionally exploding with new notions. Humans cannot help but strain towards an ideal, whether in heaven, on earth or in the winery. Otherwise we really would still make wine like the Romans, oxidised stuff flavoured with herbs, sweetened with honey, diluted with water …

On the drive back to Reims I watch the vines flip by, so calm and quiet it seems impossible they will give forth a restless wine that announces itself with a pop, then 'puns and quibbles in the glass', in the seventeenth-century playwright George Farquhar's lovely phrase. I want to see a *crayère*, one of the quarries carved by the Romans that are now used by some of the great Champagne houses as cellars. At Pommery we are too late – we just have time to stare in wonderment at Louise Pommery's Disney-like building, a *folie de grandeur* if ever there was one, and chat briefly with the winemaker. Ruinart is next door, although invisible: Louise built the winery to three storeys to ensure that. She sounds like a prize, does Louise. 'I shall replace my husband in everything,' she apparently said when he died in 1858, and proceeded to make the kind of astute business decisions that were at that time gendered male. Among the best was her donation of the land for the road into town – meaning that it is difficult to enter

Reims from this direction without passing the gates of Pommery. The house has lost much, including its independence (it's owned today by conglomerate Vranken-Pommery Monopole) and much of its reputation, and is now better known for gimmicks such as Pommery Pop, the little blue bottles you drink via a straw, like alcoholic Coca-Cola. This is a shame: along with Nicole Clicquot-Ponsardin and Elizabeth Bollinger, Louise was a role model, in a region where war meant that the so-called weaker sex often got the chance to prove that overcoming the constraints of being female was more a matter of opportunity than capability.

At Taittinger we go down, into deep-dug chalk rooms, walking into a fissure literally created by history: the building by the Romans of Durocortorum, 2,000 years ago. There are very many ways to look at this land – I spoke to vintners so steeped in the flavours of *terroir* they seemed to see it as a fruit plate, 'Épernay is more citrus while Bouzy has more pear' – but to fail to look beneath it is to miss a great deal. People talk of Champagne's porous chalk, but they don't acknowledge the less natural ways in which the Champagne soil is porous: there are 100km of caves beneath Épernay alone. Which, given that Taittinger store around three million bottles in their three kilometres, makes for a hell of a lot of Champagne.

Beneath Taittinger the bottles lie, still as corpses but live and fizzing within, as the yeast exuberantly transforms sugar to alcohol. There are *pupitres*: the hole-pocked, sloping wooden planks in which Champagne bottles, neck down, are riddled. This riddling is now often mechanised, which is certainly more efficient, although it seems strange to prioritise time-saving when your product so depends on the flavours accrued by lying atop its lees that there are laws decreeing the minimum maturation time. (For non-vintage Champagnes, that minimum is 12 months on the lees; for vintage cuvées, three years. Most quality wines are aged much longer, however.) Our relentless hunt for perfection takes peculiar forms, sometimes, yet Champagne, a fault made into an asset, suggests a better way.

You can wander from the first century AD to the twenty-first down here, past Roman quarries and stacked bottles and the salvaged doors of churches dotted at the end of arcing tunnels – lit sallow yellow, to protect the wine, and the strange light does not lessen the place's mystery. Somewhere in the middle there is – revelation. A wall breaks to reveal stairs, leading up into the dark like a metaphor for the passage to heaven. These are the remains of the eleventh-century church of Saint-Nicaise. The first church was built from the chalk excavated here in around AD 340 by the Prefect of Gauls, the '*très chrétien*' Flavius Jovinus. It later became a place of pilgrimage for admirers of Saint Nicasius, a Roman-era bishop of Reims, who was buried there. There is something mystical about this staircase to nowhere: it is easy to believe in the ghostly church, rearing out of the past, superimposed on the coolly modern Taittinger reception room above.

That early church became a beautiful abbey, where the Benedictine monks made the wine their confrère Dom Pérignon would make so famous. It was destroyed during the French Revolution, and bought by Pierre Taittinger, a newspaper proprietor and wartime collaborator turned Champagne-maker, after the Second World War. Nobody talks about his nefarious past now.

There has been no name change here, just the quiet bricking up of a passage to the past. These days, the House is smoothly corporate, with glamorous advertisements and arts sponsorship. The wines are excellent, particularly the Blanc de Blancs, called Comtes de Champagne. A recent takeover attempt was thwarted, and Pierre's grandchildren are very much in charge.

Back in the centre of town, I go into the cathedral, briefly casting my eyes down towards a stone engraved with the claim that this is the exact spot where Clovis's baptism took place; but you don't look down for long in a building where everything is directed towards heaven. This soaring stone monument to faith is sunk in seven metres of chalk and built from stones quarried in Courville, 30km away in vine country (Pinot Meunier, mainly). It is a place where the Christian is supposed to reconcile himself with God, but it's also a good place to reconcile oneself with earthly imperfections. There are many, many gaps in the fabric of this cathedral, starting with its genesis atop a Roman baths, its replacement when the first church was destroyed, and the melting, in 1481, of 400 tonnes of roof leading in a fire, which is the reason for the biggest gap of all: the top storey, which they could no longer afford to build. (In the Palais du Tau museum you can still see the gargoyles, left hollow to allow rainwater to run through, that now vomit lead.) The place was attacked by revolutionaries and bombed by the Germans. The holy relics so central to the kings' coronations have largely disappeared ... and I complain about gaps in my family story!

I walk through arch after pointed arch, like a visual echo of the words and rituals repeated here through the centuries, and I look up, at windows that range in age from the thirteenth century to the 1960s blue-grey abstractions of Brigitte Simon, descendant of generations of Reims Cathedral glassmakers, going back to the seventeenth century. A splendid triple colour-burst, given by the winemakers' association in 1954, shows traditional picking and pressing under the benevolent eye of Saint Vincent, patron saint of winemakers, but also depicts that gargantuan bunch of grapes brought back to Moses by two staggering men sent into the Valley of Eshkol to take stock of another Promised Land.

Here they all are – the winemakers, hard at work, including Dom Pérignon himself; the 44 villages of Champagne, represented by their churches; the Jews whose vinous tradition precedes Christianity's. The Wedding at Cana is there to remind everyone that Jesus was both a miracle worker and a discerning wine-lover: in that first miracle, the wine he created from water was, the Gospel according to St John makes clear, much better than whatever had run out. Here is the evidence that the true vine is a matter not of mine or yours but of stem and branch from a single root, and, as if to reaffirm that, there glows nearby an even more glorious window, by the great Russian-Jewish artist Marc Chagall. In his creation, everyone from Abraham to Jesus coexists, with the Tree of Jesse representing that direct lineage, and the colours themselves – recreated to echo the medieval colours in older windows nearby – offering an artistic pedigree of a similar kind. 'A shoot will come up from the stem of Jesse,' recounts the Book of Isaiah: 'from his roots a Branch will bear fruit.' Hard, in the centre of Champagne country, not to take that literally.

Champagne is a place of wonders, where water becomes wine, cities are resurrected and the air is visible in every fizzing glass. Other things are harder to see – roots in chalk, caves and fossils, the blood and mud of ancient enmities, the colours on a cathedral built by blind faith. I should not mind that there are so few obvious remnants of the Jews who lived here for a thousand years after Christ. They are there – beneath the soil, between the covers of books, in the descendants who returned and re-established those synagogues. It just takes a little looking.

It is time to go south, as those long-ago exiles would have done. North was no good to them: the Jews had been thrown out of England in 1290 and would not be allowed back until Oliver Cromwell's time. We drive towards Burgundy, through a succession of little villages the grey-white of chalk – or gunpowder. Would they have taken vines with them, those Jews? They were not allowed to leave with much, but a few seedlings would be light, and would appear dead until planted in soil that might prove more welcoming, and allow them a resurrection of their own.

Irancy, taken during a hillside vineyard picnic en route to
Saint-Bris-le-Vineux

3

BURGUNDY:
Rivalry

> *Deep in their roots, all flowers keep the light*
> THEODORE ROETHKE

It's a good thing there's a sign marking the crossing from Champagne to Burgundy because nothing else does. There are still little chalk-coloured villages amid cloud-dappled fields that are, in June, either warm beige or a juicy, mouth-watering green. If you stop, you'll now be offered Crémant de Bourgogne, the sparkling wine of this *terroir*; if you keep driving, the land will begin to hump into hills. Seduced by the very different wines, we tend to forget that they come from the same grapes: the sparkling Pinot Noir and Chardonnay of the north become the elegant, oak-aged still reds and whites of Burgundy. Pinot Noir is a very ancient variety that may have mutated, in Burgundy, from wild vines, while the village of Chardonnay, probably responsible for christening the grape, is in the Mâconnais.

In northern Burgundy there is a grape called César, which the locals maintain is named for Julius, Gaul's conqueror, whose power-mongering led to his own assassination and the end of the Roman Republic. The winemakers here may add up to 10 per cent César to their Pinot Noir, for a bit of extra structure, and some of the wines are all the better for it. Still, Caesar's seems an odd name to bestow on anything of which almost nobody has heard; particularly a grape whose whole existence relies on collaboration.

The pretty little village of Irancy sits in a depression like a thumbprint among the northern vines. It is less than 20km south-west of Chablis, the only northern Burgundy appellation most people know, and just below Saint-Bris-le-Vineux, which is the only place in Burgundy that grows Sauvignon Blanc. (Guilhem and Jean-Hugues Goisot's is particularly good.) The wander between these two Burgundian oddities is lovely, past fields and vineyards and across the Yonne river. Beyond Escolives-Sainte-Camille with its remains of a Roman villa and baths, including delightful, plump little cupids harvesting grapes, is another wine-producing village, Coulanges-la-Vineuse, a name said to come from the Latin *colongiae vinosae* ('vinous colonies').

Burgundy has rivers but no port; like Champagne, the region was a crossroads, although it didn't see quite as much fighting as its northern neighbour. For a long time this wasn't France but a standalone duchy so endowed with territory, and so powerful, that it might have been France that became part of Burgundy instead of the other way around. The French journalist Bernard Pivot has pointed out, slightly waspishly, that Burgundy was a colonial power while Bordeaux was merely an English colony. But, then, he was born in Lyon.

The best wines I have tried in Irancy are from Thierry Richoux, in his unpretentious little winery on rue Soufflot, named for the Irancy-born architect who designed the Paris Panthéon. Richoux makes a good rosé (and I am hard to please when it comes to rosé) and an excellent sparkling – the aforementioned Crémant de Bourgogne, lightly acidic and unmemorable, which can be opened on a whim in a way that more expensive Champagne cannot. He also has a ratafia, a sweet fortified wine. But it is his reds I really love. The César gives them a little more fullness and body than much red Burgundy, and the *lieux-dits* – single vineyards – of Les Cailles and Veaupessiot are a great way to compare the small but telling differences in *terroir* for which Burgundy is famous, without paying Burgundy prices, since we are still 130km from the famous Côte d'Or.

Burgundy is both the simplest and the most annoyingly complicated wine region in the world, but the best of the wine is worth any effort and even, sometimes, a little dishonesty: Voltaire used to serve his guests Beaujolais while secretly pouring good Burgundy for himself. The Sun King, Louis XIV, loved these wines, while Napoleon, forced by gastric cancer to cut down on drink at the end of his life, opted for Chambertin, by the bottle, and – like the Romans whose Empire he had tried so hard to resurrect – watered it down. The women around these great men surely enjoyed Burgundy, too, if they got the chance, although it seems entirely possible that many, like Voltaire, refused to share.

Almost all Burgundy red is pure Pinot Noir, the white Chardonnay, but as usual with wine there are exceptions: Sauvignon Blanc, César and the even rarer Sauvignon Gris up north; Aligoté, a frequently lacklustre white grape mainly used to top up crème de cassis to make the Burgundian cocktail, kir; Pinot Beurot and Pinot Blanc, still found on the Côte d'Or; the lighter red Gamay grape in Beaujolais, on Burgundy's southern borders. (There are exceptions to Aligoté's dullness, too; Domaine Ponsot in Morey-Saint-Denis makes a Premier Cru from it, and the version that grows in Bouzeron, 160km or so south-east of Irancy, skirting the lovely Morvan regional park, is so good that it has its own *Appellation Contrôlée*.) In between these northern and southern oddities is some of the best wine country in the world, chopped into tiny parcels by generations of inheritance, each sliver of soil treated a little differently by its owners, with those differences then blooming into remarkably individual bottles. Perhaps this is unsurprising, in a place that has been made by rivalries – between Romans and Gauls, old and new religions, strict Cistercian monks and more hedonistic Benedictines, the Burgundians and the French.

In his book on his successes here, *The Gallic Wars*, Caesar, clever but humourless soul that he was, blamed his enemies' defeat partially on wine: his Gaul is divided into three parts, of which the northernmost is inhabited by the bravest people. The Belgae 'are furthest from the civilization and refinement of [our] Province, and merchants least frequently resort to them, and import those things which tend to effeminate the mind' – and since those merchants were, as we have seen, already making a fine living off the thirsty Gauls further south, there are no prizes for which things he meant.

Barbarians, being incapable of the civilised use of the accoutrements of cultivation, should just steer clear: otherwise, their behaviour becomes paradoxically more uncivilised. What an irony, then, that the defeat of these so-called drunkards would lead to their home becoming the greatest wine-producing land in the world.

Later, monasteries sprang up; the monks who needed wine for the Eucharist found themselves in a land of plenty. Just as Christianity's roots grew strong in the soil assiduously tilled by monks, so the ancient varieties of Pinot Noir and Chardonnay have flourished here as nowhere else. Most wine-lovers are familiar with Chablis, 20km north-east of Irancy; the Côte d'Or further south is world-famous. Between the two lies an area where the vines destroyed by phylloxera were never replaced. Unfortunately, that's the patch I live in.

From Irancy, it's 150km south to Beaune, the medieval walled city that is at the centre of Burgundian wine, historically if not geographically. Administratively, you soon enter the Côte d'Or, but it is a long drive to the little ridge of hills, divided into the Côte de Nuits and the Côte de Beaune beneath it, where the grapes for great Burgundy grow. Côte d'Or translates as golden slope – but some think it is a truncation of Côte d'Orient, so important is that eastern orientation, the Pinot Noir and Chardonnay grapes sucking as thirstily at sunlight above as the roots do for water, below. (Never plant your vines to face the setting sun, advised Virgil, and the advice, it seems, was sound.)

I could keep going directly south, through Burgundy towards Lyon, capital of Roman Gaul. This was the city from which roads spread north to Paris and west to Bordeaux and the coast, and south to Marseille and Italy, or Narbonne and Spain. It was also the city poised at the northern end of Roman Gaul's most vital and efficient highway: the Rhône. Wealth and sustenance, information and wine flowed in and out of Lyon, as did people. No conurbation is an island: the places we settle are those best suited to connecting with others. Civilisation is communication, which means that our preferred locations in which to keep still are invariably based on their ability to facilitate moving around. Most great cities are on ports or highways: either we must trade goods or we must be able to shift ourselves – and defend ourselves from others' movements.

Instead, I linger. Away from the vines and towards the setting sun lies a beautiful, neglected land where the light is dying in other ways, too. 'West of Dijon', wrote sixth-century historian and bishop Gregory of Tours, who not coincidentally chose to reside in Dijon, 'are fertile mountains covered with vines that provide the inhabitants with a wine as noble as Falernian.' He is referring to the greatest of the Roman wines – not something that he would have had a chance to taste, but still clearly a benchmark for great wines in the early Dark Ages. Those vines he wrote of are, however, long gone. A vineyard outside the exceptionally pretty medieval village of Flavigny-sur-Ozerain; another at Thorey-sous-Charny, a couple of stubborn, obsessed loners here and there: this is what remains, brave attempts at reviving a moribund tradition (or, perhaps, at defying Caesar: who are you calling a barbarian?). The Chablis producer Simmonet-Febvre has 15ha in Villaines-les-Prévôtes and Viserny where they make some very good whites but the others I have tried from this forgotten patch of *terroir* are, at best, drinkable: nobody would worship them as they do the great Pinots and Chardonnays of the Côte d'Or proper.

The Flavigny vineyard, in a tactical move that Julius Caesar would surely have approved, has named itself Flavigny-Alésia, the latter being the location of the final battle between the Gauls and the Romans, and so one of the area's better-known sites. It has a nice tasting room, but it is a remnant, not a vanguard, and seems to know it.

My part of Burgundy has few railway stations or motorways. It is a beautiful backwater, where cows graze and mistletoe tangles in straggling trees, where flat green fields rise to wooded slopes and birds of prey hesitate above roads so straight they are surely vestiges of the Roman craving to connect the world. The Canal de Bourgogne, an attempt to link the Atlantic with the Mediterranean via portless Burgundy, is a later reflection of that same desire, but these days most of the Auxois sits quiet, its glory days, like its vines, long gone.

I have no roots in this place but I do, in a sense, have offshoots: C's children are growing up here, so I now spend more time in this vineless patch of one of the world's most famous wine regions than anywhere else except England. I am just one of the millions who, for reasons that include politics, religion, economics and personal entanglements, have ended up here instead of elsewhere, while others have picked up and left. Call it chance or fate or predestination, depending on your allegiance – although the serendipity that gave and then revived the great wines of the Côte d'Or is enough to make an atheist believe in God. And, in fact, God is partly responsible, even for those who don't believe in Him, because one of several reasons why the vines were replanted from the valleys to the less forgiving hillsides was that the Catholic monks saw, in the conversion of sterile hillsides to fruitful vineyards, producer of Christ's blood in the form of the Eucharist, a symbolic equivalent of the pagans whose sterile souls were being planted with the true vine: Christianity.

Is this part of Burgundy so great because of the happenstance that the right grapes were planted on the right slopes at the right time? Or has our taste in wine formed around what we were given? Just as I can, given a whimsical moment, and perhaps a glass of wine to fuel the imagination, speculate on who I might have been had different circumstances arranged to produce me, so can you look into that glass and wonder about what, exactly, you find there. A spectacularly successful retail product, a benediction, a cure for homesickness, or for all the world's ills. The elixir that melds savages into sophisticates. How has the past formed our tastes? There is no real way to know.

We are not even terribly sure what the wines of 150 years ago tasted like, never mind those of 2,000 years ago; the Romans' preferred additions sound abominable to modern ears, but how can we judge the sensitivity of palates that had never tasted potatoes, or tomatoes, or coffee, or processed sugar? These are the gaps we fill with imaginative reconstruction. Without them, there would be no stories: wine is the libation we pour on our own ignorance, an offering to whichever gods of completion and satisfaction we happen to believe in.

The word rivalry comes from the Latin *rivalis*, 'taking from the same brook', and that sense of fighting over the same patch of territory feels very appropriate in Burgundy, even if northern France rarely wants for water. The Napoleonic inheritance laws, still in place, forbid parcelling out more land to one child than another, and somehow the Burgundians have never found the corporate loopholes that have enabled Bordeaux, for instance, to keep large properties intact. The result is tiny patches of land, and names that proliferate across the region, making it hard to know which Morey or Boillot you're buying. While my family were moving and changing monikers, these people have stayed still, and proliferated.

Wonderful, impossible Burgundy, beautiful and temperamental, where every rule has an exception, a little like French grammar only more so. The weather alters from one valley to the next; the vines give way to undulating fields thick with corn or rape or grass, which then go back to vineyards again. Canals interlace the region, intermittent reminders that, natural as it looks, this is a man-made landscape. The Dukes of Burgundy once held land from near Geneva to modern Belgium and the Netherlands – the pretty multi-coloured tiles on Dijon's older roofs are a reminder that nothing here is homogeneous. The Romans and their subject Gauls planted vines but it was the industrious and thirsty Church that enclosed the land, and there is no great Burgundian vineyard without its own minor version of Jesus's first miracle. The turning of water into wine, wrote the American farmer-poet Wendell Berry, is a very small wonder: 'we forget the greater and still continuing miracle by which water (with soil and sunlight) is turned into grapes'. It is safe to say the monks did not forget. The whole cycle, from planting to harvesting to winemaking to transubstantiation, to say nothing of the very fact of it being a cycle, constantly renewed – all of it was a miracle, so why not give thanks by trying to make the wine as good as it could possibly be?

Those monks were jealous of their miracles, though. Burgundy's Jews, like those of Champagne, were vintners and moneylenders, and when both occupations became replaceable by Christians, they were thrown out, just as they had been in Champagne a little earlier and in England before that. Traces of those ancient communities (as opposed to those who crept back after the Revolution) are, as I've already seen, very hard to find. Nonetheless, this is the patch of France that holds my heart. My last bottle, if I have the choice, will be red Burgundy, and it will be good. I'm not sure what I'll eat with it: that will depend on the season, the location and my capabilities at the time. I will ingest a trace memory of those long-vanished ancestors, in a reversal of the ceremony of the Eucharist: ashes to ashes, dust to dust. And, as the first, less used part of that Book of Common Prayer quotation has it, earth to earth. (Genesis: 'You return to the soil, for from it you were taken. For you are dust and to dust you shall return.')

The Auxois is beautiful, with its creamy pale brick houses and its rich green fields tilting gently towards the sun – or sometimes the rain, hail or snow. Like mine, its history is almost forgotten: the wine that once grew here, the medieval dukes more powerful than the Kings of France, the industry that, in the nineteenth century, made even my small town, Vitteaux, wealthy and respected. In a hilltop village, chatting with the wife of the village mayor, I hear of vines grown in the next plot until the 1960s, when the owner died and his inheritors could no longer be bothered. The grapes were white, she said, not Chardonnay, although she didn't know what they might have been. (Perhaps Aligoté, or Pinot Gris.) The land can still support vines, even if most of its inhabitants have forgotten there ever were wines made here. That fight, to coax an elixir from the reluctant soil, has been abandoned. What is remembered is the great battle fought at Alésia.

Before he was a barely known grape, Caesar was the Emperor who vanquished Gaul. Round here, Gaul is conveniently personified by the fierce leader Vercingetorix, particularly in a spot now marked by a rather peculiar, if interesting, 'Muséo-Parc' which has a round building with a good explanation of the war, live re-enactments, and some spindly outdoor wooden reconstructions of the Roman fortifications.

Vercingetorix was a leader of the Arverni who drew together the disparate Gaullish tribes in a vain attempt to swat back the Romans. Defeated, imprisoned and eventually strangled on Caesar's orders, he was a charismatic young man 'whose father had held power over all Gaul, and had been put to death by his fellow-citizens, for this reason, because he aimed at sovereign power', according to Caesar's *Gallic Wars* – hardly an unbiased source on a people Caesar defeated (he calls the Gauls 'men unaccustomed to toil'), but it's all we have.

'Until the lions have their own historians,' said the great Nigerian writer Chinua Achebe, 'the history of the hunt will always glorify the hunter.' Vercingetorix was certainly a lion, but was he a hero, a nationalist *avant la lettre*, uniting disparate Gauls against the Roman invader? Or was he a nuisance with a barely formulated plan, who caused many deaths, including his own? Certainly, several tribes united under him and fought off Caesar for an impressive length of time, with inferior weapons and strategy: even the Aedui, so loyal they were known as Rome's 'brothers', briefly joined the Gaullish side (but only briefly). Still, it was Napoleon III, Emperor of France from 1852 to 1870, who revived Vercingetorix's reputation and made a nationalist cult out of him. A seven-metre-high statue he commissioned, near Alésia, sports drooping Asterix-style moustaches, a resigned expression – and Napoleon III's features. A moving, patriotic phrase, supposedly taken from Caesar's book (and so already unreliable, for how would Caesar know what the enemy was saying to his own troops before battle?) has been cunningly tweaked from the conditional ('he would, by his exertions, bring over those states which severed themselves from the rest of the Gauls, and would create a general unanimity throughout the whole of Gaul, the union of which not even the whole earth could withstand') to the definite: 'United Gaul, a single nation animated by a single will, can defy the universe'.

Napoleon III remade the fight for Gaulish self-determination in his own image, to reinforce the message that he was the leader France needed, although given that he turned himself from President into Emperor it was surely Julius Caesar he should have been channelling. Still, the temptation to reshape the past into something more palatable can become overwhelming when the future looks less than bright. 'Isn't that just how virulent nationalism works?' I ask C. He is preparing a Burgundian dinner, of baked rabbit with peppers and potatoes, and I am opening a Domaine des Clos Beaune 1er Cru 2000, which was made by Grégoire Bichot (another surname that crops up a lot) although the bottle doesn't say so. This is wine from the part of Burgundy the whole world knows, and while Beaune Premier Cru wines are not as highly regarded as some from villages further south, ours is savoury and earthy and delicious, and is mature enough to need drinking. I raise my glass to the light so the contents glow ruby with the edge of brick orange that signifies encroaching age, and wonder aloud what the difference is between the frequently toxic nostalgia of retrograde nationalism and the purifying movement towards more natural winemaking. 'You have to differentiate between tradition and nostalgia,' C replies, flipping the rabbit on to a platter and arranging the vegetables prettily around it. The increasing rejection of pesticides, the focus on harvesting by hand, as winemakers go back to methods that Pliny would have recognised, is very different from reshaping the past into a myth. 'Tradition is a living inheritance from our forebears,' he says; 'nostalgia is recreating a past that, more often than not, never was.' The root is Greek: *nostos*, the return home, and *algos*, pain: nostalgia actually means homesickness. 'But what was spatial has now become temporal: we hanker for a time, rather than a place' – and both are, to some extent, of our own imagining. When the future is frightening, the temptation is to turn backwards and reinvent the past: glorious Britannia, all-powerful America, Gaul the righteous warrior, splendid even in defeat. It is no accident that Hitler named his regime the Third Reich, in deference to the First Reich, the Holy Roman Empire that arose in the ninth century and lasted for almost a thousand years.

Next day, we leave home once again – an Anglo-Australian Jew and a London-based Canadian, departing rural Burgundy for winelands that have largely forgotten their Roman heritage, so powerful is the Catholic tradition (or should that be myth?). Thanks to the Burgundian hierarchy of wine, in which Grand Cru vineyards – the top designation – show the vineyard name on the bottle, while the next designation down, Premier Cru, takes the name of the village plus the vineyard, travelling through Burgundy is a little like driving across a giant premium wine list. We stop briefly at Bruno Clair's winery in Marsannay-la-Côte, but it is lunchtime and the French are strict about such things, so we quickly purchase a couple of bottles and move on. Just below Dijon is Gevrey-Chambertin, which the Romans called Gibriacum. A first-century villa with accompanying vineyard has been disinterred here, delighting archaeologists and historians with tangible proof of the writings of Eumenius. That prominent citizen of Autun (then called Augustodunum, the hill of Augustus, after its founder) wrote in AD 312 of the region's vines, describing them – already, in the fourth century! – as 'ancient and admirable'.

Those vines were probably planted on the flat land. As well as the religious imperative, it was economic necessity – the need for wheat, which can grow only on the flats, while vines, like goats, thrive on inclines – that impelled the monks to send their vines, like their cathedrals, climbing towards the heavens. Further south, the Romans were the first to plant hills, and maybe in Burgundy they tried both, and the realisation came gradually that the stressed vines on stony slopes made more luxuriant wine. Then came the Christians, with their belief in the literal truth of Jesus's metaphor that he was the 'true vine'; their desire for converts and their view of the suffering of the plants and the bleeding and crushing of the grapes as a re-enactment of the Passion – followed, of course, by their resurrection as wine.

We are travelling south to Beaune, past vines fanning out from pretty villages – Chambolle-Musigny, Nuits-Saint-Georges, Savigny-lès-Beaune – whose names I can taste. Beaune, founded by the Romans or possibly before, is a walled city, its treasures carefully enclosed by those who knew that the end of the *Pax Romana* had resulted in barbarian encroachments and enemy neighbours multiplying like weeds. Just outside the encircling ring road there's an upmarket *chambres d'hôtes*, Les Jardins de Loïs. It is a magical place, with a large private garden and a wine cellar, in which the owner, promises me a tasting of his wines; first, however, there is Bouchard Père & Fils, across the road in a castle built into the city ramparts. In the early eighteenth century the Bouchards were sheep traders, crossing Burgundy to get to Belgium, picking up a bit of wine to sell along with their flock. Pretty soon the live wares were jettisoned, they bought this fifteenth-century château and they have been here ever since, although an uprooted tree still waves its branches across their coat of arms. Bouchard is the biggest owner of land under vine on the Côte d'Or but contributes to the general confusion of names via a nineteenth-century schism, where an eldest son went off and founded Bouchard Aîné & Fils, across town. There is really very little point in trying to untangle such things in Burgundy – just give thanks that you barely have to worry about grapes, even if Pinot Noir's infinite variety does mean that a bottle of red Burgundy can be anything from thin, acidic and pitiful to luxuriant and loamy as a well-planted garden.

The grounds at Bouchard are beautiful and so are the views: Nuit-Saint-Georges is visible, and Corton forest with Pernand-Vergelesses peeking out, and on a clear day you can see all the way to the Alps. We climb a tower that was once used for gunpowder and now holds barrels of ageing wine, and pop out into raised gardens planted with lavender and topiary that look out towards the pale stone curve of the ramparts and down onto a complex of buildings that once housed the Bouchard family. The business has belonged to the Henriot family, makers of excellent Champagne, since 1995, although there are still around 30 Bouchards employed here.

In his catchily titled 1855 book *History and Statistics of the Vine and the Fine Wines of the Côte-d'Or*, the Burgundian botanist Jules Lavalle, who was responsible for the first classification of Burgundy plots, or '*climats*', looks back to the proliferation of the vine in Gaul under the Romans. (There are about 1,200 *climats* – not bad for a mere 5,300ha.) He talks of Domitian's edict of AD 92, ordering swathes of vines pulled up – an extreme form of protectionism, although whether he was trying to protect the Italian vineyards, as Lavalle suggests, or foreign land that would be more usefully planted with nourishing wheat, is hard to know. Most people agree that this edict was never really enacted – certainly, Gaullish vineyards continued to multiply, even as Domitian shrank from the unpopularity his gesture had helped ensure. There is a wonderful story in the histories of Suetonius, who was alive in Rome at the time, that Domitian's fear stemmed from reading the verses circulating through Rome: 'Go ahead, cut down all the vines; you won't be able to prevent there being more than enough wine left to drink at your funeral!' And he was right to worry. There probably was plenty of wine for the celebrations when he was assassinated in AD 96.

His edict remained on the books until the third century, when it was repealed by Emperor Marcus Aurelius Probus to enable his soldiers to plant vines; he had a healthy mistrust of idle warriors. That didn't help him, either: those same soldiers, perhaps not keen to transfer their military skills to the hard graft of vine-tending, murdered him in AD 282 – in a vineyard.

Bouchard, like our lodging, has wonderful secret gardens, enclosures within the city for those wealthy enough to create a tame version of the agriculture that made their wealth. I am very fond of Bouchard's wines: I first visited this beautiful place in 2006, tasting the 2005s still in barrel (a lucky break, since it was a great year) and standing in the stone tasting room drinking – it was too good to spit – Les Perrières Meursault 2002, a wine so pleasing that one fellow journalist claimed he was going to name his soon-to-be-born daughter Chardonnay in its honour. In 2014, Pierre Garcia of Burgundy University organised an archaeological dig on Bouchard land in Savigny-lès-Beaune (in fact, in their car park) in search of ancient vineyards, and found traces of vines that he believes date from Roman times. He has found others from the same era at Gevrey-Chambertin, and certainly, Beaune was a centre of viticulture, once there was viticulture.

The tasting room is unchanged and the Bouchard wines are still very good with, now, an extra layer: these particular combinations of sights and scents and flavours are taking me back to that last tasting, a decade ago. We try three of the four levels, from regional – simple Bourgogne Blanc or Rouge – to commune or village, then Premier Cru, including Vigne de l'Enfant Jésus, a great red wine made on land given by Anne, Louis XIII's Queen, to the Carmelite nuns. They had predicted a long-awaited son for the Queen, then 37 years old and blessed only with daughters. Sure enough, a year later she gave birth to the future Louis XIV who would build Versailles, and whose likeness – shades of Napoleon III! – Anne's other gift, a statue of the baby Jesus, was said to closely resemble. No Grands Crus are opened, but then they make up less than 5 per cent of all Burgundy production and several, like Domaine de la Romanée-Conti, are now more famous for their prices than for their flavours, mainly because almost nobody can afford to taste them.

Ten minutes' walk away, the cellars of Joseph Drouhin contain the tell-tale fishbone pattern of Roman building; a road ran through here at that time, export director Christophe Thomas tells me. Like Bouchard, Drouhin is a *récoltant-négociant*: a big company that buys in grapes as well as growing them. This is fairly atypical for this region. Most growers here are self-described peasant farmers, if ones whose slivers of land – some so poor that they say a chicken could die of hunger during harvest – are nonetheless rich in the infinitely various welcome they offer Pinot Noir and Chardonnay vines, and rich in what they are worth, too.

This is the greatest *terroir* in the world for Pinot Noir, and probably for Chardonnay, although both are fecund travellers, planted everywhere, thriving in many places, so that they are ideal purveyors of nostalgia, the longing for a mythical home. We know that this is not Burgundy, they tell me in southern Australia, 10,000 miles from France, but we do think there's something Burgundian about our Pinot Noir ...

I find Thomas at Drouhin headquarters, on rue de l'Enfer. It's the former home of the archbishop, he says, which is odd given that Enfer means Hell. Deliveries are sometimes a problem, apparently: the company thinks he is joking. But rue du Paradis (Heaven Street) is close by, and those early monks were not ones to turn away from the unpleasantness of the afterlife. Immortality meant something different to them.

The Romans planted here but there is no question of the monasteries' importance: wine and the Church, spreading together across the land. It was the monks, as we have seen, who planted the hillsides; who enclosed certain particularly precious plots, or *clos*, such as the legendary Clos de Vougeot; who continued the Burgundian tradition of loyalty to a higher power that those long-ago Aedui had begun – except that now the power was higher still. So assiduous were they in planting the best sites that it is said they licked the soil, to check how the wine that came from it would taste, and I hope that is true.

Thomas takes us to see an ancient *pressoir*, the machine for crushing the grapes, in a dark room across the street from the monastery, 'to make life easy for the monks!' It is sixteenth century, although the technology had not changed much in a thousand years. They still use it, occasionally, although the timescale is from a bygone era: it takes two months of watering for the wood to swell enough for the contraption to function. The filter is a basket. 'It doesn't work like modern winemaking equipment,' muses Thomas, staring at it. 'The first time we tried to use it, the wine oxygenated before fermentation and we were very disappointed' – however, the freshness returned later in the process. Observation is vital, he says: 'Now we live more and more in the instantaneous but wine is in time ...' So it is: just as adulthood is the logical moment between childhood and decrepitude, wine is a delicious interlude between grape juice and vinegar. I think of Bede, the eighth-century English monk who had vexed me back in England by failing to give coordinates for the country's vineyards. In *The Ecclesiastical History of the English People*, he wrote:

> The present life of man upon earth, O King, seems to me in comparison with that time which is unknown to us like the swift flight of a sparrow through the mead-hall where you sit at supper in winter, with your commanders and ministers, and a good fire blazing in the midst, while the storms of rain and snow rage abroad. The sparrow, flying in at one door and immediately out at another, whilst he is within, is safe from the wintry tempest, but after a short space of fair weather, he immediately vanishes out of your sight, passing from winter to winter again. So this life of man appears for a little while, but of what went before or what is to follow we know nothing at all.

The *pressoir* was used to make 1,000 bottles each of red and white wine from Clos des Mouches, one of the company's oldest parcels of land, next to Pommard at the southern end of the Beaune appellation. The odd name (*clos* is an enclosure but *mouche* means fly) comes from the bees – honey-flies, or *mouches à miel* – whose hives once stood there. The Romans, as we have seen, also put honey in their wine, and Bede's analogy for human life, which was intended to persuade the king to convert to Christianity, took place in a mead-hall (mead is fermented honey); it is probably no coincidence that honey, which never rots, is the only immortal foodstuff. Virgil and the Bede both mention honey, I tell Thomas, and he nods, unsurprised: 'People who like wine all speak the same language.' C brightens instantly and starts quoting the great French writer (and sometime monk) François Rabelais, who would have been contemporaneous with that *pressoir*. '*Buvez du vin et vivez joyeux* [Drink wine and live joyously]!'

We leave the protective walls to return to our temporary home, Les Jardins de Loïs, for a tasting of owner Philippe Dufouleur's wines, which he labels Loïs Dufouleur. In the large house, opposite that beautiful private garden, they point us down to the cellar where Philippe, white-haired and well-fed with a kindly, suntanned face, is waiting. Like so many Burgundian winemakers, he has tiny fragments of famous vineyards. 'The soil here allows us to have fun,' he maintains. He was a *négociant*, a seller of other people's wines, 'but I have been liberated for ten years now!' he cries jovially, raising a glass of blackcurranty Clos des Perrières 2011 to his good fortune, and ours. Clos des Perrières is another Premier Cru from a small, high vineyard very near the border with Savigny-lès-Beaune; both are at the northern end of the Beaune appellation, but they are very different. We try a couple of Philippe's lesser Beaunes, which are still good; 2015, he tells us, will be a great year, when it is ready. Then he waves us out through the enormous gate – big enough to drive a horse and carriage through, as it would have needed to be. He found an expert to fix it up when he and his wife bought the dilapidated property in 1980: 'We need to save the old crafts. If it costs a bit more, never mind – I only want to employ people who are good at their job and adore it.' He points to the peephole, enabling inhabitants to view would-be incomers before letting them in, then winks at me: 'You know that in French this is called a Judas?'

We have dinner in Caves Madeleine, a wine shop with trestle tables. A superb, very young sommelier serves us a Crémant de Bourgogne by Céline and Laurent Tripoz, who are proudly biodynamic (they sport a Demeter mark – apparently the goddess of agriculture, Greece's Demeter or Rome's Ceres, now certifies wine). It's excellent with little mustardy squares and good sourdough. We say we want to drink Burgundy, *naturellement*, and a succession of wines by the glass follows: a Saint-Aubin Chardonnay, La Pucelle, from Pierre-Yves Colin-Morey (he's the Colin, his wife the Morey, both famous names in endlessly confusing Burgundy); a Pinot Noir from Maison des Belles Lies in Santenay, five kilometres south of Saint-Aubin; a second Pinot from Régis Rissognol-Changarnier, a simple Bourgogne (that is, the most basic appellation) but from Volnay, further north, near where we are eating, that is rustic and drinkable. The food – carrot soup with *espelette*, a local pepper; bean salad with lemon dressing; cod with carrots – is superb, the vegetables so good that C notes down their supplier, a local allotment, for a lightning detour to rake up whatever the restaurants have left, on our way home. This is the way to try Burgundy, unless you're going to devote your life to learning about individual patches of vines. A conversation with a good sommelier, like a dialogue with a cherished dining companion, is one of life's great pleasures, and it has always puzzled me that depictions of the world to come don't include such earthly joys – with the exception of Islam. In the teetotal religion, fine wine is set aside for the faithful in the afterlife. But, really, can't we have both?

Before we head south through the Côte de Beaune I want a quick look at my favourite Apocalypse. In the 1440s, Rogier van der Weyden was commissioned by tax collector Nicolas Rolin to paint a triptych for the charitable institution he was setting up: Les Hospices de Beaune. Beneath the distinctive multi-coloured tiles of Burgundy, you can see the beds where the sick were laid and the altar where Nicolas and his wife attempted to turn a lifetime of wealth accumulation to good account for the hereafter. And, certainly, they have a lasting renown here on earth: the Hospices own vineyards, and hold a charitable auction every November which sets the year's wine prices, and while the Hospices itself is now a museum, there is a modern hospital where the work of caring for the sick – those whose mortality is all too evident – continues. As for that afterlife, van der Weyden's altarpiece, *The Last Judgement*, is wonderful in its detail, and an enormous magnifying glass on rails running from one part of the nine panels to the other enables the modern viewer to peer far more closely at the delights of heaven and the torments of hell than any medieval worshipper could have done. Against a golden background, Christ looks down impassive as saints, angels and kings pray and rejoice; humanity, meanwhile, climbs naked from the earth and stumbles off towards eternity or damnation. Is it fanciful of me to see an analogy with the town's finest creation in that moist earth and the bare but promising creatures popping out of it?

We pass through Pommard, the Romans' Polmareum, possibly named for Pomona, goddess of tree fruit. In his *Metamorphoses*, the Roman poet Ovid writes of her successful wooing by Vertumnus, 'a dresser and pruner of vines'. It is so beautiful here: all these small villages, the ribbons of vines rising in orderly fashion away from them. I once cycled from Beaune, via Pommard, all the way south to Chalon-sur-Saône, and the best part of the trip was this first day of cycle paths through the vines. Since the steeper the slope, the higher the wine quality, the paths are cut through cheaper land, making it excellent cycling for lazybones: very flat.

It is a peculiarity that Pomona's orchards are said to include vines, but then in Roman times vines were trained up trees – a process known as (and considered contiguous to) marriage. In the words of Ovid's contemporary Horace, 'On his own hillside each man spends the day, and weds his vines to waiting trees' – and Vertumnus accordingly uses the example of a vine and an elm to push his courtship of Pomona. 'There was a specimen elm opposite, covered with gleaming bunches of grapes. After he had praised it, and its companion vine, he said: "But if that tree stood there, unmated, without its vine, it would not be sought after for more than its leaves, and the vine also, which is joined to and rests on the elm, would lie on the ground, if it were not married to it, and leaning on it".' It's amazing that Pomona responded to such unsubtle wooing, but apparently she did.

We have seen this confusion of grapes and tree fruits before, in the theory that the fruit that caused the exile from the Garden of Eden was not an apple but a bunch of grapes. In Vézelay, just the other side of the Morvan regional park from Vitteaux, a gigantic twelfth-century basilica presides atop a hill; it's an important stop on the pilgrimage to Santiago de Compostela, and everything from its majestic exterior to the three semicircles of detailed sculptures above the inner doors and the light that shines, at summer solstice, down the central aisle is designed to impress the humble worshipper. But the devil is in the detail – in a mischievous medieval sculpture, one of many, high up on a capital. A snake entwines round the Tree of Knowledge – and, sure enough, the fruit he offers Eve, while Adam looks on with hand to mouth, is a plump cluster of grapes. Vézelay is a wine-making village, with its own Chardonnay appellation and the remains of a temple to Bacchus beneath the church, so the mason may have been playing to his audience, reminding those who took full advantage of the grape's powers of comfort and rejuvenation that temptation, too, is always close at hand.

Pommard has the richest red wines of the Côte de Beaune; the wines of Volnay, just next door, are lighter, surpassingly elegant. Volnay, wrote Jean-François Bazin, a Dijon-born politician, 'leaves a trace of lipstick on the Côte de Beaune, like the outline of a kiss'. We stop for lunch at L'Auberge des Vignes, between the two: a proper old-style Burgundy purveyor of *la cuisine bourgeoise*, with homemade *jambon persillé* (ham terrine with a parsley-flecked jelly) and excellent *oeufs en meurette*, or poached eggs in red wine sauce. And we drink the Pommard such hearty fare demands, from vines we can see out of the window, served in a *fillette*, which can mean a little girl, or a mid-size (50cl) bottle of wine, a size that really ought to be more popular than it is.

Albert Boillot has a pretty house and small tasting room in Volnay; his four hectares are divided in slivers scattered around the two villages. Apart from a basic Chardonnay, they are all Pinot Noir. Boillot is another very Burgundian name – Jean-Marc and Henri Boillot both make wine – but his is far from the most famous moniker in Volnay: the late Hubert de Montille, irascible star of Jonathan Nossiter's 2004 film *Mondovino*, probably has that honour. In the film, he likened the US's attempts to shape the wine world to the Roman Empire: Rome, too, he maintained, tried to impose its tastes. To which I'd respond: yes, but imposing your taste for wine on barbarians was surely less cultural imperialism than an act of kindness. And force, as we have seen, was hardly required. We taste several wines, buy a few. It is so much more pleasing, and memorable, a way to purchase wine than soulless online clicking, and if the latter does at least offer the choice of the whole world, sometimes it's nice to buy a little of the soil you're standing on and, months or years later, drink and return to that particular moment, that particular spot.

Next stop: the Château de Meursault, a proper pre-revolutionary castle, with some vineyards that have been here a thousand years. Others are more recent: when André Boisseaux bought the estate in 1973 he pulled down houses to plant vineyards, which are therefore (as Jean-François Bazin has pointed out) surely the world's only vines that can boast telephone lines and mains sewerage. The name of the village comes from *muris saltus*, which means mouse-leap – a charming description of the small stream known as the Ruisseau des Clous, or brook of nails. There are still the remains of a Roman fort on the hill, and the stream's entertaining nickname – and so, ultimately, the label on a thousand coveted wine bottles – was the invention of Roman soldiers, amusing themselves as best they could between the battles that conquered Gaul.

The château, which owns roughly as many red vineyards as white, is that rarity: a good Burgundy producer that is set up for tourism. You pay for a tour and a tasting, but both are worth it, from the caves, going back to the twelfth century and smelling sweetly of gently steeping barrels, to the kitchens, which also peel back through the centuries (although some were destroyed by floor tiles above so heavy they broke the ceiling). As for their wines, I have had a very decent half-bottle of their basic Pinot Noir at the Auberge des Vignes and the bill didn't ruin my lunch but you can, for the price of many dinners, buy one of several Premiers Crus or their only Grand Cru, a patch of Corton just south of Vosne-Romanée on the Côte de Nuits, and still a great deal cheaper than that village's aforementioned legendary Domaine de la Romanée-Conti.

Like most people, I can't afford the best Burgundy and wouldn't get an allocation if I could: the tiny quantities mean that top producers can play favourites with buyers. Instead, I go to one of the better village *caveaux* and pay to taste a few open wines from various local producers, and also play a pleasurable game of Wine Bingo with their extensive list. I buy what I like and can afford, or what I can afford and think that I might like. The people who serve are steeped in Burgundy and can advise me, and their manners are so good and their priorities so well aligned that in Chassagne-Montrachet, one of the best of these *caveaux*, I have seen a young woman weather, unblinking, a major fight between a 10- and a 14-year-old (no bottles broken, thank goodness) and go on to sell me two mixed cases.

One of those cases contained a beautiful Chardonnay from Domaine Hubert Lamy. Now, in Saint-Aubin, in the domaine's ridiculously small winery, I am learning about close planting from Hubert's son, Olivier. He stands between giant oak casks that come up to his shoulder, swirling Chardonnay. 'Before phylloxera, vines were planted very close together,' he says. He has gone back to that: 'it is good for the vine roots to have to compete for minerals'. Lamy, whose family have made wine here since at least the seventeenth century, has grubbed up some of the vines he did not feel were on the best sites, and sold others that were a bit too far away for him to oversee properly (by 'too far' he means 20km). He is uncompromising, but not unfeeling. When I start talking about the pain and upheaval of phylloxera that still echoes through the wine world, from grassy, vineless Burgundian hills to the extraordinarily recent revival of Priorat, in northern Spain, he nods soberly. 'Phylloxera was the biggest challenge we ever faced, although mechanisation is hard, too.'

Of those mechanical changes, he is withstanding some while adopting others, prioritising the need 'to retain the ability to taste and smell the changes around me'. It's the attitude of a proud, self-confessed peasant – if one whose wines can reach hundreds of pounds a bottle. And they're wonderful: an iodine Premier Cru Chataignier, a creamy lemon La Princée 2010, the oak perfectly integrated, a Chassagne-Montrachet, from Le Concis du Champs, also from 2010, all hazelnut and butterscotch. It was an 'exotic vintage', he tells me, with hail and thunder; the grapes had noble rot, the fungus that makes sweet wine in places like Bordeaux, but is unusual here. They had to harvest quickly and so lost a bit of the citrus freshness in the wines – but gained an interesting tropical note, I think. It's amazing how different the wines are, even when the *terroirs* are side by side. It's rather like a large family, where you can see fleeting resemblances but each face and personality is distinctive. We also try Olivier's St Aubin 1er Cru 2015 Clos du Meix, from vineyards near the old church in this impossibly picturesque village, where even the post office is backed by gently ascending vines. A *meix*, he tells me, is a word from Roman times, similar to the southern *mas* – it means the property, including vineyard, of the most important person in the locale. The wine is racy and elegant, tasting strongly but not unpleasantly of the hard limestone on which it grows.

In summer, driving through the Côte d'Or is pure pleasure. Serried slopes of dark green, with clusters of purple or golden grapes peeping out, silently observe your passing; away from the vines, early morning mist wisps past the grazing cows beneath slopes that were once grape-covered, too. I love both parts, the lost winelands and the thriving ones, although I feel a closer affinity with the former.

Eumenius's praise of the region's vines as 'ancient and admirable' was written in a letter to the Emperor Constantine, in a significant year. In AD 312, the Emperor fought the Battle of the Milvian Bridge against his brother-in-law and rival Maxentius, and attributed his great victory to the God of the Christians. (Apparently he was visited by Christ in a dream, and marked the sign of the cross on his soldiers' shields.) This led to his conversion, and marked the beginning of the end for the view of Judaism as a peculiar little religion that was no threat to any gods-fearing polytheist, however bellicose the Jews themselves might at points become. For the Christians and Jews were true rivals, in the Latin sense, both taking from the brook that was the Old Testament, and so differentiation was vital. Even before Constantine's conversion, edicts forbidding intermarriage and blessings (Christian landowners had a habit of getting their crops blessed by both Jews and Christians, which probably made them twice as saleable) were being drawn up; the fact that Christianity had retained and transformed the Jewish blessings of the bread and the wine made dining together particularly problematic, because if you countenance the Jewish blessings aren't you making a mockery of the new, improved Christian version? 'There are many in our ranks who say they think as we do,' John Chrysostom, Archbishop of Constantinople, was preaching by the end of that century, 'yet some of these are going to watch the festivals and others will join the Jews in keeping their feasts and observing their fasts. I wish to drive this perverse custom from the Church right now.' And so the Jewish customs were uprooted, like vines with an insect-borne plague, and the memory of that former kinship eventually scrubbed from the record. This is how things are: the monks are remembered here with gratitude and honour, the Jewish vintners largely forgotten. History is written by the winners, and they build monuments to their victories, to distract from the sadder stories buried beneath.

We have been travelling straight down, at Beaune rejoining the A6 or Autoroute du Soleil, the modern incarnation of a highway to sunshine that has been followed by wan northerners since conquering Romans began the weary tramp home – and probably before. But I want to visit Eumenius's Autun, which is back in that western hinterland, on the edge of the Morvan, so we turn off. My deliberate wiggle, to take in the places most interesting to me, turns out to have Roman antecedents, too. Despite the famously straight roads (I have a tendency to chant 'Roman road!' every time we start down miles of straight tarmac in Burgundy, and surely sometimes I'm right), the Romans were pragmatists, and when the best spot on the plain – at the crossroads of the Rhône and the Saône rivers, the Arroux providing a connection to the Loire Valley and the Yonne leading to the Seine basin – turned out to be slightly off the Via Agrippa, they diverted their road to accommodate. Augustodunum, founded by Augustus probably a few years before the birth of Jesus, was built to replace the Aedui capital Bibracte, provide a focus for trade and honour the loyalty of the Aedui. It was a walled city, and a couple of the gates are still visible, great imposing arches designed to remind those entering and leaving of the power of Rome; and if you look down on the rue de la Jambe de Bois (a wonderful name: Wooden Leg Road) you still see the large grey stones of the Roman Cardo Maximus, or main street.

We have brought the children, so we wiggle a little more en route to the Roman theatre to show them the cathedral, which once contained the relics of Lazarus, raised by Jesus from the dead. Surely there could be few more appropriate saints for wine country – and in fact, the twelfth-century tympanum above the western door is also an improbable survivor, resurrected from beneath a layer of plaster slathered atop by disapproving eighteenth-century churchmen, serendipitously just in time to save the scenes from the Revolution. The north tympanum, which was still exposed, was destroyed, as was Lazarus's tomb: his second, naturally.

The high arch that remains is carved with another Last Judgement, even more gruesome than Beaune's: angels reach down to smite the unworthy, hands wrench off a sinner's head, and a thin, naked mortal covers his face in impotent regret. The carved borders, delightfully for me, include vines and tiny stone vignettes of the Labours of the Months, many relating to the vintage: vine-waterers and grape-pickers celebrate an annual resurrection, and I feel that thread stretching back through the millennia: not just the winemaking process, which hasn't changed in essence, even if it has in particulars, but the Christians, Jews and Romans, all invoking their deities via the magic of grape juice transformed into wine.

We run along the sandy avenue to the theatre, which held 30,000; the city's population is now half that. It is well enough preserved to conjure enthusiastic Romans and Romanicised Aedui, avidly cheering or booing the plays before them. Even theatre has its roots in wine: the word comedy comes from Komos or Comos, Greek god of drunken revelling and son and cupbearer of Bacchus's Greek predecessor, Dionysus. My vinous musings are interrupted by a drama of our own: all four children are yelling in protest as C strides up onto the stage (modern, but in its rightful place, judging from the ancient moss-choked stones of the curved seating) and begins declaiming Shakespeare's reimagining of Mark Antony's speech in *Julius Caesar*, now more famous than anything Caesar really said – with the possible exception of 'Veni, vidi, vici', if indeed he said that.

'Friends, Romans, countrymen, lend me your ears,' C roars, with the voice projection of an academic – or a Senator. The kids howl with mortification, a bird or two chirps and the ancient stones wait indifferently for this, too, to pass. Several incarnations of my own father crowd into my mind, all of them embarrassing: correcting a sommelier; showing up late, always, to collect me from some school trip; dancing. He would have known, and applauded, this speech, and I listen, glad that these children have the unappreciated luxury of being embarrassed by their vigorous and unabashed – and very funny – parent.

But the phrase he is declaiming has strong echoes of Autun's devise. *Roma Celtica, soror et aemula Romae*: Autun is the Gaullish Rome, sister and emulator – or disciple, or possibly rival – of Rome. The friendship may have been a little forced, but the Aedui were the countrymen of Rome, whether they liked it or not.

We leave north via the Porte d'Arroux. This ancient entrance, once matched across the city by the long-vanished Porte de Rome, is now two arches straddling the road topped by a hunk of curved stonework. Across a bridge, in an empty field, sits the remains of the Temple of Janus, Roman god of gates and doors, and beginnings and endings. (The month January is named for him.) He was worshipped at planting and at the beginning of the harvest, which is also the end of the grape's life as a plant, and the beginning of its transformation. He signified transition, including the changes of adolescence, and his two heads look back and forwards, to the past and the future, barbarity and civilisation, the country and the city, childhood and adulthood – all rivalries of one kind or another. That his temple should be a tall, battered, half-ruined shell in a field, on a site that was once sacred to a Gaullish deity and is now a haunt for history-hungry tourists, seems entirely right. We photograph the two older girls – an adolescent and a child, back to back, of course – in a jagged hole overlooking the city and head back to the modern world, in search of lunch.

Later that evening, we eat five-spice grilled duck with plums and open a wonderful, berry-and-spice Armand Rousseau Clos St Jacques 1er Cru 1996, to mark the end of the Burgundy section of my trip. It's appropriate wine on several fronts: one of my father's, and a beautiful example from a legendary producer, grown in a small plot (less than seven hectares) that is nonetheless divided into strips belonging to five different wine-makers. The *clos* is named for the statue within it of St Jacques, signifying that this, too, is a stop on the route of Santiago de Compostela, walked by pilgrims (from the Latin *pelerinus*, or traveller) to the site of the apostle Saint James's tomb in Galicia. (Like so many travellers, he has different names – Saint Jacques, Saint James, Santiago – in different languages. And, as we already know, he has a symbol: the scallop shell, its distinctive shape imprinted on Proust's madeleine.) I am glad to raise my glass of wonderful wine to James, a fellow Jew who wandered out of our shared religion and into a younger one, and kept on wandering: even after he was beheaded in Judea, his remains continued travelling, to Spain. There is already too much rivalry in the world, and, after all, we still share a common cup.

Eve plucks the fruit of the Tree of Knowledge: a bunch of grapes. Carving on a capital in the basilica in Vézelay.

PONT DU GARD.

Drawing of the Pont du Gard near Nîmes. From *South Eastern France* by Augustus J. C. Hare, 1890

4

THE RHÔNE:
Roots

*To be rooted is perhaps the most important and least
recognised need of the human soul*

SIMONE WEIL

At Lyon, the road surrenders precedence to the Rhône.
I know no river as appealing as this one, its wide, flat
surface rippling with power that once drove conquest as well as trade but has been leashed, these last
two centuries, by dams, dikes and weirs. The Romans
were always good at harnessing external forces to their
own ambitions; they turned tribes into allies and the
Rhône into a highway, and settlements grew along the
river banks as all Gaul basked, more or less, in the peace
and wealth of the *Pax Romana*. That route is now laced
with bridges, and a few days' wander south through the
region's vineyards means weaving from one fertile bank
to the other, each crossing a reminder of the complex
mesh of mastery and dependence that is Rhône history.

In this valley, the Empire seems to burst out of the
soil, like those still more ancient fossilised creatures in

Champagne. Mosaics and amphorae and statues pop up everywhere, far more consistent in form than the soil they have lain in for 2,000-odd years. Rhône *terroir* varies from schist to clay to the south's *galets roulés*, the great round river-smoothed, heat-retaining pebbles found most famously in Châteauneuf-du-Pape. These stones may have been deposited by the river, or they may have been rained down by a beneficent Jupiter to help his son Hercules fight the fierce local Ligyan tribe. Whichever version you prefer, the stones are there, warming the soil and the roots of the vines, helping the plants to ripen faster, both in Châteauneuf-du-Pape and across the river in Lirac.

To travel north to south along the Rhône is to move backwards in time, reversing the Romans' trajectory from Greek Massilia (Marseille) north to cooler lands and fiercer barbarians. It also involves moving from the famous single varietal wines of the northern Rhône – red Syrah and white Viognier – to blends of Grenache with Syrah, Mourvèdre, Carignan and sometimes Cinsault, and an array of white grapes including Grenache Blanc, Clairette and Bourboulenc.

Before driving south to Ampuis, I pause briefly to pay homage to a piece of bronze – one discovered, fittingly, in a vineyard. This tablet in the Gallo-Roman Museum in Lyon is the record of a speech (well, half of it; the top of the tablet is lost). It bears witness to the Emperor Claudius's determination to open up access to the Senate, in defiance of the incumbents' objections to allowing Gauls, even wealthy ones, to join their number. Claudius was born in this city in 10 BC, when it was Lugdunum – still young, but already the second greatest wine port in the world after Rome. He wasn't a member of the local tribe, the Allobroge (which gave its name to the local grape, *allobrogica*), but a Roman who believed that this was not a difference that much mattered: 'Persicus, that most high-born gentleman and my friend, is not ashamed when he finds the name Allobrogius among his ancestors,' says Claudius on that bronze fragment, and he clearly felt the reverse should be true, too: no Allobrogian ghost should feel his descendants slighted by Rome for their lineage. The speech recorded here was given at the Senate in Rome in AD 48, and it worked: wealth and merit, not birth, became the criteria for the highest level of citizenship, which was access to high office. All this happened while Claudius's troops were subduing Britannia, although even when they succeeded, the land at the end of the world never did achieve a seat in Rome's Senate – a failure for which, thanks to Claudius, the British must blame their forebears.

Vines have generally been more acceptable immigrants than the people carrying them, although the soil has sometimes proved less welcoming than the locals. In the first century AD, Columella, our greatest remaining authority on Roman-era agriculture, wrote of that Rhône-born Allobrogica grape that the agreeableness of the wines was affected by a change of region. This notion, that where a vine puts down roots influences the wine it will produce, is one of the earliest references to *terroir*.

Down the Sunshine Highway I go, road flirting with river bank, on my way to the Côte-Rôtie, or 'roasted slope' – a reference to the sun that bathes these hills, thanks to their angle, and also shelters them from the wind. This well-cooked, well-protected *terroir* produces Syrah with a spiciness and firm structure that is noticeably different from the same grape (sometimes also called Shiraz) grown elsewhere. Similarly Viognier, the principal white grape (with Roussanne and Marsanne) of the northern Rhône, can be as overblown and over-perfumed as a dying rose – but in these parts, particularly just below Ampuis in Condrieu, it can also make an extraordinarily elegant and exotic wine. Here, you can drink the truth of the observation that where you are planted makes a difference. The great achievement of Claudius, as for likeminded winemakers, was to state that those roots may define but should not limit you.

Until recently, there were just fields, the bright, fresh green and brown of new-sawn wood, until past Vienne. That, as we shall see, has altered, but this is still mainly agricultural country, with relatively few slopes that receive enough sun to ripen the grapes fully, and hills so steep and hard to work that the price of the finished wine climbs, too. There are good fruit and vegetables down near the river: Ampuis is also famous for a type of apricot called an *ampuisais*, and, as in Burgundy, the vineyards presumably terraced the hillsides precisely because they were more adaptable than the fruit and cereals that took precedence further down, on flatter, more fertile land.

The ancient stone terraces remain, along with the habit, in the northern Rhône, of training vines up a single pole – useful for workers stumbling between steep-planted vines and harking back, perhaps, to the custom of coaxing vines up tall trees that Roman writers mention; a practice that led those vineyard workers who weren't slaves to demand, as part of their pay, the potential price of their burial.

They are all long dead, in the line of duty or elsewhere, those peasant grape-pickers: they have crossed the Styx, never to return. And the fruit they picked is long drunk, but their masters have left their mark, as if this land were too beautiful to leave, just because you happened to be dead and buried within it. Just as the hilltop castles and ruins of the Middle Ages still survey the vineyards and lavender fields below, so the Romans are still there, as matter-of-fact as neighbours, their arches poking out of the soil at St Rémy or Orange, their roads bumping past the museum at Saint-Romain-en-Gal, their towns as visible as exposed roots at Vaison-La-Romaine. There are two complete temples, one at Nîmes, the other at Vienne, both of which survived, like the Mars Gate in Champagne, thanks to the unintended benevolence of the Church. These Christians incorporated the pagan houses of worship into their own, either as a gesture of domination or out of mystical belief in the power of a religious site, even one from a misguided religion. Either way it's a lovely irony that the great power that finally subsumed Rome should then protect the last vestiges of those gods the Church Fathers thought to destroy.

The Greeks of Massalia may well have planted the first Rhône vines, but they drafted in Roman help to fight the local tribes and the Romans, as usual, did not go home afterwards. Ensconced, they carried on the good work of propagating the olive and the vine, and those tendrils of civilisation have long survived them. Philippe Guigal has dug pottery tubes, like ceramic vine roots, out of his vineyards and, while not everyone agrees with his claim that they indicate ancient irrigation channels, nobody denies that they are ancient, the remains of a signature imprinted on the landscape, like a flourish on a deed of ownership.

Eve Guigal, Philippe's wife, shows me round their winery's public area, with its cool marble, genuinely ancient mosaics and replica Roman boat filled with amphorae and *dolia*, the gargantuan clay containers that served as ballast – unless one broke, at which point 900 litres of free-flowing wine could capsize the ship. She lets me peek into their private study, where ancient Greek *kraters*, the large vessels in which wine and water were mixed by the civilised, line the shelves alongside the sinuous vessels from which those *kraters* were filled. Then we descend to the large cellars beneath Ampuis where the Guigals store their wines, from here and from Châteauneuf-du-Pape, Gigondas, Tavel and Côtes-du-Rhône. They are enormous – three hectares, or about two football fields – and as I walk past orderly rows of oak barrels I am reminded that it was the Gauls who invented the barrel, rendering the amphora obsolete – and so making life more difficult for historians, since amphorae endure while wooden barrels generally do not. Before they age and die, their gift is to permit tiny amounts of oxygen to enter, enabling their contents to age, too, first gloriously and then fading into sourness and obsolescence. I think of the words of Horace: 'O Plancus, remember wisely to end life's gloom and troubles with mellow wine ...'

The Guigals buy in grapes for their cheaper, wider-circulation wines, and the obsession with the ancients does not extend to trying to emulate their wine-making methods – which sounds obvious, but you'd be surprised. There are a few people trying to make wine 'just like the Romans' and I plan to meet them, although I think they're insane. The Romans sealed their wine vessels with pitch; their additions of herbs, local or exotic, and honey, marble-dust and resin may have been intended to improve the flavour – or possibly to disguise it. The waspish first-century AD poet Martial praised wines of Vienne made from the Allobrogica grape, which apparently tasted naturally of pitch; the statesman Cato recommended feeding the squeezed-out grapeskins to cattle, which seems reasonable, or moistening them with seawater to make a drink for slaves, which doesn't. If, as Louis Barruol of Château de Saint Cosme, further south, remarked to me, all wine dreams of becoming vinegar, it seems highly likely that most Roman wine achieved that dream. Who would want to replicate that?

Philippe and his father taste incessantly – they make 3.5 million bottles of Côtes-du-Rhône, and they have 800 domaines' worth of grapes from which to choose their blend. Tasting them all must be impossible, but 'my husband and father-in-law are not reasonable people,' Eve says wryly, so evidently they get through a fair few. The result being that this crowd-pleaser wine has what all blends were initially intended to offer: consistency.

That was Dom Pérignon's gift to the Champenois: sameness and continuity, an assertion of superiority over time, weather and nature, an indulgence of overweening ambition akin to damming the powerful Rhône. Consistency: don't we all dream of it? We harness nature, find gods to supplicate, blend the juice of one grape with that of another, all in the service of

knowing where we are and where we will be tomorrow. And yet great wines, even great blends, are varia-
ble, as is everything living. If you really want to taste,
you must first embrace uncertainty, accept that nothing
stays the same, nobody knows much and today's circumstances may change without warning. Wine is both
a buffer against those fears and a reminder of them.
Those enormous grapes from the Promised Land that
were presented to Moses were themselves a promise.
This place is fertile: you will eat, drink and bloom here.
But the very fact that they had been carried away was
also a reminder that what is rooted can be pulled up
and banished. I like to think that Moses made wine
from those Eshkol grapes, and so tasted the place he was
destined never to set foot in, and savoured, at the very
least, the promise of an end to exile and the opportunity to care for your own land, and drink its fruits.

Philippe's grandfather Étienne Guigal knew where he
was – the family has been at home here for centuries, maybe
millennia. Still, that didn't protect him from upheaval. He
started working aged eight, after the war; the *ampuisais*
apricots and wines were his trade, and he must (although
this is not how Eve frames it) have scraped together the
wherewithal to buy his own vines through sheer determination and, quite possibly, bloody-mindedness. When he
went blind, his 17-year-old son Marcel became his eyes;
Philippe is Marcel's son. It isn't hard to comprehend why,
for the Guigals, consistency might be enticing.

And their entry-level wines are certainly good enough
to merit replication. The 2015 Côtes-du-Rhône white

is rich and creamy, with great acidity, the L'Hermitage 2012, also white, sweetly rounded and mineral. Moving towards idiosyncratic individuality, I try two of their three so-called La La wines – La Mouline, La Landonne and La Turque – single vineyard wines with which the Guigals helped revive this area in the 1960s and 1970s. (The Roman irrigation pipe was found in La Mouline, which is in the form of an amphitheatre, although nobody knows if there's any significance to that.) The 2012 La Mouline is delicious, almost smoky; La Turque, of the same vintage, is full of raspberries. These are produced in tiny quantities – about 5,000 bottles of each.

While I taste two wines from Saint-Joseph, Eve airs the theory that Saint-Joseph was actually once part of the legendary hill of Hermitage. Both are about 60km south of Ampuis, and close, if on opposite sides of the Rhône; Hermitage, unusually for a northern Rhône appellation, is on the east side of the river, which wiggles obligingly there to give the slopes better exposure to the sun. But 'it's the same soil!' cries Eve. '*Granite à dents de cheval*' – which translates as granite with horse's teeth.

She is happier to admit heterogeneity above ground. 'We have walls from all eras in our vineyards,' she laughs as we walk through the cellars, pointing out a giant stone with a Latin inscription that promises payment, for reasons unspecified, to a long-forgotten widow. This was found here in Ampuis, while the shards of tombstone surrounding it were dug out of those horse-teeth vineyards at Hermitage.

Before leaving little Ampuis, its houses painted the pink and brown of the surrounding sun-parched rocks, I stop for lunch in the kind of modern bistro/wine shop that France used never to have, and still doesn't quite do with conviction. Two winemakers are waiting for me, wines untouched before them while a cool beer, accompanied by tapenade toasts, rapidly disappears. Pierre Gaillard and Yves Cuilleron are both big, solid men, balancing precariously at a high table when they should be elbows down at a refectory bench. I hoik myself on to a stool opposite, and am instantly poured a glass of a Viognier called Taburnum. The name comes from Pliny, who also talked, flatteringly, of those other pitchy Vienne wines, Sotanum and Heluicum.

The Viognier I'm given is lovely but is not, of course, Pliny's wine – nor would I have welcomed the taste of tar with my asparagus terrine. But the land it grows on may be the Rhône's newest and oldest *terroir*. Abandoned after phylloxera because the vineyards here were so steep, says Yves, that 'people did not have much energy to replant', they stayed fallow as the city encroached, until these two plus another local winemaker, François Villard, got together to try to resuscitate what proved to be that rarity: great *terroir* that nobody wanted.

'We are the generation who revived these vineyards,' says Yves. 'My family has been here for three generations but my father had to go and work in a factory – you couldn't make a living from wine then.' How times have changed. The distinctive rectangular border on Cuilleron's labels (like Guigal, he makes wines in several places, although on a much smaller scale and using his own grapes) is visible in plenty of British shops; and, meanwhile, he and Pierre are obsessed with bringing Sotanum, Tabernum and other such forgotten fragrances back to life, in the ancient vineyards they call Seyssuel.

Pierre is the quieter of the two, although appearances may be deceptive. At the Roman museum at Saint Romain-en-Gal – a fabulous place just outside Vienne, with beautiful mosaics and an actual Roman road running through the grounds – the guides inform me that every last weekend in September, for the re-enactment of the Roman harvest festival of Vinalia, this bulky and soft-spoken man dresses up in a toga and pulps grapes old-style, with his feet, before vinification in a genuine (well, genuine imitation) Roman press. All this in the museum garden, with the wonky but smooth-worn stones of that ancient road below and the vineyards of Seyssuel above, and modern Vienne across the river. There is a Roman garden with more than 100 herbs planted here, and various grape varieties thought to be ancient. The artefacts in the glass-walled museum were found in the 1960s, during a perfunctory root around before a school was due to be built on the site. It was known that Vienne had been larger in antiquity – it had 30,000 people to Pompeii's 40,000 – but the scale of what was here surprised everyone. After Rome's fall, the soil had crept over the vestiges, hidden and protected them, and waited for the spade, or the plough.

Cuilleron started with four hectares; now he has 60. The three original winemakers (who banded under the name Les Vins de Vienne) have been joined by almost a dozen others, including big Côte-Rôtie names such as Michel Chapoutier and Stéphane Ogier. The talk is of an appellation of their own – at the moment, the wines must be classified as Vin de Pays, which is much less prestigious, although the prices are fairly high. Still, they want the official stamp. 'It will be the most northern appellation in the Rhône Valley,' says Stéphane Ogier, who has called his (excellent) Seyssuel L'Âme-Soeur, which means Soulmate. In a land where every other hill is topped with a crumbling piece of history, warm stone seemingly burnished gold by the sun, these winemakers are taking a chance on history hidden beneath the ground.

We try the Sotanum, which is 100 per cent Syrah and exceptionally rich, like a blackberry and granite viennoiserie, and talk about land. Pierre and Yves point out that the soil here is schist, just like the Côte Brune, which is, with the Côte Blonde, one of the two slopes that make up the Côte-Rôtie. We discuss the grapes exported to the New World, and planted on entirely different soils. The theory of *terroir* says that they will produce very different wines there – and so they do. The wines of the Old World, particularly Bordeaux and Burgundy, may still be the world's most respected, but there is a warning here: learn to adapt where necessary, or, no matter how great your hegemony, you will crumble. Your influence, like Rome's, may long outlive your glory – but most winemakers, I think, would prefer to retain the glory. Wines come and go: 'Vineyards, like states, have their rise, their greatness and their fall,' said Pliny the Elder, back in the first century, and the enormous holes in our knowledge of ancient wine bear this out. Still, we are all the losers if a great wine dies, and, with the changing climate, that risk increases all the time. Let's hope that the Old World can learn from the New – or, rather, that the latter can remind Western Europe of the techniques of adaptation, forgotten here through long disuse, that all new arrivals need to make themselves at home.

The bottle empties; the afternoon rambles on. I learn that Syrah is a cross between Dureza and Mondeuse Blanche and that Durif, known in California as Petite Sirah, used to grow in Chavanay, ten kilometres down the river from Ampuis, when Yves was growing up there. He thinks it is ancient, possibly one of the Allobroges' grapes. Later, when I look it up, I will discover that Durif may be known as Petite Sirah but not all Petite Sirah is Durif – sometimes it's Syrah and sometimes something else. I will, not for the first time, roll my eyes at grape nomenclature and remind myself that whatever travels will change its name, that one of the things I love about wine is its complexity, in background as well as in flavour, and that if that changes I am always at liberty to start studying fizzy pop.

By the time we have moved on to discussing Cuilleron's other recent planting, the red grape called Persan, which grows in Savoie and neighbouring Isère and is, according to my companions, another possible Allobrogica variety, I am late for my next winemaker. Fortunately, Gilles Barge is only a minute away: he has a tasting room on the high street. I am also rather full of wine, which turns out to be a plus, because Gilles piles me into his car, aromatic with cigars and sweat, and drives me over the Reynard stream that separates the Côte Brune from the Côte Blonde, up into the vertiginous hills and stops at – a small steel contraption attached to a single rail, heading almost vertically up the terraced hillside. It swiftly becomes apparent that the sideless metal crate at the back is my chariot and that my blithe companion (now puffing on a Vape) is the driver, although that feels like rather a fancy name for the job required. I look at his weathered face, realise it may be the last human visage I see before falling to my death among some of the world's best-loved vines, and wish fervently that I'd drunk even more at lunch.

This primitive apparatus is 200m long and cost Barge €45,000, but he would like to lengthen it when he can afford to: the sheer slog of getting up the hill to work the vines and then bringing the grapes back down probably only barely made economic sense in ancient times, when an unlimited supply of slave labour was available. 'In some wine regions, you can plant fifty hectares in a year,' says Barge: 'we took ten years to plant a single hectare!' Nonetheless, viticulture lasted here until the First World War. Then, says Barge, the combination of war, Prohibition and economic misery defeated the locals, and the forest reclaimed the land. In fact, by the 1960s there were only about 60ha still planted with vines in the whole of the Côte-Rôtie. Today, that figure is over 270ha, but complacency is not an option. He gestures to the trees fringing the path. Give it a couple of years, he says, and the forest would take over again.

The sheer difficulty of making these wines, even with a monorail or a horse to work the vineyard, makes me wonder about the sanity of those ancient Romans. How thirsty they must have been, to plant and maintain these hillsides! Even for those who sat back and ordered the work, the financial outlay would have been considerable. They could have bought in wine early on from those avaricious Italians who charged a slave for an amphora, later from the Empire's Spanish colonies, or from elsewhere in Gaul. But they must have wanted the taste of these hills, unlike any other, the rich wines from roots sunk deep in the schist of the Côte Brune and the lighter, sandier, limestone of the Côte Blonde. Only then could they reassure themselves that, no matter where they or their parents may originally have come from, they belonged here: not exiles, destined only to taste others' nectar, but twice-born, like Bacchus.

I'm wandering further down the Rhône, still in Syrah country, past Tain l'Hermitage brushing the river and Saint-Joseph opposite. Past Saint-Péray, which demonstrates the truth of Pliny's remark about the rise and fall of vineyards, with a mere handful of producers of sparkling white wine left, in an appellation once so renowned for that style of wine that the nineteenth-century American writer Edgar Allen Poe mentioned it several times. 'In his seclusions the Vin de Bourgogne had its allotted hour,' he writes of the restaurateur Pierre Bon-Bon in one short story, 'and there were appropriate moments for the Côtes-du-Rhône. With him Sauterne [sic] was to Médoc what Catullus was to Homer. He would sport with a syllogism in sipping Saint-Péray, but unravel an argument over Clos de Vougeot, and upset a theory in a torrent of Chambertin.'

Alberic Mazoyer, winemaker and co-owner of Domaine Alain Voge (Monsieur Voge, once the village distiller back in an era when every village had one, is now in his late seventies with health issues), has vines in both Saint-Péray and Saint-Joseph, as well as Cornas, a tiny, sun-stroked village indelibly associated with rich, red wines. His duties range widely: when I show up at his Cornas winery he is outside the tasting room, vacuuming the car. 'I have to do everything,' he explains good-naturedly, abandoning his cleaning to drive me up into the hillside vineyards. They are certified biodynamic, and the grasses wave gently between the vines, fringed by cedar trees and sloping down to an incredible view of the Rhône Valley. 'The Romans settled here because the river was so useful for transport,' Alberic says, admiring the panorama. 'It was by far the easiest means to carry heavy amphorae or barrels of wine.'

The soil is 80 per cent granite, so even after a downpour you can walk without squelching, yet the vine roots can always find water. (And you can taste that granite in the wines, framing the fruit and keeping it in check. Fruit, unlike the vines that bear it, should not wander too far. If it does, the result is what is known as a fruit bomb: the unpleasant sensation of having your tongue colonised by invading blackberries.) Alberic was born a little further south, but he is fully assimilated; he, too, has put down roots. This, he tells me, looking around him and down into the village that gives his wines their fame, is the heart of the appellation. He sighs with satisfaction.

There is a further outcropping: a tiny, nineteenth-century chapel that was once above the vineyards, built to honour a miraculous spring that apparently cured fever. (Prosaic explanation from this Jewish atheist: maybe getting away from polluted water in the towns had something to do with it.) Now, thanks to global warming, the tiny stone building at 370m is surrounded by vines, a confluence of God's two favourite liquids, both miraculous in their way. The chapel is named for Saint Peter in Chains, like the world's most famous basilica, in Rome.

We brush through the grasses, flowers and butter-flies as we make our way back to the car, turning for a last look down onto that dramatic panorama designed by geological accident but nurtured by the Romans. 'I think we are very close to the Romans now in the Western world,' says Alberic thoughtfully. I'm not sure whether he means our fascination with them or our equivalent status as a power in decline. Perhaps both. That said, he acknowledges that, in other ways, we can never really get close to them: they have crossed that mythical river, far less fordable than the Rhône, to the land of the dead, and even our senses cannot bring them back to us. Alberic would love to taste their wine, although he knows that that is impossible. Well, so would I, even if I do doubt I'd want to finish it. The Romans did not just bring wine with them, Alberic points out: like any culture on the move, they took their music and their customs. Yes, I add, and that fusion of all three: religion. And yet polytheism has vanished from the former Roman colonies I'm travelling through, except in the form of lovely relics whose preservation does indeed seem like a miracle.

I taste Alberic's wines, which are exceptional. Saint-Péray Harmonie 2015, a still white that's 100 per cent Marsanne (as are all the whites except the sparkling, which has some Roussanne), has a lovely stone fruit nose and gentle acidity; it should be drunk young, says Alberic, which wouldn't be hard. Terres Boisées 2014 is more rigorous and longer lasting and must, Alberic explains with the precision that only a Frenchman can muster, accompany smoked salmon or scallops with olive oil and lemon, unless you're keeping it for a couple of years, in which case open it with chicken in a cream sauce. I nod and try the Fleur de Crussol 2014, from 70-year-old vines planted in a single vineyard on the former bed of the Rhône, then mellowed in barrel for 17 months. I really like this, I tell Alberic: I can taste herbs and flowers, and there's a light bitterness like a spritz. He nods, unsurprised. I refresh my mouth with his sparkling wine, Les Bulles d'Alain, and think of Poe: this would surely merit his 'sporting with a syllogism', if I knew what one was. ('Two premises, one major one minor, which lead necessarily to a logical conclusion,' C informs me. 'So: Socrates is a man, all men are mortal, therefore Socrates is mortal.') There is one Saint-Joseph, a lovely herby violet Syrah called Les Vinsonnes, and three Cornas reds of which the Vieilles Vignes 2013, all granite and dirt, was so delicious I wanted to tuck it under my arm and run off with it. Thierry Allemand, perhaps the most admired Cornas vigneron, has said that if you don't want to work hard, you don't make wine in Cornas, and that exertion ripples through the wines, which are perfumed yet muscular.

They are hard workers and humble, the winemakers of Cornas. When I visit Auguste Clape, whose name is one of the appellation's most famous, he tells me that when new oak became a trend, and lots of local winemakers started softening their wines' fierce tannins in new barrels, he consulted Tim Johnston of Juveniles Wine Bar in Paris on whether he should do the same. The horrified reaction – 'No, no, don't change anything!' – is something to be grateful for, and in fact that particular trend is fading. 'For my grandmother,' says Auguste, the latest of many generations of winemakers, 'it was a fault to taste wood: they put peach leaves and salt in new oak to get the taste out' – which rather makes me think that the Romans might not have been so crazy with their additions after all. His 2002 is full of mulberry but still has lots of tannin: I'd like to taste it again in a few years. Oak softens wine but so does time, and if you don't know how to wait you have no business being a winemaker.

Somewhere around Montélimar we cross into the southern Rhône: different soils, different grapes, although those differences do not at first show in the landscape. (Both sides, of course, can make wine they call Côtes-du-Rhône.) Outside Bourg-St-Andéol, down a small lane, sits a sixteenth-century house with a very modern banana tree. Raphael Pommier of Notre Dame de Cousignac considers it his weathervane: when we venture outside after a rainstorm, he fingers the leaves glumly and points to the banana sack, which isn't ripening: 'the grapes will be the same. It is too wet and cold for Grenache, although Syrah doesn't mind.' We have left the pure Syrah country of the northern Rhône for the hot south, where the red grapes Grenache, Syrah, Mourvèdre, Carignan and Cinsault form different combinations and proportions. Today, in late June, it isn't very hot and Raphael isn't very happy; he, however, is certainly a man who knows how to wait. 'Farmers think ahead,' he says. 'When we build terraces they last thousands of years.' When we walk past his vineyards we see them, shored up by ancient walls half hidden under foliage. At the edge of the vineyard is a tangle of scrub, enclosed by barbed wire; the remains of Roman baths hide among the brush. Currently it's unexcavated, and nibbled by grumpy goats.

Raphael has been thinking ahead in other ways, too. He has converted half the house into a *chambres d'hôtes*, chaotic but comfortable, and has built a pool and a jacuzzi. He has five young children, at least one of whom he hopes will take over his vineyards. Although just now they are more interested in the pool.

His family have been farmers a long time: 'we tilled the bishop's land before the Revolution.' We walk up a hill, past the buried source of the nearby stream, more vines and a smart house that used to be part of the family property but now belongs to second-homers. This was a sacred place, he tells me, and at first I think he is referring to the water source, for what is more important to a farmer than water? But then I see, among the trees, a very old chapel, its altar a Roman lintel, its distinctive cornerstone, according to Raphael, possibly part of a Roman wine press. Apt, really, since a cornerstone is a kind of root: the basic contact with the earth, from which all else grows. Looking at that stone, limestone white, with its central depression that might, or might never, have held the screw of a Roman wine press, I am struck by the many shapes taken by our need for stability, certainty – foundations. Rome is the foundation (one of them) of modern Western society; Christianity is one of the West's central religions. Judaism is the basis of Christianity, in turn, and wine – the benediction and the sacrifice, the symbol and the promise – a founding tenet of both. I think of the Book of Isaiah, where God lays a foundation stone in Zion: 'a tried stone, a costly corner-stone of sure foundation'. Zion is the mount where the Temple stood, as well as the ideal of a homeland; that cornerstone was reappropriated, in the New Testament, as the foundation of the Church. ('The stone the builders rejected has become the cornerstone.') Wine is the crossing point, the river and the bridge, between Christianity, Judaism and paganism – not the only one, certainly, but surely the most flavourful, and perhaps the richest in symbolism, too. Nothing is really pure, which is why a pagan tool has become the cornerstone of a house of worship for a people who turned a blessing over the fruits of the earth into a celebration of sacrificial suffering. Every church, really, has a pre-Christian cornerstone, and all house pagan temples and Jewish rites. How right that this stone should sit there reminding us of the needs we all share, for roots, for validation – and for myths, since almost none of these things is quite as firmly grounded in reality as we would fervently wish them to be.

Raphael tells me about Alba-la-Romaine, which was abandoned by the Romans around the fourth century in favour of the more easily defended Viviers, or Vivarium – that is, a place where livestock and other animals were held; about the port of Alba's stout trade in wine, on boats to Arles, Marseille and even Rome.

We walk back to his summer kitchen and he tips out some sharp, tasty little Provençal black olives, pours me a glass of wine named for Vivarium (Côtes du Vivarais blanc, a third each Clairette, Marsanne and Grenache Blanc, tropical and very drinkable), and begins making *soupe au pistou*, the traditional Provençal minestrone enlivened by a powerful crushed paste of basil and garlic (pistou is the local word for a pestle). The talk turns to *terroir* – to the uprooting of people and the things, like wine, or customs, they can or cannot take with them, and the changes those movements make. 'It's like Grenache,' says Raphael, pounding until the twinned scents of sharp garlic and heady basil almost bring tears to my eyes. 'You can plant it somewhere else and it will bring something. But the grape it is *ter-roir* and it will change ... And eventually you will have something different. But it will still be *terroir*.' Quite so, I agree, popping olives. That replanted Grenache will have something of where it came from and something else of where it is right now. This is surely part of our attachment to family, I say to Raphael and to C, who has now joined us. Between them, they have nine chil-dren. In the most fundamental sense, wherever you are, you can look at family and see where you came from. We discuss friendship, the cornerstone of atheist lives. 'A friend,' says Raphael, as he seasons our supper, 'is what you have after sharing a hundred kilos of salt.'

If you are interested in time passing, says Raphael, come with me to see La Grotte de St Michel. Early humans sheltered here; then the caves were covered over, and were only rediscovered by a hunter in the 1830s. Neanderthal and bear bones were found, among the graceful stalactites and stalagmites. There are basins and natural statues (one bearing a remarkable resem-blance to Father Christmas) that really have been filed away by time, an endless unwearying motion of water that caused this rock to yield.

I concertina my neck and stare up into those stone spikes reaching down into the underworld, just as vine roots do. These caves are not devoid of interest for the wine-lover: several barrels of local product are ageing discreetly under the entrance, some of them Raphael's. He and other local winemakers hold tastings down here, he says – it makes it much easier to explain the soil types when you can point at them, just above your head. He brought his kids here on one of many summer visits and the pleasing coolness struck him as cave-like not in the sense of cavemen but in the sense of *caves* – French for cellars. So he whipped up support from the owners of surrounding vineyards and gained permission from the local administration to age a few barrels down here, and now you can drink his Vinolithic Côtes-du-Rhône Villages, a Grenache-Syrah-Carignan blend, after its maturation in these natural cellars, more ancient than Champagne's, if not than the rock that surrounds them. The wine label includes the only Neanderthal drawing found here – replicated on a convenient wall of the grotto, since the original is too fragile and too far from the entrance for public viewing. It has a cluster of odd dots above it – what are those? Raphael smiles mysteriously. An hour, a lot of chilly, moist caverns and a couple of *son et lumière* shows (the French can never resist adding filtered lights and pop music, even when the subject in question needs neither) later, we surface and he enlightens me, handing me a bottle as a farewell gift and pointing to those strange dots with a bashful grin: 'I think they're grapes.'

I rather like the idea of Neanderthals carefully decorating their painted bison with a fruit that would come to mean so much to their descendants. And, really, they do look like grapes. But more, I like the imaginative power that has reached across so many years to share an interest beyond warmth, food, shelter. Here is the gap in time, as deep and unfathomable as those miles of ancient caves. There are far more centuries separating Neanderthals from Romans than divide the Romans from us, but the gulf is not just a question of years; it is the olive and the vine that bring us and our classical predecessors close. Wine is the cornerstone of our civilisation, and those Neanderthals exist on the far side of a river more unbridgeable than the Styx. What did they love, those distant ancestors, apart, presumably, from one another? Since we will never know, let's retrospectively offer them the comfort of a liquid so beloved by the locals who succeeded them. I don't like to think of anyone, not even a 100,000-year-old predecessor, being deprived of wine – particularly when the shelter of stone walls and intermittent bear flesh were, to our knowledge, their only treats.

At Vaison-la-Romaine, I pick my way through the extensive ruins in a downpour and flee for the museum. There's a statue of Emperor Domitian looking worried, as a man who attempted to curtail the burgeoning winemaking capacities of his Empire should. Two items stand out among the amphorae, the glassware and the mosaics (including a very large and beautiful tile floor featuring peacocks): an enormous carving of Dionysus/Bacchus, bearded and fearsomely staring, vines woven into his hair; and two limbless statues, probably captives, carved from the calcareous stone that serves the local vines so well. Sculpted to perfection, they seem to gaze longingly at one another, and their entrapment – in stone, in the past, in enslavement and in the immobility of those missing limbs – feels like a metaphor for human inadequacy. Why am I stuck, gazing longingly at figures from the past, unable to truly understand them?

I turn back, as usual, to wine. I'd better be careful, I think, as I pull into Domaine de Cabasse, in Séguret: looking for the truth in the bottom of a glass can end badly. But then I get out of my car before an elegant building with a pool beside it and vines at every compass point, and a wonderful spicy scent hits me. Later, I'll try Casa Bassa 2011 and realise that it's the smell of the very old parcel of Syrah behind the house. The immediacy, the portability of this, cheers me instantly: no matter how many bottles I drank in London I would never know that the whole property was perfumed with it, and now, no matter how many bottles I try back home, I will never fail to see this house and vineyards, the round hill of Séguret flanked by the honey-coloured village, before me as I sip.

And then there is dinner with the property's owner, Benoit Baudry, who is as happy to share information as good wine. 'Nobody knows Séguret,' says Benoit cheerfully. 'We are very proud of our village but we are alone!' His vineyards are on the border of Sablet and Séguret, with vines in Gigondas, too. Here is a decent man enjoying life. He has found what he wanted right here, and his contentment soothes my restlessness; it doesn't make me want to stay still, but it does reconcile me to my travelling. 'Tomorrow there'll be the *Mistral* wind,' he says, by way of farewell, 'which is annoying perhaps for you but good for the vines: it prevents mildew.' And he is right: at the castle of Suze-la-Rousse, an enormous, twelfth-century monster that looms over the small town, doors bang open in protest at the powerful gusts. 'The *Mistral* is the best friend of the vigneron – it fights disease for him!' cries Jacques Avril, who works for the Wine University housed in the château. He wrestles the door open against this importunate best friend in order to show me an incredible panorama of the Drôme vineyards, then leads me back inside to an interesting little museum in those imposing rooms, with amphorae to admire and a series of exhibits on the wine of the living, the dead, the gods and the Greeks. A cutaway of a boat shows the amphorae clustered in straw – a reminder of the Rhône's twin functions, as giver of life to the surrounding vineyards and mode of transport for the fruits of their harvest.

The vines of Gigondas, planted by Rome's Second Legion, suck flavour from the jagged, calcareous Dentelles de Montmirail mountains and moisture from a subterranean reservoir that may have given the village its name: *gignit undas*, springing forth from water. Most people prefer the story that a landowner nicknamed Jucundus, or 'joyful', bestowed his cheery designation, like a blessing. It is certainly a happy place, green and sunny, producing rich, rounded wines.

Louis Barruol of Château de Saint Cosme reckons that the centre of Gigondas life in Roman times was a villa on his property, and while these sorts of histories are hard, if not impossible, to separate from wishful fiction, there are certainly substantial Roman vestiges in his cellars: what looks like a horse trough carved out of the sandstone he calls *saffre* is, he says, a storage vat for wine 'although it was a bit complicated because wine doesn't like oxygen'. Well, ours doesn't. Louis is the winemaker who pointed out to me that all wine dreams of becoming vinegar.

The Barruol family has been here 400 years and likes history: there's a mini museum next to the Romans' vat, with ancient oil lamps and prehistoric statues dug out of the vineyard. Louis's uncle is an archaeologist, his grandfather was an eminent historian and the Barruol men seem accordingly at ease with their ancestors' pain: there are implements on the wall for making silk, which is what many winemakers were reduced to once phylloxera hit. More competition for the Jewish silk-weavers of Lyon, a misfortune to add to the decimation of the vineyards needed for their sacred ritual.

The Barruols' interest in the history of the Rhône vineyards has nothing to do with the vogue for trying to make Roman wine that I'm planning to look at further south. 'That's just business,' sniffs Louis, and of course he is right, since those wines are tailored to please modern palates. It's something else as well, though: a hankering to really experience, even taste, the vanished past. I think back to my two limbless statues in Vaison-la-Romaine, gazing yearningly at one another as I gazed yearningly at them, and sympathise. Maybe for a man whose family has been here so long that painful tug is lessened, although I can't quite believe it, given that Barruol has clearly spent a lot of time thinking about the Romans' activities here. They planted fruit trees and vegetables, and 'vines for a bit of fun', he says, but probably not on more than 10 per cent of their land and the wine was all, he believes, drunk locally. He has carefully calculated how much land the Romans would have needed to make winemaking viable here; around 11 or 12ha, he reckons. Château de Saint Cosme, he adds, is 15ha.

He talks about the *Pax Romana*, and the chance to build settlements in economically astute but militarily disadvantageous places, like the edge of the Rhône ('It's flat! Next to the water! It's undefendable!'), safe in the knowledge that Roman order would be maintained. He is adamant that the Gauls made wine before the Romans came. 'People travelled around. The climate is so favourable … you think they had wine forty-five kilometres away [in Massilia] and not here? I don't believe it.' He adds impatiently, 'We have a tendency to trace history in straight lines but that isn't how it happens. The vine spread across the world and nobody can say that it went to one place and only then to another – the same is true of other events.' In other words, the famous view of history as one damned thing after another is all wrong. I couldn't agree more. We try his 2016 Gigondas Hominis Fides (Latin for 'Man of Faith'), from the barrel. It will be bottled in spring 2017. It is gorgeous, full of cloves and raspberry and bay. He returns to the subject of modern-day Roman wine, repeating himself: 'It's all business and wishful thinking!' But, laughs C, surely wine *is* wishful thinking …

We walk out of the cool, ancient cellar onto a large, tiered lawn and talk turns to Pliny. 'The trees he described here were deciduous, he didn't mention pine,' says Barruol. 'Now we have both but perhaps soon there will just be pine.' It's inevitable, he thinks. Obviously climate change exacerbates everything, but this is not necessarily a man-made phenomenon: 'in the Bible they describe a landscape quite a lot like this one, with cereals and rivers – nothing like Israel today'. The world changes, and humankind tries to keep up.

We drive away from Gigondas, the honey-coloured village backed by pale mountains, towards Cairanne, the plain rolling out before us, its flatness matched by a featureless blue sky. At an otherwise ordinary round-about in Orange on what was once the Via Agrippa, a triumphal arch rears: 'That mighty monument of a great and warlike people,' the early twentieth-century travel writer Theodore Andrea Cook called it, 'set at the head of the vast highway by which their legions marched towards the conquest of the north.' It was probably built by Augustus to honour the veterans of the Gallic Wars, then updated by Emperor Tiberius a century later, in celebration of his Germanic battles. It is enormous, and incongruous, head-to-head with the trees, its curved spaces framing the circling cars, etched with the stories of triumphs no longer remembered. The Romans seeded the land so assiduously with statements of their presence that even the windy little village of Caumont-sur-Durance, where we stop for the night in a lovely seventeenth-century *chambres d'hôtes* called Hôtel Le Posterlon, turns out to have a Roman garden, with the recently discovered remains of a bath-house now lovingly surrounded by little patches of greenery symbolising various gods. Jupiter's tree is, I learn, the oak; Bacchus has the ivy as well as the vine, which is not surprising given the ancient tradition of the thyrsus or ivy-coated stick, symbol of fertility and hedonism, carried by Dionysus/ Bacchus and his fellow revellers. Back at Le Posterlon, my young host brings me a glass of *vin ordinaire* to accompany a simple dinner of sliced meat, pâté and the tiny sour gherkins that the French love so, and tells me he is starting a cellar, to sell local wine.

The architecture ranges from monumental, like that arch in Orange, to rambling, like the extensive ruins at Vaison-la-Romaine, or quietly visible, like this little Roman garden. Sometimes it's even smaller. 'We still find tiles among the vines, and sarcophagi and fragments of *dolia*,' says Jean-Pierre Meffre of Saint-Gayan as we taste the Gigondas he calls Origine, a predominantly Grenache blend with Syrah and Mourvèdre that's full of berry, spice and chewy tannin. The Roman road from Vaison-la-Romaine to Carpentras goes just past his vines and there's a stream that probably inspired the

Romans to plant here. At nearby Domaine du Pesquier, vine-growers have found a Roman-era oven for baking tiles, abandoned so abruptly there were still tiles in it.

But it is not just the Romans who are more visible here than they were further north: at last, the Jews are, too. 'Everyone from Carpentras has Jewish blood,' says Nancy Gonthier, casually: 'Our family name was once David.' During the papacy's absence from Rome during the fourteenth century – a sojourn sometimes referred to as the 'Babylonian captivity' – Carpentras, along with Avignon and the nearby towns of Cavaillon and L'Isle-sur-la-Sorgue, was the home of the Pope's Jews. This small area, the Comtat Venaissin, became a place of refuge both to displaced popes and to the descendants of the original Babylonian captives, although if the Jews' commercial usefulness was validated and protected by the Holy See it was in a manner ranging from kindness through tolerance to outright persecution, including designated places to live, 200 years before the Venetians invented the word 'ghetto'.

What an odd combination that must have been: the endlessly displaced Jews and the temporarily ousted popes. There is nothing on the scale of the Popes' Palace or its namesake, the village of Châteauneuf-du-Pape, yet Carpentras has a beautiful Rococo synagogue, with chandeliers as well as menorahs, the seven-branched candlestick that is a distinctive symbol of Judaism. Below, there are the ovens, for bread and for matzoh (the unleavened bread of Passover, a reminder of the occasion on which the Jews, led by Moses, were forced

to flee Egypt so abruptly they had no time to let the
bread rise). There is a vat for wine, which was made
here; grapes were also sold to pay for paupers' graves.
And there is an amazing 30ft-deep *mikveh*, or ritual
bath, with steps descending into emerald water. This is
the oldest synagogue in France, and still in use, if with
a very small community. Cavaillon has another, a little
later, restored in the eighteenth century, and even more
gorgeous: pink and gold, with a little museum about
the Comtadin Jews. There are small vestiges – another
mikveh in Pernes-la-Fontaine; the information that
there is a Hebrew name for Avignon (which may have
had Jews as early as the third century): *ir ha-gefanim*,
City of Grapes. Here, at last, are the three objects of
my quest united, and it surprises me not at all to learn
that Carpentras was once known, to the Jews who
were temporarily safe here, as *la petite Jérusalem*: Little
Jerusalem.

As I drive into Carpentras my first glimpse is of the
church spire, a menacing finger pointing upwards. The
barbarians may have overthrown Rome but it was the
Church which inherited her power, and that's very
obvious here: when I ask the owner of a gift shop near
the church for directions to the town's Roman arch,
she has no idea what or where it is. After much wandering around the centre, I find it – right beside the
church, in its shadow in every sense. Even the synagogue is better signposted, although its beauty is invisible from the square outside. In 1367, when its first
incarnation was built, ostentation by Jews would have
been neither advisable nor legal. Once again, I'm put
in mind of Pliny's comment: empires as well as vineyards have their moment of glory. Perhaps, in a few

centuries, those who wander in my footsteps will have
to ask directions to the church, too.

Nancy and her sister Alexandra run Domaine de la
Camarette, which is the opposite of a ghetto: around 40
grape varieties cohabit here, the result of their father's
career as owner of a nursery – for grapes, naturally.
They have a shop, a few guestrooms and Nancy's husband cooks in their restaurant, which is so good that the
tables in the domaine courtyard fill, on a balmy Tuesday
night, with local diners. Their lightly herbaceous rosé
slips past my tongue with the unremarkable ease of a
stream flowing downhill; it's a fine accompaniment to
tempura, then pork. Despite all the unusual grape varieties, their best wine is a Syrah-Grenache-Mourvèdre
blend, 80 per cent Syrah, and I like to picture the experiments, the trial and error, that led to this happy combination: which came first, the realisation that the fruity
Grenache that grows so happily here could benefit
from the north's Syrah, or the wish to leaven that Syrah
with something a little rounder and friendlier? Maybe I
should feel less kindly towards this successful combination and this entire overproductive region, given that its
sunny ability to gush forth rivers of easy-drinking wine
was one reason my part of Burgundy could never revive
its wine industry after phylloxera, but wine and churl-
ishness make a terrible combination.

There are arches in this part of France that are far harder
to ignore than Carpentras or even Orange: Aurore at
Domaine de Poulvarel has promised to show me the
Pont du Gard. I cross the Rhône yet again and find

myself driving past the Avignon Palais des Papes. It is stunning: tiered and crenellated and gigantic in an entirely different manner from the hulking disproportion of Suze-la-Rousse. I'm hard put to keep my eyes on the road. And surely the line of descent from Rome to Roman Catholicism becomes as intertwined here as my criss-crossings of the river, for the popes who built that palace and gave their name to Châteauneuf-du-Pape (the New Palace of the Pope) may only have come because of their love for the local wines – or at least, so the fourteenth-century Italian writer Petrarch scolded, calling Avignon 'the Babylon of the West'. Here, he wrote, 'reign the successors of the poor fishermen of Galilee; they have strangely forgotten their origin'. Most migrants want the taste of home; these princes of the Church steered their banishment towards the earth that tasted best to them, then built a palace to memorialise their exile. Did any aroma reach them of ancient Rome, the pagan Empire that had originally brought these grapes here? Or were they, as would befit their calling, happy to be where they were, content in the knowledge that God had willed it thus?

It is hard to feel Petrarch's righteous rage on the beautiful drive from Domaine de la Camarette to Sernhac: the sunny roads and magnificent river, as supple as a panther; the climb up past blue-grey rocks to the plateau, are enough to bring on revelation in the soundest atheist. If I were a fourteenth-century pope, I'd have come here, too.

Before the Pont du Gard there are the Vins de Pays du Côteaux du Pont du Gard: the appellation of Aurore's family's wines. 'We have around forty hectares; that is what you need to make winemaking practical here,' she says. The garrigue, the local scrub, brings complexity – 'and freshness, which is really important here where it is so hot!' – and the soils, ranging from red to pocked with those large, warm stones, the *galets roulés*, give variety. The wines are mostly intended for good-quality easy-drinking, particularly Les Perrottes 2013, which is 40 per cent each of Grenache and Syrah and 20 per cent Carignan, has a lovely blackcurrant quality and is, it turns out, named for a Roman tunnel, excavated by slaves, that is as deserted as the nearby Pont du Gard is busy. Of course, it's a lot less impressive than a three-tiered bridge rearing above the river that must look, thanks to a little restoration, almost exactly as it did two millennia ago; but still, this tunnel too bears testament to the Romans' talent for making scarce water resources obey them, whether for reasons of transport, human thirst – or thirsty vines.

It's dark in Les Perrottes, hidden within the quiet earth, an introvert to the Pont du Gard's whizzbang extrovert. A Roman oil lamp would have lasted 11 or 12 hours, which would have been the working day down here, cutting this soft (but not that soft) soil into a channel. There used to be a divide down the middle but the medieval inhabitants took the stones to build their homes. We surface after 11 or 12 minutes, glad (not for the first time) to have very different lives from our predecessors, and stop for a picnic under the dry, rustling trees. Then we head to the Pont du Gard, the three towering storeys of arches that seem so excessive for the admittedly important task of bringing water into the city of Nemausus, now Nîmes. As we walk across the bridge beside them, I crane my neck trying to view the structure's entirety and wonder to what extent its magnificence, like that of the triumphal arch at Orange, was intended to impress not enemies but subjects. There must have been so many who called themselves Roman citizens without ever having seen Rome; civic pride for an unseen *civitas* would not seem hard when looking at the power of the Empire carved three storeys high in local stone ...

That power has waned but it has not disappeared. Now, however, it is often seen through a sentimental haze. Diane and Hervé Durand of Mas des Tourelles kept finding amphorae shards in their vineyard, so at great expense and effort they decided to nourish the heritage they were treading on, and like a giant vine out of the shard-strewn soil came ... a Roman wine press. Built to the detailed specifications that Cato so considerately left in his writings, supplemented by the visual descriptions in the Saint-Romain-en-Gal mosaics, it is a truly extraordinary thing: a whole tree trunk, seven metres long and weighing 2,500kg, pressed into service to crush the grapes that are then fermented in great clay *dolia* that sit buried in the nearby ground, their sides glittering with tartaric crystals. 'We stir the wine with a fennel brush,' says Diane, neglecting to mention that it has first been pressed by young men in togas – but, then, the little film she shows does that for her, and it's so absorbing that even a couple of American children who have been dragged in here by wine-loving parents sit quietly. The resulting wines contain thyme, cinnamon and honey, as the originals would have done: the Turriculae, following a Columella recipe, has fenugreek and even seawater. They are curiosities, but very drinkable ones; how close they come to the originals is impossible to know, but then, as a Rhône winemaker pointed out to

me, 'even our grandparents made wine differently: society is much more in love with sugar now!'

Before quitting Gaul, I stop just outside St Rémy de
Provence to pay my last respects to the mysterious,
mythic figure who tried so hard to keep it out of Rome's
clutches. Caesar's arch there commemorates the Gallic
Wars, and a figure who is very probably Vercingetorix
stands, hands tied, calmly accepting his defeat. He looks
nothing like the giant with the Asterix moustache near
Alésia. He is another sculpted slave. His defeat was my
gain, I suppose, as regards the wines of Burgundy, but still,
it's sad to see this powerful pagan so subdued: another
casualty of the Romans, almost written out of history.
Mind you, the arch has lost its cap and the figure holding
him has lost his head – Rome's primacy has crumbled,
too. The Church has overshadowed both stories; history
grinds on, in anything but a straight line, and much is
worn away by its inexorable motion. It is such an odd
shape, the St Rémy arch: thick at the sides and slender
on top, and Theodore Andrea Cook believed that too
much earth had been scraped away at its base, too. He
admired it greatly nonetheless but, while I appreciate its
more human proportions, and the stories picked out on
its sides, it feels empty, this boast of victory over a long-
forgotten enemy. It can't compare with the majestic presence of the Pont du Gard, which brought life, in the form
of water, rather than venerating death and destruction.
That enormous structure has become, paradoxically, part
of the landscape for locals and tourists alike. I remember
the road and the mosaics at Saint-Roman-en-Gal, cush-
ioned for centuries by the soft enclosing soil, protected

and nurtured like vine roots. And I wonder how long, exactly, a person or a people must stay put before they can rightfully claim that land as home.

A quick stop in Nîmes, to walk round the almost intact amphitheatre, Les Arènes, and see the Maison Carrée. I find I prefer the former, which seems more real than the cool classical perfection of the temple. Perhaps that is because the amphitheatre has been put to fairly gritty use for its entire 2,000 years: first, as entertainment site for the bloodthirsty residents of the colony of Nemausus, carefully emulating Rome in their leisure activities as in this beautiful circular stone venue for them; then as fortress, protecting those erstwhile citizens from the barbarians; and later as habitation, with houses and shops built into the venerable curved stone, as they also were in the amphitheatre at Arles. In contrast, the Maison Carrée has been restored to a columned faultlessness that is probably appropriate to its original function as a temple to youth (specifically, to Caius and Lucius Caesar, Emperor Augustus's adopted heirs). The building feels sterile, inorganic – as perhaps it should, given that the two boys it honours retained their youth forever, both dying in their early twenties without issue.

Less complicated to amble down the city's calm, narrow streets: there is a peculiar joy to wandering, not quite aimlessly but without severe time constraints, in a city you know not at all. I keep my eyes open for the little brass buttons sporting the city's coat of arms: a crocodile chained to a palm tree. The design mocks Mark Antony's passion for the Egyptian Queen Cleopatra, and celebrates Octavian's victory over them both at

Actium in 31 BC – a triumph that transformed Octavian into Caesar Augustus and the Republic of Rome into an Empire. This was, presumably, what Augustus's predecessor and adoptive father, Julius Caesar, had been aiming for, but it took his assassination to achieve it. The Republic had acquired the land on which to plant vines, but it would be the Empire that would truly enable the ebb and flow of wine, from *terroir* to territory.

As I circumnavigate Les Arènes I look across the road and see a woman in heels and a black gown tipped with white fur – a magistrate, a judge? – sipping a fizzy drink outside the Palais de Justice: progress, unless you count the drink. And as I head out of town, south towards Spain, I pass a sign: *Vous Longez la Via Domitia!* – You are travelling down the Via Domitia, the road, the first the Romans built in Gaul, which links Italy to Spain via France. That sign feels like a congratulation from the far-distant past, a message from the ghosts of one peripatetic people to the living representative of another: you are on the right track.

Bacchus supported by his mentor Silenus on a third-century
sarcophagus in the Gallo-Roman Museum in Lyon

The vineyards of Celler Bàrbara Forés, Catalonia

5

CATALONIA:
Trade

*Breath of balm from phials of yesterday ... perfume of
apples ripening in their winter chest, of the field lavish
with the leafage of spring; of Augusta's silken robes from
Palatine presses, of amber warmed by a maiden's hand; of
a jar of dark Falernian shattered, but far off ...*

MARTIAL, *EPIGRAMS* (Trans. Walter C. A. Ker; amended by
the author)

As France becomes Spain, so the Via Domitia takes the
name of the first, more successful Emperor, in whose
reign it was laid. Down the Via Augusta I go, faster than
any Roman could have dreamed, back to an earlier, fiercer
incarnation of Rome, still fighting more for survival
than for glory. In the early third century BC, Emporion
was already a city of 300 years' standing; a Greek port
whose name would live on long after its life was over, as a
byword for trade. Much of that commerce was with the
Phoenicians, great sailors and traders, fanning out from
their main city, Carthage, on the Gulf of Tunis, to bases
all over the Mediterranean, including southern Spain,
where they exchanged their oil and wine for Spanish

silver. Their impressive reach worried the Romans, who fought a series of wars (called, confusingly, the Punic Wars), which eventually achieved Cato's desire. '*Carthago delenda est* [Carthage must be destroyed]', he had repeatedly shouted at the Senate, and so it was. And so was the Punic presence in silver-rich Iberia, although the Greeks stayed for a while, sharing space with a Roman city, Emporiae, which soon overwhelmed them.

The Phoenicians had been selling oil and wine for Spanish silver, but that would change with the arrival of the thirsty and enterprising conquerors. Hugh Johnson, in *The Story of Wine*, suggests that victory, over the Carthaginians and others, brought security, wealth and an increasing interest in luxuries such as wine. Certainly, by the middle of the second century AD, twenty million amphorae of Spanish wine had been shipped into the city of Rome.

The cities along the Catalonian coast ebb and flow: Emporion gives way to Emporiae, Tarragona rises then falls, Barcelona arises and stays risen – more or less. That first Greco-Roman city tumbles, eventually, into ruin. But the Romans did not head back out with the tide. They put down roots so deep that the Catalan language is still closer to Latin than to any of its neighbouring tongues including Spanish, and they changed the way the Spaniards think of themselves – which was not, until they arrived, as Spanish. Even though they divided the Iberian peninsula into Tarraconensis in the north, Baetica in the south and Lusitania, now Portugal, Hispania was their creation. In all that comes after, from Sepharad, the name given by Jews of that era to their Iberian home, via the Moorish kingdoms to the plundering of the New World by Christian Spain, a little of Rome mingles, like sediment in the bottom of a wine glass. And, in fact, the Romans' very presence here may have been due to wine: some historians say that Cato's venom was partly a response to Carthage's pre-eminent vineyards – certainly, the only book the conquerors saved, of all the written knowledge of that older civilisation, was a treatise on vine husbandry by an agriculturist named Mago.

If wine encouraged them to flow in, the Romans certainly returned the favour, making of Spain a wine emporium that has lasted 2,000 years. Veterans of Caesar's campaigns were given land and planted vines; the Jews, whose presence in Spain dates from at least this period, would also have needed wine for their rituals. The Iberian peninsula already had native vines, and the Phoenicians, down south in Gades, now Cadiz, may well have had a little home-grown wine, but it was thanks to the Romans that Spain became a vineyard, at the same time as she became Spain. By the time Pliny was writing his *Natural History* in the first century AD, the *balisca* grape – its growing patterns and weather preferences – was known in Spain as *coccolobis*: 'its wine is apt to go to the head,' wrote Pliny, 'but the yield is abundant'. And some think it likely that *balisca* travelled to Bordeaux (which, thanks to its fine port and poor soil, started its wine life as an emporium for others' wines) to become *biturica* – which then began the Bordelais project of conquering the world. How much duller our dinner tables would be if people and vines had ever learned to stay still!

'There are two Spains,' says Xavier. 'One is Castilian, and those are the conquerors, Fascists, Catholics, and

oppressors. We Catalonians are the other: we are deal-
ers, Communists, anarchists and revolutionaries.' We are
reliving the Spanish Civil War in Plaça de Sant Jaume
in Barcelona's ancient Gothic Quarter, outside the
city hall. Xavier, who works for the Barcelona History
Museum, has just conducted a walking tour of the old
city that ended here, atop the centre of Roman Barcino,
a walled city with 76 defensive towers, its forum later a
monastery ('Wherever you see a square in Barcelona,
there was once a monastery or convent,' says Xavier)
and now, the main square. 'Why so many towers?', I ask
Xavier, '76 seems like a lot'. He snorts. 'Barcelona was
built on the vanity of the people,' he replies. It was a rich
city, a trading city, even then, and one of its main exports
was wine, most of it terrible. As Rome grew to a million inhabitants – more than any European city would
manage again until the nineteenth century – Barcino
and Tarraco (Barcelona and Tarragona) profited from an
Italian thirst that had far outgrown home production.

These were the traders – and Rome facilitated that
trade, with peace, security and roads to supplement the
Mediterranean's function as a route to market. 'The
Catalans are the richest of Spaniards, because they work
and produce the most,' wrote the Englishman Richard
Ford, in his 1845 *A Handbook for Travellers in Spain*,
adding revealingly: 'The Tarragona district, as in the
days of Pliny, furnishes wines, which when *rancios*, or
matured by age, are excellent … red and full-flavoured
wines, which are exported by Cette [Sète] and the
Languedoc canal to Bordeaux to enrich poor clarets for the English market: the liquor, when new, is as
thick as ink, and deserves its familiar appellation, "black
strap".' Clearly some things had changed little in the

1,900 years between: the Spaniards were still purveying wine, the Catalans were trading around and across the Mediterranean and Spanish grapes were supplementing what the poor soils of Bordeaux could supply.

There are several ways to look at the idea of two Spains, but in Catalonia you can't ignore it, because of the language divide. Is the city Empúries (Catalan) or Ampurias (Spanish)? Who decides? Whatever you call it, this vast remnant is amazing: two great cultures, side by side, the Romans further back from the thriving Greek conurbation on the coast, like the rich guy who comes in and builds a higher building in order to keep the view. This is the only place on the peninsula where you can touch both cultures within a couple of steps and it is spectacular, with the bright sea just beyond. The Roman city is only 20 per cent uncovered but there are baths, a forum, the carefully mosaicked floors of former villas. It is odd how we see Roman culture, these days, from the ground up, and not far up, either: with the lack of walls and roofs, we wander cities no higher than a vine, punctuated by the odd column or statue. Empúries is beautiful, a grid of sunburnt stone just brushing the Mediterranean that made it glorious, its back turned to the road that destroyed that glory. The Via Augusta marches from France all the way to Cadiz, via the trading mecca of Narbonensis and what was, at the time of the road's building, newly established Tarraco; Empúries, a true port city, was rendered obsolete.

Empúries suffered the fate that so often befalls the first in line: glory followed by irrelevance. This golden coastline was *terra remota*; the Roman civilising machine altered its power structure and its economics without changing its essence. If the Catalonians are traders, geography explains why – the Greek emporion, a trading place or market, comes from *emporos* meaning merchant, particularly one who trades on a large scale, usually by sea. That is to say, the word originally signified a traveller.

There is still *terra remota* north of Barcelona, in a wine-producing region that was destroyed by phylloxera: in fact there is now a winery called just that. On our way to the city, we detour for a look. There are disconcerting numbers of vines fringing the polluted highway, but Terra Remota, only a few kilometres from the turn-off (and so far north that Google, until recently, thought it was in France), is shielded by winding small roads that lead up to a deceptively plain cement block, pleasingly low-lying against the blue-misted Pyrenees. Emma Bournazeau is not so much a blow-in as a blow-back: her grandfather left Catalonia after the Civil War, and her father made a fortune in silicone implants in France and was, until his death, a co-owner of the winery she and her husband Marc, also French, have built.

The money may have come from artifice but there's little sign of it here. The winery is built into the hillside on three graduated storeys, so gravity can send the grapes where they need to go; it is designed to admit the cooling, drying northern *Tramontana* wind while shielding trucks of cut grapes from harsher weather. In a region, Empordà, that the nineteenth-century Catalan poet Joan Maragall described as the palace of the wind, the Bournazeaux have designed their own palace of wine, and, while those winds aren't necessarily benign to humans (here, as in Provence a little further north, they are held responsible for madness and suicide), the winemakers have wisely made their accommodations with nature.

Despite adhering to organic rules, with a low-energy winery ('no neighbours have pesticides, either,' points out Joan Frei, a Swiss-German who moved from a salesman's life in his homeland to winemaking in this distant, wind-scoured place), the Bournazeaux are not terribly interested in local varieties; there is Garnacha and Tempranillo in Camino, their spicy, curranty principal red, but also the ubiquitous Syrah and Cabernet Sauvignon.

Everything here is done by hand, which puts me in mind of those make-believe Romans at Mas des Tourelles, effortfully pulling the lever that used a man's weight to crush grapes. What was once the only way to create a product that requires a fair bit of human interference is now the luxury option, in a mechanised world, and I remember Olivier Lamy in Burgundy, comparing the disruptions that technology causes with those brought about by phylloxera. It makes sense that you can't make something as sensual as good wine without a fair bit of human touch, just as it seems logical to put the emphasis on really good wine when you're less than an hour's drive from two of the world's finest restaurants: El Celler de Can Roca, in Girona, and Ferran Adrià's legendary El Bullí, which closed in 2011. In no era have the rich drunk plonk, even if the definition of plonk has changed. Wine is a social tool and so an instrument of differentiation. I can demonstrate power, if I have any, by the quality of the drink I offer – or by withholding that drink entirely.

Terra Remota's wines are few but excellent, with an eye to the market that's reflected in the spare but welcoming tasting room and the offer of a bike tour of the vineyard with a picnic of local foods and, of course, a bottle of wine. The room's open fireplace should be used for barbecuing, I think wistfully: their Clos Adrien red would make it a party. Still, the 100 per cent Grenache rosé is one of the nicest Spanish pink wines I've tasted – usually they are too dark pink, too powerful. Perhaps it's the proximity to southern France, home to the world's greatest rosés, or Emma's family's 70 years of exile there, which has made the difference.

The Romans may have quickly overrun the peninsula but it took them until Augustus's time, the first century BC, to take full control and organise everything in their inimitable way. (A nice fact, for those of us in need of a little collective pride: by 19 BC, when Augustus's general Agrippa subdued the last part of the Iberian peninsula, only one legion was needed to keep order, compared with Britain, which required three, despite having only a quarter the land mass.)

Once they did get organised, wine flowed from Spain to Rome and beyond, to the Loire and northern France, to England and to the troops on Rome's German frontier. The Romans didn't introduce the vine into Spain but they surely propagated and systemised it, and there are fragments of Spanish-made amphorae across Europe that bear witness to that ancient thirst. A lot of the wine was plonk – ideal, as Ovid says, for getting the porter of your mistress drunk – but some, from around Tarraco, was good. Pliny, as Richard Ford noted, mentioned them, and in very flattering terms, as the best of the foreign options – and he was Procurator there so would have had the chance to do his research. His contemporary, the poet and Consul

Silius Italicus, claimed that these wines could compete with any save the finest crus of Latium, in Italy, while Martial wrote that 'Tarraco, that will yield only to Campanian vineyards, begot this wine that vies with Tuscan jars' – although he was Spanish (born 300km inland, near modern Calatayud), so may have been a little biased.

Wine's civilising influence (to say nothing of the taxes it reaped) became part of the Romanisation project, the one that ensured that Martial and Columella, and even the Emperors Hadrian and Trajan, would be born in Spain but come down to us as, unquestionably, Roman.

Back in Barcelona, in a medieval building on Carrer Paradis (Paradise Street), just round the corner from Plaça de Sant Jaume, three nine-metre Corinthian columns tower, unlikely living-room ornaments. This was the Temple of Augustus, and the columns survived erect because some gentleman, a secular version of the churchmen who saved Champagne's Porte de Mars or Nîmes' Maison Carrée, decided they'd make a nice decoration and built his house around them. Barcino is also visible elsewhere: an ancient arch pokes out of the side of a tower; the chapel of Sant'Agata, part of the royal palace, sits atop a Roman wall. My hotel, the Mercer (the word comes from the Latin for commodity), has one of those 76 towers embedded in its basement: a defence tower in the modern business centre, which doesn't feel like such a change of occupation. Ostentation from one end of civilisation to the other, I think, looking round my plush surroundings, but there's no denying it feels grand to cohabit with the Romans this way. And the wine list in the hotel restaurant is appropriately fantastic, as good as the one in the Michelin-starred Restaurant Gaig we ate at the previous night on a winemaker's recommendation. The latter had sections for DO Empordà, where I've just been, and DO Montsant and DOQ Priorat, where I'm going next (DO stands for *Denominacíon de Origen*, Spain's equivalent to France's *Appellation Contrôlée*). At Gaig, I took a vinous meander 60km inland, to the tiny DO Pla de Bages, which is, apparently, the location of a Roman city, Bacassis, named for Bacchus – and so, probably, a winemaking site then, too. A 2002 Cabernet Sauvignon Gran Selecció Reserva from Enric Solergibert was deep and spicy and intense but didn't swamp a long rectangle of boneless suckling pig with strawberries and spring onions – an odd combination on all fronts, but a successful one and, anyway, oddity is underrated.

Next day, sitting in La Vinya del Senyor, a tiny bar opposite the beautiful Santa Maria del Mar church, tasting wines from all over Catalonia that range from the famous (Sot Lefriec, from Penedès) to the more obscure (Castell del Remei, from Costers del Segre, 120km west of yesterday's Pla de Bages), I tell C that there is one last Roman vestige I need to visit before travelling further south. In Spain, the year that is of overwhelming importance is 1492. Every schoolchild knows that this was when Columbus sailed for what turned out to be America; fewer are aware that this was also the year that the last Moors were expelled from Spain, after nearly 800 years of partial occupation, or that in 1492 King Ferdinand and Queen Isabella signed the Order of Expulsion that forced every Jew in their extensive territories to convert or leave. The reasons vary from political pressure to parsimony (the Jews financed Columbus's trip; this way they never had to be reimbursed. And if you think that's unlikely, consider this: Columbus was never paid all that he was promised for his explorations, either.) The effects were far-reaching, for Spain's economy and for the Jews who were, once again, on the move. They had been pretty well integrated, and there are ghostly traces of them all over Barcelona (which, with 3,500 Jews, now has the largest concentration in Spain). The hill outside the city, once the Jewish cemetery, is still called Montjuic (the hill outside Girona, 100km further north, has the same name for the same reason); on the city tour, Xavier pointed out Hebrew writing carved into stones in the Gothic Quarter that were swiped from synagogues after the expulsion. Down a tiny street in the *Call*, the former Jewish quarter, is a building that some claim as ancient Barcelona's synagogue. It is tiny, which it would have been – the law forbade a synagogue to be larger than the smallest church – and its slightly skewed position, out of whack with the buildings around it, means it faces Jerusalem, as a synagogue must. It became defunct after 1391, when a massacre of Jews took place all over Spain, like a precursor of future miseries, but was restored and reopened in 2002, and people have married here, although it is not a synagogue with regular services – and it looks like no religious building I've ever seen. Downstairs, where the ground would have been 2,000 years ago, there's a tiny space full of what my father would have called *tchtochkes*: jumbled items, all donated, including scrolls, menorahs, books, a stained-glass window featuring the 12 tribes of Israel. Nura, our guide, points to a large stone etched with Roman numerals; the marks, she claims, commemorate the destruction of the Temple. Is this true? There's no way of knowing, but I sense the longing to believe that it is.

The city itself is so amnesiac, in this regard, that I will find almost everything Nura tells me on our Jewish city tour hard or impossible to believe. Still, it's oddly moving, this room full of old things looking for a place and a purpose. The impulse to gather them here, to try to imbue them once again with meaning, seems similar to my own quest. There is a glass case with silver Kiddush cups among the religious paraphernalia, and I look and imagine them filled with wine, and wonder where those vines grew …

As we walk back round the corner to the Mercer, to pack up and check out, I find the photograph on my phone of a plaque near La Sagrada Familia, the (still) unfinished twentieth-century cathedral by Antoni Gaudí that's as gargantuan and fêted as the Sinagoga Mayor is tiny and forgotten. It's a fragment of a poem by nineteenth-century poet-priest Jacint Verdaguer I Santaló, called 'The Emigrant':

'O Sweet Catalonia, homeland of my heart, to be far from you, is to die of homesickness …'

We continue down the AP-7, although diverting quickly to see the extraordinary Pont du Diable. This first-century aqueduct is neither as high nor quite as long as the Pont du Gard, but it is still magnificent – a water conduit in the form of a signature, branding the territory in stone. How the Iberians must have marvelled to see what their new masters could do! And with what gusto they then joined those who had beaten them: traces of Celtiberia are harder to find in Catalonia than vestiges of the early Spanish Jews.

That is not an issue when it comes to the Romans. Tarragona is astounding: one of the most fully integrated

Roman cities in the world. The way the modern city has grown around the Roman puts me in mind of a grand old tree I once saw, which had calmly encircled metal park railings with its ancient trunk and continued, unharmed and unperturbed, into the street. The houses built just inside the Roman walls, the cathedral constructed atop a Roman temple, the amphitheatre, spread out beside the Mediterranean – it seems appropriate that the beach just beyond the last of these is called the Playa del Milagro (Miracle Beach), although apparently it is miracle in the original sense of something to look at, i.e. a place with a lovely view (the Spanish for 'to look at' is still *mirar*) rather than in our modern sense of a scarcely believable wonder.

Tarragona may have survived so well because it fared so badly – Rome's capital of *Hispania Citerior* was neglected by the Visigoths in favour of Barcelona, then destroyed by the Moors. Some of it, surely, is luck. The Church's drive to supersede Rome means their temple has vanished beneath the cathedral, which is itself so hemmed in by houses that it's hard to see. But in the middle of the amphitheatre, the remains of another church are visible. Those early Christians will have taken surrounding stones in order to plant themselves in an arena where their brethren were martyred; it seems pure serendipity that they didn't take too many, and that the church has evaporated while the surroundings have not.

The city is still very proud of its Christian heritage, though: St Paul is said to have preached here, and personally converted the girl, St Tecla, who is the city's patron saint. There's a Pontius Pilate tower, too, a century older than the first-century Circus to which it is

attached, and mostly overlaid with a medieval structure: Pilate supposedly saw service here, or maybe he
was born here while his father was serving in the city.
Or maybe not.

The Circus now has a modern road for a neighbour
but the tell-tale curve around which charioteers would
have steered, sawing frantically at the reins to control
speed-maddened, foam-spitting horses, is still apparent.
Part of it sits beneath nineteenth-century houses, but a
formidable amount remains in plain view, and the city's
history museum is now inside. The linked vaults that
would have connected the Circus to the nearby Forum
have served multiple uses: shelter during the Civil War,
housing, abattoir, even beer storage for the bar the Circus
used to house, 30-odd years ago ('wonderful sandwiches,'
reminisces our guide). A couple are still bars – not ones I
want to drink in, but I do like the ancient, curving walls.

Tarragona has been a city since 218 BC and it is
easier to project yourself back in time here than anywhere else I've been: so much is still visible. You walk
along the tops of Roman walls and imagine yourself
a soldier, or lean out over the parapet (or mirador –
we have taken the Spanish word back) at the end of
the grand boulevard called La Rambla Nova, staring
at the amphitheatre and the ageless ocean, and conjure Roman ships. Or, you eye the curve of the Circus
and wonder how many spectacular chariot crashes the
occupants of those seats witnessed. I look at their living spaces and places of entertainment and government
and wish that their drinking and dining habits were as
flamboyantly on show.

The contrast with the Jewish presence here is even
more striking than in Barcelona; the *Call Jueu*, or Jewish

Quarter, has been pretty much destroyed, and a community that had been here over a thousand years by the time of the expulsion in 1492 has left few traces. There is a basin, or possibly a child's sarcophagus, with inscriptions in three languages – Hebrew, Greek and Latin – found here that's now in the Sephardi Museum in Toledo. As with the Roman temple beneath Tarragona's cathedral, the Christians have left their mark: it has a hole in the bottom, from being used as a baptismal font.

This was the capital city, and the fount from which flowed wine both good and mediocre in immense quantities. Today, the most famous wine in Catalonia comes from a slate hill, two curlicueing hours' drive inland from Tarragona, beneath imposing crags cut out of a hot, milky sky. Priorat's big, deep reds are a very long way from the kind of rotgut that Ovid expended on his mistress's porter: it is Spain's only DOQ, the country's top designation of wine quality, apart from Rioja. Prices are high, unsurprising when you stand at the edge of a vineyard, as I did at Ferrer Bobet, with your toes curling over its lip, staring at the top of an employee's head as she examines buds at the bottom of the same vineyard, ten metres down. So hard is winemaking here that one vine will yield a bottle or sometimes even half a bottle of wine; down the hill, in less rarefied vineyards, you get five bottles per vine.

There are theories about Roman winemaking here – Christopher Cannan of Clos Figueras has a Roman wall in one vineyard and has found a stone he believes was part of an early wine press – but very little solid information. Six centuries after Roman influence in Catalonia ended, a clutch of monks escaping heavy taxation – 'they didn't want to pay for the king's wars any more,' says Cannan – founded a monastery here and, presumably out of the usual desire for solace both spiritual and material, planted vines on land so steep that, even today, tending by hand or donkey is often the only option. Appropriately, they named their monastery Scala Dei, God's Ladder. Certainly, this is a special place: there is nothing quite like Priorat, with its vineyards threaded in single-file zigzags up the steep hill made of a special, glittering schist, called *licorella*, that is apparently the reason for the unusual quality of the wines.

The modern-day faithful are the clutch of winemakers who turned up in the 1970s, long after phylloxera had devastated what was left of the industry, and founded five wineries, originally vinifying their grapes all together in one ramshackle barn. They believed that better wine could be made on these vertiginous slopes than the bulk swill that was all that remained to Catalonia after the louse's depredations had led to the uprooting of vines and corresponding displacement of vine-growers. And they were right. Isabelle Barbier drives me round Clos Mogador, the most famous of those pioneering estates. She is a Frenchwoman from Nantes, which is a nice rest for my schoolgirl Spanish: '*Nous voulons refaire la vie du terrain* [we want to make the land live again],' she tells me, talking of planting wheat as well as vines, just as they would have done long ago.

Isabelle's husband René Barbier is, despite his name, Catalan, for the last few generations, anyway: the family arrived from southern France after phylloxera had ruined livelihoods there, the kind of migration in muddy boots that was presumably one of the ways the louse travelled south. Few of the founders of modern Priorat are native – Daphne Glorian of Clos Erasmus is Swiss-German, the Palacios family comes from Rioja, far from the trading shores. It is obstinacy and belief in this *terrain* that binds them, rather than a shared past on this or any other soil. Back in the 1970s, René Barbier wasn't daunted by the difficulties of making wine here; he was just enraptured by the land. Even now, Isabelle points to their grassy, flower-strewn vineyards, the single rows of vines shining in the sun as they wend their way down the hillside, and waves a dismissive hand towards a neighbour's squeaky clean rows. That is not the way, she says. 'This covering of vegetation [she calls it a *tapis végétal*, a carpet of plants] keeps the freshness in the soil. We have enormous respect for nature.' A good life requires space, she adds, looking at the vines, but this clearly applies to the Barbiers, too: Isabelle worked as a dance choreographer while her husband was making wines. I still remember my first taste of Clos Mogador, several years ago, at the house of a wealthy friend who had challenged me to find him a wine that would 'blow his head off', in the sensual rather than the fruit-bomb sense. It was a 2005 and it blew us both away. Isabelle offers a 2013, which is too young ('after five years it will be good and after ten years better,' she says, making me wish, not for the first time, that I had a gigantic cellar and a lot of spare cash to spend on top, unready wines) but full of red and black fruit and thyme, a bit of liquorice – and fennel. 'Oh yes,' says Isabelle, 'there is fennel everywhere here!' And she offers me their Clos Nelin 2013, a weird yet wonderful white that's a blend of 50 per cent Grenache Blanc, the other 50 per cent a mixture of Viognier, Pinot Noir (vinified as a white), Roussanne, Marsanne, Macabeo, Pedro Ximénez and Escanya Vella, a local grape whose name translates as 'the old lady strangler' – probably because eating the grapes raw is a little like being throttled. That acridity is still perceptible in the wine, but softened to the point where it is simply saliva-inducing, and mixed with apricot and spice. It is unlike anything I've tasted, before or since, and that shock of the unexpected – assuming it tastes good – is a great attribute in a wine.

Clos Figueras was originally a collaboration between Cannan and Barbier, whose property is just across the road; part of the winery with rooms in which we stay used to be a restaurant run by the Barbier children, the other part a chicken farm. Cannan, who is a jovial, white-bearded wine importer originally from Gloucester (another blow-in), loves history: 'I told them not to dare touch it,' he says of that Roman wall in the vineyard, and in Montsant, down the hill, he named a wine he makes Laurona, in honour of the local vineyard that Pliny is supposed to have praised as Tarraconensis's finest – although others think that Laurona was modern Lliría, 280km south near Valencia. Cannan is also experimenting with amphorae, like his brethren across the border in France: they are interested in the way the amounts of oxygen that seep into the wines differ, depending on whether the container is clay or wood. His Priorat reds are Grenache-Carignan-Syrah with a touch of Cabernet Sauvignon and, sometimes, Mourvèdre, and they are restrained and herby with that lick of Priorat slate: I try two of the second wine, Font de la Figuera, a fine-grained 2013 and a 2011 that actually tastes younger because, says Cannan, 'it got very hot at just the wrong time that year, just before harvest, so we didn't make the top wine at all and the grapes from the old vines went into this, instead'. The Clos Figueras 2012, his top wine, is rich yet light, and tastes a little of strawberries. There are worse ways to ensure success than to set up shop across the road from the most successful winemaker in the area, but Cannan's enthusiasm is very genuine – and he, unlike any of his neighbours, has had the sense to offer keen drinkers of these fairly alcoholic wines somewhere to stay.

Down the road from Falset to Gratallops, the only directions being to turn left after the palm tree, is another winery, Mas Martinet, belonging to one of those five original pioneers. 'The idea behind the five families was one wine with different labels but it was too hippy, it didn't work out,' says Sara Pérez cheerfully, ushering us towards her car for a tour.

Pérez looks glamorous enough to be at home in a Madrid salon, but she found the eyrie that is now her favourite vineyard in 1995 while out chasing eagles, and as her battered jeep bumps towards it around hairpin bends, and I garble a silent prayer for survival to an unspecified deity, I am obliged to reassess. She may be Priorat royalty, daughter of one of the five founding winemakers and married to the son of another, but Pérez has very definite ideas on everything, from the sensual importance of touch – she sometimes jumps in the vat to crush grapes with her feet, the old-fashioned way, because she believes in 'contact with the wine, not just with eyes and tongue but also with hands and feet' – to the vitality and ongoing relevance of history.

That sensuality is very far from the monks who made Priorat a thriving vineyard of thousands of hectares, most of it intended for transubstantiation into the blood of Christ ... or is it? Drinking your god's blood is a pretty sensual thing to do, after all. We zigzag higher and then higher yet, the vine-coated hills stretching ever further and steeper beneath the jeep's wheels. The monks planted in places that ensured that they, too, would suffer – like a martyred prophet, or the son of God, or, for that matter, a well-placed vine. They chose to plant themselves here because a twelfth-century shepherd boy had had a vision of a ladder reaching to heaven, and they took that ladder – Scala Dei – seriously, striving ever upwards from the glittering rock. There is a Catalan saying, *de las piedras sacan panes* (you can get bread from rocks), to which the monks might reasonably have added, and wine.

Pérez also strives ever upwards although I don't think her reasons are religious, or not in the conventional sense. There is certainly something spiritual about the connection she feels to her wines. 'We fell in love with this vineyard,' she says, as we stand at last atop a hill, Escurçons (worryingly, it means viper in Catalan), whose soil – still the famous *licorella* of Priorat – is threaded with red from iron oxide. 'But people thought we were crazy to try to buy it, because the land registry had burned down during the Civil War so nobody knew who owned it.' Three years and a trail through seven families later, it was theirs. Pérez points to a pile of crumbling brick: there were people here once, making wine. 'We found little houses, they must have picked and fermented right here. I need to do that, one day.' She feels her debt to the past, both immediate and distant. So she is bringing back the finicky local Garnacha grape, including Garnacha Peluda (literally, 'Hairy Garnacha') that became too hard to cultivate after phylloxera, as well as planting the Cariñena that replaced it. And she is also, after some soul-searching, keeping the Cabernet Sauvignon that helped make the area's name but has now fallen victim to the trend towards more 'local' grapes: 'That is what my parents planted, I am here because of Cabernet Sauvignon. So I need to give thanks to Cabernet Sauvignon.'

Her respect extends much further back. 'We can understand a lot of the things we do or make, the things we are, through history,' she says. Her vineyards have been organic since 2000 ('we understand that one vineyard is one world and must be more or less enough by itself. It needs insects, and the nutrients and defences provided by the cereals and other plants and animals that like to live together with vines') and now, like Cannan, she experiments with making wine in amphorae and in demijohns, glass bubbles that are usually about knee-height, unless you're Sara Pérez and decide you need an enormous (54-litre) one 'so I found someone who still had the expertise to hand-blow it for me ...'

She and Barbier live here, between the villages of Falset and Gratallops, in a primitive loveliness: no electricity or piped water, just solar power and a generator ('when it's not working that's okay, it's not working') but with raked hills all around, a reservoir below, jars of *rancio* wine – the drink, deliberately oxidised, rich as fruitcake, that Richard Ford so admired – ageing on the roof and a spectacular cellar where past vintages, whitened by dust, face shelves empty in anticipation of future bottles. 'Every generation has something to explore,' she says thoughtfully, eyeing those bare and patient shelves: 'every generation is searching for a wine style that explains that moment.'

Her wines are like their maker: strong and full of personality. They soften with a few years' mellowing, she says, opening a 2005 Clos Martinet for us. It is still full of black fruit, but in contrast to the younger wines, which shove blackcurrants and blackberries at you, this wine offers them, sweetly, as a host to a guest.

From the wine aristocrats on the hill, we descend a little way (still 170m above sea level) to the self-confessed peasants in its shadow: four farmers making wines in the Montsant DO, in a corner of the local cooperative building in the village of El Masroig, under the Orto label. Joan Asens has almond and olive trees and is, he says, a farmer not a winemaker, which is a little disingenuous since he served as Alvaro Palacios' technical director for 17 years, yet he is less Sara Pérez's opposite than her mirror image, equally in love with his land and with a similarly tactile sense of history. 'I didn't know my great-grandfather,' he says, handing me a glass of his aromatic Les Tallades de Cal Nicolau 2012, which is named for that gentleman, 'but I drink the same wines and I work the same vineyards.' This impels him to nurture indigenous grapes – Nicolau's wine is made of Picapoll Negre – in vineyards that buzz and murmur just as they would have before the invention of pesticides: 'If you have just one plant, the vine, that's all the insects will have to eat,' he points out.

Asens and his cohorts have gone so far in the other direction that it isn't just insects who feed well in his fields. A fragile old lady smiles and waves from a field so full of whispering grasses it is a little hard to see the bush vines among them. Her younger companion has a basket and the two women bend like reeds, picking – 'peas,' says Asens. 'They give nitrogen to the soil … and this soil makes them so sweet!' This is how his ancestors would have tended their vines, but Asens' deference encompasses the churchmen who grew wine here in the Middle Ages, too. He ferments his wines in wood because 'monks 900 years ago had no inox [stainless steel] or cement tanks'.

He is too steeped in his strokable, plantable, drinkable kind of history to have much time for mine. 'We don't know about them – those traditions were lost,' he says impatiently when I ask about the Romans. If you cannot in some way touch it, this son of the soil isn't interested in talking about it. Perhaps Christopher Cannan's interest – his belief that the Romans were responsible for most of those steep terraced vineyards – has something to do with the large chunk of Roman wall in his own fields. Or perhaps he just has a different kind of historical imagination.

Before the Romans came, the Phoenicians who dug tin, silver and lead from these slopes also planted grapes. The lead they probably needed for anchors: a different kind of rooting for a peripatetic people. (It was the Phoenicians who had founded Carthage, too, so their influence on Spain's wine runs deep.) That young shepherd whose visionary ladder led to the monastery's founding was only continuing a trajectory that began on the ocean floor: with our feet in the soil and our heads tilted heavenwards, we are all trying to move and remain still at the same time.

Winemaking here had more or less stopped when Barbier and his friends turned up. The land under vine was down to 600ha and children were leaving to find work elsewhere – always the sign of a dying economy. Now those children's children are returning. There is an industry, and tourism, although that is still fledgling – so far, Gratallops has just one hotel, Cal Llop, plus Clos Figueras's three nice bedrooms, but needs much more to accommodate the modern part-time wanderers who are the making of so many wine regions. 'There are still more people in the winery than in the village,' says Cannan. The village of Falset is livelier, but retains its medieval character: when a window opens above, as I wander the narrow streets in the silent heat of the siesta hour, I am gripped by a sudden fear that someone will empty slops on my head.

And I love Falset's Hostal Sport, despite its awful name: it is neither sporty nor a hostel, but a sort of Swiss chalet meets country inn with spacious, comfortable rooms and a cavernous dining room that serves Catalan specialties – *pa amb tomàquet* (bread with tomato), *truita amb suc* (omelette in a salt-cod sauce), botifarra, a local sausage, with white beans. Everything is delicious; nothing is light. But we need some insulation from the wines, because the list is fabulous: lots of Catalan options at splendid prices, including the wines of Tomas Cusiné, a winemaker from Costers del Segre, and Scala Dei, the reincarnation of the monks' winery. These are both wines I have tried and liked in England, via the Wine Society, but I'm happy to taste them here, on their home soil. There are also plenty of Priorat aristocrats – I could break the bank on Clos Erasmus 2006 or Alvaro Palacios' famous L'Ermita 2004 in magnum, if I liked – but instead we try drinkable, if unmemorable, wines from the Enomatic, that clever machine which allows a bottle to remain open for several days by filling the emptying space with inert gas to exclude the oxygen. And I experiment, in honour of our botifarra, with a glass of Garnatxa Blanca from Viñedos de Ithaca called Odysseus, because Homer's epic of that early traveller is one of the first, if not the first, surviving work to mention sausages.

We are having a lot of fun: if there is a better game than experimenting with combinations of food and wine, in a place that excels at both, I have yet to find it. Still, between copious courses we note the mismatch between a mid-range place like this and the expensive, small-production, limited-availability wines that have drawn tourists to Priorat in the first place. Sometime soon, the boutique hotels will move in, and the place will change – not necessarily for the worse.

It is a beautiful region, whether or not you're interested in the wine, or the ghosts of Romans and monks who were the area's main visitors for so long. The grey crags of the 'holy mountain' – the Montsant mountain range, so named for all the hermits and monasteries it once sheltered – point towards the sky like a promise, or a threat. We are up high, and God must seem very close, for those who might be seeking him.

Not all of whom are Christian. Ten kilometres south of Falset, past a sparkling, pretty stream, is Capçanes, the cooperative that makes wine for much of Barcelona's religious Jewish community. This is a recent development, and an odd one, given that nobody in the village is Jewish, but it was the saving of the winery, which was selling off its grapes for bulk wine before the approach from Barcelona came. Now they have the wherewithal to bottle their own, non-kosher wines, thanks to the

frummers (religious Jews) who move in for a week during harvest. And here is one of the great paradoxes of a
religion that survived 2,000 homeless years by a combination of ruthless practicality and immovable stubbornness. Wine, in Judaism, is essential: ritual, from the
weekly Sabbath to the annual Passover meal, relies on
it, and so it must not be sullied by Gentiles. This means
that only Jews can make it. To quote the Capçanes web-
site: 'Wine, more than any other food or drink, represents the holiness and separateness of the Jewish people.'

It is also a reminder of our very problematic relationship with our God. On the one hand, wine is a gift, a
miracle, and every Friday night, to usher in the Sabbath,
the observant says a prayer (one of the few I actually
know) that praises God as the creator of the vine. On
the other hand, it is a substitute for the lifeblood that
Jews are forbidden to eat, and Judaism, like its descendant, Christianity, uses blood to represent suffering. In the
time of the Temple, wine was poured upon the altar as a
libation, or offering, along with the animal sacrifice; the
latter represented God's gifts, freely received, the former
the blessings that must be worked for – planted, tended,
harvested, pressed and fermented. That giant vine that
Josephus tells us twined around the Temple's entrance
would have left worshippers in no doubt as to the grape's
importance. And after the Temple's destruction in AD 70,
wine, like its creators, had to work harder still, becoming
the substitute for the blood that had been spilled there.

Wine requires human interference to exist. However,
for observant Jews that interference is complicated
because a bottle opened by a Gentile is no longer kosher,
no matter how carefully the wine inside was made. This is
not a biblical prohibition but does seem to coincide with

the beginning of exile. Presumably other religions' habit of pouring libations meant that any wine not made by Jews could, potentially, have been used to sacrifice to foreign gods – a live danger for those living in foreign lands.

It is permitted to buy in grapes, which must have been important for a people who couldn't always bank on staying in one place long enough to grow their own. After that, it's all up to the *frummers*, and the vinifying that would presumably have been carried out at home, once upon a time, now finds a temporary home in complaisant wineries – another metaphor, surely, for the Chosen People's squatting in others' homelands.

Capçanes is an airy, unbeautiful building with young winemakers wandering in and out; when I was there they were preparing for a party in a downstairs room that reminded me a little of a classroom. The winery's non-kosher wines are really good, and excellent value: Mas Collet 2012, a Garnacha blend, is silky yet austere; the more upmarket Cabrida (with a beautiful label of simply sketched goats) is 100 per cent old-vine Garnacha and is a big, rich wine, more bull than goat, that needs cellaring for a while to gentle its tannins.

The kosher wines are different: harsher, brasher, less elegant. This is partly because the oak barrels used are also a blend of dogma and practicality: they would like, says Vanesa, the marketing manager, to change them all every year, since contamination of any kind is such a preoccupation, but that would be insanely expensive, so they change a third annually. This still means very new oak flavours in the wines, although for any observant Jew brought up on a liquid diet of Manischewitz, the grape juice-sweet American kosher wine that is the market's major player, any Capçanes wine really would be manna.

Vanesa has never seen the kosher wine being made, even though she has worked here two years: her outsider status forbids it, although that's about religion, not gender. Unlike the Romans, who at one point permitted a man to kill his drunken wife and suggested that men should kiss their female relatives to check for wine on the breath, Jews do not have strict rules about women and wine; there is no law against a female winemaker although in practice they have been few. And even the Romans, unlike their Greek predecessors, permitted respectable women at the *convivium*, or banquet. So both these ancient peoples were arguably more advanced than certain Burgundians, who until just a few decades ago forbade women to be present in the winery for fear their presence would turn the wine.

Despite the preoccupation with disease and uncleanliness, purity is paramount. Jews are forbidden to use any product except copper sulphate on the grapes, Vanesa tells me: 'It is even more complicated than biodynamic farming.' Why are these wines made here, of all places? I ask her. She shrugs: 'We have a train station, a direct line to Barcelona. It's as simple as that.' Just as the Romans planted vines along the Rhône, their equivalent of a railway line, these Jews are ensuring their wine can travel to where they need it to be. But, but … why go to all this effort and expense when you can just buy in Manischewitz? She looks surprised. 'Because every peoples loves the good wine!'

We drive back past little El Masroig (the name means red, because of the soil, Asens told me), with its bold graffito: '*Ni frontières ni racisme*' (Neither frontiers nor racism), the point surely underlined by the decision to write in French. Further inland, we enter Terra

Alta, another DO, and in the slightly larger town of Gandesa we stop for lunch. The Hotel Piqué dining room is vast, windowed onto a parched road, almost stunning in its absence of atmosphere, like being forced to stare at a white wall for an hour. But the food is really good: slices of octopus studded with purple suckers top a truffley potato puree, and the wine, which has the charming name Somdinou, is a pleasant Garnacha Blanca from the local cooperative. There are two reasons I'm here and that cooperative is the second one: the first is Celler Bàrbara Forés. Both are housed unconventionally, to say the least. But before we go inside, Manolo Sanmartín, who with his wife Carme Ferrer owns Bàrbara Forés, shows us around the vineyards. This takes time: they are dotted in different places, like domaines in Burgundy, although here it is not others' vines that sit between them but a very Mediterranean mosaic of herbs, cereals, olives, almond and hazelnut trees. He picks his way, somewhat gingerly, across a sunny field of Garnatxa Blanca fringed with broom: he recently broke a leg in a cycling accident. The glasses he carries are set down on a barrel that has clearly been left here for just this purpose, and we taste the fruit of last year's harvest, pouring the excess back onto the soil, offering a libation of our own. It's a lovely wine, herbaceous and scented – I can taste the broom that I can see, and this is to me one of wine's greatest delights: it is sensuality purified, liquefied. I look out over the assortment of crops, and it all seems to belong so easefully to this land, as if it had been here forever, which I know it has not.

Why is there so much white Grenache here? I ask Manolo. Because, he says, it is a grape with less strength than red Grenache so it needs more nutrients; the glinting *licorella* in Priorat can't provide them. Here, in a climate between continental and Mediterranean – 'we get two winds, one dry and cold from the land, the other moist, from the sea, which refreshes the canopy of vines,' he explains, 'so they suffer but they don't suffer too much' – these vines, which arrived with a French soldier in 1647, thrive. The wine's restraint, its acidity and almond flavours, all testify to the happiness of the home it has found – with a little human help. There is great continuity, some ancient – amphorae have been dug up here from the second and third centuries BC, so it's possible that even before Roman occupation the Phoenicians traded the local wines – some more modern. Carmen is the fifth generation in the family business: Bàrbara Forés herself was born in the town in 1828. The wine is made in their home, a set-up so odd it's hard to appreciate without seeing it. In a classically proportioned eighteenth-century townhouse, down a tiny Gandesa street, the gracious staircase presumably leads to ordinary accommodation but the ground floor's main room is full of wine vats and the cellars have clusters of oak barrels. It's a tiny space. 'You cannot do things fast here but we are not looking to do them fast, just well,' says Manolo. And they do manage to squeeze in a further instance of continuity: the amphorae they use for the Morenillo, an ancient local variety, because, says Manolo, 'they give micro-oxygenation without woodiness' – that is, they let a little oxygen leach in to gently aerate the wine, which barrels do, but without the oak taste.

The Morenillo goes, with 30 per cent Garnacha, into the silky El Templari 2014, which tastes of juicy dark-green leaves like myrtle or bay, with a touch of redcurrant. I want to grill some red meat to go with it, but Manolo is more specific: grilled duck, he says, or pork cheeks stuffed with thyme.

We talk about the trade that has made this region what it is. The family, after all, is continuing that tradition, their wines sold all over the world and appearing on the lists of top restaurants such as Heston Blumenthal's three-Michelin-starred Fat Duck in Berkshire. Again and again down the centuries, trade has saved the Catalans from the consequences of injudicious political choices, most recently Catalonia's fierce opposition to Franco during the Civil War. There was serious fighting in Gandesa in 1938, says Marc, Manolo's cellarmaster, but the area has certainly recovered: one impetus behind the Catalonian desire for independence is the amount this rich region pays into the communal Spanish pot. I ask them about the problem of Catalonia's disproportionate wealth. 'For Spain it is a problem,' says Marc: 'not for us.' It is strong leaders who forge unity among disparate peoples, but they rarely do so gently. It was a considerable achievement that the Romans did not squash the nations they conquered: obey their rules and pay their taxes and you would be left in peace.

We finish with the equally lovely Coma d'en Pou 2013, with its clove and balsamic and aromatherapy-strong nose, and I regretfully replace my glass, leave the good wine and good conversation and head out of the front door into the sunlight, towards a winery that's less a home than a place of worship. In Falset, before sitting down to lunch in a restaurant so dark I wanted to breathe in some sunlight first, I had wandered down the main street, rounded a corner and found a building resembling a Modernist cathedral, with arched entrance, tall, narrow windows and two immense symmetrical side arms like the long vertical lines of an imposing doorway: an entranceway, perhaps, to a holy realm. And so it was: Celler Cooperatiu 1919 was blazoned on the triptych frontage, and the glorious lines of the vaulted arches above the wine vats seemed to arc in hymn-like praise of wine's original creator. The architect of this marvellous building was César Martinell, a student of the legendary Gaudí; it is one of several such wineries now known, aptly, as wine cathedrals. Gandesa has one, too, and it is extraordinary: a giant white building held aloft by brick arches within. Like all great avant-gardists, Martinell respected the past, and the roof echoes the shape of both oak barrels and amphorae (there is also, to me, a Moorish touch to that white-windowed exterior). Like any self-respecting member of a union movement, Martinell wanted to make life easier for workers – and winemaking can be this well lit and beautifully appointed almost nowhere else. This is what Camille Peters, militating for workers' rights in Champagne, could only dream of. You cannot walk past one of these buildings without understanding the abiding love for wine, and pride in making it, that has powered the industry perhaps since the Phoenicians first pulled in the anchors they had gouged from these hills, loaded their amphorae and sailed off to tell the world about Catalonian wine – and, like all good storytellers, profit from the telling.

It is, I think, no accident that they are called cathedrals. Not just because of wine's holy function, but also because of religion's affinity with trade. It demeans the fervour of Christian belief not one jot to point out that the Church grew wealthy and mighty selling religion. The trader looks forward to profit on earth, the believer to reward in heaven, but both preserve the past in their different ways. In Conca de Barberà, just east of Tarragona, Miguel Torres – owner of one of Spain's best-known wine brands, which bears his name – has been nurturing a plan for over 30 years. 'In the nineteenth century, there were more than a hundred types of vines in Catalonia,' he tells me, when we meet in London. 'Many were lost through phylloxera, and only varieties with high yields replanted. The market was there for quantity, not necessarily quality, so that is what was provided. But a vine never dies ...'

So old vines lurk, in vineyard corners or in nearby forests or bushes. By patient research, Torres, whose company is based in Penedès, a little further east, has managed to recover about 40 of these forgotten varieties since he began his programme in 1983. 'The most successful method is running small ads in the local Catalonian newspaper, telling local winemakers that if you have a vine and you don't know what kind it is, get in touch. We get calls all the time and occasionally it is something of interest.' With the help of the nearby universities of Montpellier and Tarragona, they study the DNA of the vines, look through the ancient books and try to figure out what they have found. 'Usually that doesn't work, so we call them after local places ...' Which is just what the Romans did, thus losing the ancient names; now their names must be replaced in turn.

Here, then, is the vine twice-born in yet another sense – and through the imperatives of trade. We don't think of business, that relentless, insatiable ebb and flow of goods and cash, as an agent of preservation, although if tourism is a form of trade (cultural experience for money, in a world where more and more goods are virtual), then we really should. Torres is doing this because he is a businessman – a very successful one, making wines in every important region in Spain. Two of the rediscovered varieties, Querol and Garro, now make up part of his Gran Muralles wine, along with the better-known Garnacha Tinta (Grenache), Cariñena (Carignan) and Monastrell (Mourvèdre). But he is not only a businessman, any more than Caesar was only a soldier. He is partly, surely, an opportunist – a believer in *carpe diem* (a phrase from a Horace poem that actually means to pluck the day, as you would a grape – it's the same verb used for harvesting vineyards. Press a Latin-based language and drops of wine squeeze out.). He really is plucking the day – and making wine out of it.

So do shoreline traders look both forwards and back-wards, like Janus, the two-faced god I met in Autun. In this vibrant and dynamic part of Spain, even the past becomes a propulsive force. *Terra remota*, once the end of the world, becomes the treasure chest of Spain. Vertiginous vineyards are replanted, and their wines gain worldwide renown. Kosher wine becomes a trade for Gentiles. And the wineries are cathedrals that glo-rify the common man. (And perhaps, now, woman.)

It's exciting – but also, frankly, exhausting. The more sensual, mystical aspects of wine – those that Martial evoked when he wrote of the fragrance of remembered kisses – are hard to find here, except of course in the glass. I am delighted that the vine is proving, once again, its capacity to survive and thrive and conquer oblivion. Still, I need to move on, to a more backward-looking place: down the Via Augusta from the traders to the dreamers, from those who market the past to those who are still inhaling it.

Sara Pérez of Mas Martinet tests the wine she is ageing in amphorae and demijohns

The 'cathedral' of Bodegas Barbadillo in Sanlúcar de Barrameda

6

ANDALUSIA:
Yearning

A palm tree stands in the middle of Rusafa
Born in the West, far from the land of palms.
I said to it: 'How like me you are, far away and in exile,
In long separation from family and friends.
You have sprung from soil in which you are a stranger;
And I, like you, am far from home
May dawn's clouds water you,
streaming from the heavens in a grateful downpour.'

ABD AL-RAHMAN, FIRST EMIR OF CÓRDOBA

(Trans. D. F. Ruggles)

'Since the fall of Carthage, Baetica has been famous for the beauty of its many vineyards,' wrote the Greek geographer-historian Strabo in the first century BC, and, probably, that wasn't a coincidence. Those Carthage-dwellers whose talented vine-tending had made Cato so viciously envious that he had clamoured for the city's destruction would have crossed to the southern third of Spain, and planted vines there. Beautiful, sun-stroked Baetica, which became the Jews' Sepharad, the al–Andalus of the Arab Moors, and now our Andalusia: the Carthaginians were only the first of many to love this land while thinking wistfully of somewhere else.

Right now I am occupying the space next to an upended oak barrel beneath a cohort of pig limbs in El Rinconcillo, a dinky Seville bar so unashamedly appealing to the tourist eye that I imagine it must be authentic. Before we turn back to the past, a moment to contemplate present glories: the slippery, sensual wonder that is *jamon de bellota*, the deep pink, fingernail-thin ham from pigs whose tell-tale *patas negras* (black hooves) have ranged daintily beneath oak trees, fattening in spacious luxury – the rules decree two acres per pig – on the acorns that they somehow transmute into savoury flesh laced with melting white fat. To be an observant Jew or Muslim is to call this delight an abomination, and if shapely dark pig legs hang from bars all over Spain, and every other dish seems sprinkled with ham, that is testament to the ascendancy of the one religion that has no problem whatsoever with pig meat. Under Ferdinand and Isabella, the Spanish Inquisition tried to make sure that all Spain was Christianised, by converting the willing and killing the reluctant, and the *mozarabes* (Arab converts) and *conversos* (their Jewish equivalent) must have sprinkled herds' worth of ham and choked it down to demonstrate their change of faith – a bitter parody of the function of food to preserve life. I will always remember food writer Claudia Roden's description, in her book *The Food of Spain*, of Torquemada, the first Grand Inquisitor, standing on a hill of a Saturday, surveying rooftops to see if there were smokeless chimneys: secret Jews, observing their Sabbath by abstaining from lighting a fire (work forbidden on the day of rest). I imagine he checked ham consumption, too. His calculating murderousness is only made more sinister by the knowledge that he himself came from a family of *conversos*.

There is no chair to go with my barrel, which is probably a good thing since otherwise I'd be sitting below my food: tangy *boquerones* (fresh anchovies in vinegar), creamy *croquetas* – with ham, of course – and terrible little dry breadsticks that look like fodder for pigs. I'm drinking Manzanilla sherry and inhaling the ocean. Manzanilla is only made in Sanlúcar de Barrameda, the little coastal town from which Magellan sailed to circumnavigate the globe (carrying, they say, more sherry than weaponry, in an echo of William of Normandy's arrival on the Sussex coast laden with casks of wine). There is no reasonable explanation for the fact that wine aged here smells and tastes saltier than those aged down the road in Jerez de la Frontera. But that in no way lessens the pleasures of either.

Wine was an abomination to the Muslims yet rarely did a Jew or Christian force it on them, although some of them certainly drank of their own volition, and al-Motamid, last Moorish king of Seville, would publicly mock water-drinkers. Nor was it banned, although production certainly decreased, during the centuries of Moorish rule, between the eighth century and the final expulsion in 1492. When, that same year, the Jews were expelled from Spain, they still owned sufficient vineyards for 30 *aranzadas* (just over 100sq.m) to be confiscated and given to the Royal Convent of Santo Domingo.

There is one man I know of who was forced to drink alcohol in contradiction of his faith, and that was in Spain, in Valencia, halfway between my first stop and my second. However, his persecutor was a fellow Muslim. Ibn Jubayr was secretary to Granada's ruler in the late twelfth century, when the Moors who had first flowed across the Mediterranean 400 years before ruled half Spain. His royal boss forced him to drink seven cups of wine, then remorsefully filled the emptied goblet seven times with coins in repentance, and that money fuelled an eventful pilgrimage that has survived via his writings. This was wandering powered by vines – but, mainly, those who wanted wine, who needed it for their religious festivals and believed in its transcendent power, were not obstructed. The Moors were making so much money taxing non-Muslims with protected status that a special word, *dhimmi*, was used for them – and perhaps they calculated that everyone would eventually convert, anyway. Certainly, there were financial and social incentives to do so, as well as periodic use of threats or force. When the Moors arrived in the eighth century – Umayyads from Syria, fleeing a transfer of power – the vast majority of Iberians were Christians. Two hundred years later, most were Muslims.

Culinary evidence of ancient persecution aside, I love the layering of one culture, one religion, upon another in Andalusia. Even before I reach the famous Cathedral in Córdoba, it is everywhere. In Seville, I visit Santa Maria la Blanca, a church, decorated in the gorgeously excessive curlicues of the Andalusian Baroque, which has been both mosque and synagogue; it reminds me of the early Church's passion for building its places of worship on top of Roman temples, as it did in Tarragona. I see it as both an assertion of supremacy and a tacit acknowledgement that the other lot may have been onto something, if only geographically – rather like planting vines where your forefathers did, even if your winemaking methods are entirely different and you rather despise theirs.

I travel a few kilometres north across the Guadalquivir river, the Romans' Baetis, for which they named the province. Italica, one of the first cities the Romans founded abroad, is impressive, even if the earliest vestiges are inaccessible beneath the modern satellite town of Santiponce, although, as I discover later, there is one way to see some of that buried treasure.

Like so many others, this city was founded by victorious Roman generals rewarding their veterans with land – in this case, by Scipio Africanus, after defeating Hannibal in the Second Punic War. Three hundred years later, in AD 98, two natives of Baetica became Emperor in succession. Hadrian, who succeeded his cousin Trajan, had a fondness for the grandiose gesture that will be familiar to anyone who has seen his wall between England and Scotland: in his birthplace, then a town of 8,000 inhabitants, he built an amphitheatre big enough to hold 25,000 people – so, half the size of Rome's. Still, it has outlasted him by 2,000 years, in surprisingly good condition given the Sevillanos' long-standing tendency to use Italica for building materials. The floor mosaics up the hill have survived, too, and some of them are surprisingly playful: even the animals being hunted in one black and white composition appear to be having fun. These former internal floors of wealthy houses look now like the unearthed roots of this city, unintentionally exposed to the elements. Which, while I'm there, are much in evidence: it pours, obscuring the hardy remains of an ancient metropolis and turning the amphitheatre sand (the Spanish for sand is still *arena*, from the Latin) to yellow-grey soup. We hop puddle after puddle in that bare, round space where men once conducted intimate battles they termed entertainment. I am aware that complaining of rain in southern Spain is like whingeing to a starving person that you need to lose a few kilos, and you can't, in theory, love wine and hate rain, since without it there isn't any, but that's just theory: I am a Londoner and I find rain a bore, particularly when wandering round a city that hasn't owned a roof since the second century AD.

We drive back into modern Seville, the city of orange blossom, via a bridge overlooking a gargantuan Carthusian monastery that was once Christopher Columbus's burial place. He has since been moved several times, and there is ongoing debate about which sets of bones – one in Seville, one in Santo Domingo – are actually his, meaning, arguably, that the discoverer of the New World is now in both worlds at once. ('There are two Spains', Xavier repeats in my head.) What would Columbus have thought of the changes his discoveries set in motion? The secular equivalent of that Carthusian monstrosity is the eighteenth-century Royal Factory, a tobacco factory that resembles a palace, complete with moat. It would have had guards to protect the wealth flowing in from New World tobacco plantations, and been the fount of thousands of livelihoods. Many, many lives and loves would have played out within its influence. No wonder the nineteenth-century French writer Prosper Mérimée made his gypsy Carmen a *cigarrera*, one of the feisty cigarette girls 'not noted for their chastity' who worked there, and Don José, the man who so disastrously falls for her, a factory guard.

Impossible to ignore this pseudo-palace but very easy to miss a genuine one, with an even more surprising story. At the beginning of the last century, the Condesa de Lebrija, a wealthy arts lover, acquired some ancient mosaics. Her purchases were legal, an Elgin-like attempt to save these artefacts from raiders and construction in Santiponce, and she probably succeeded, although as with Elgin and the Parthenon Marbles, removing chunks of the national patrimony would not be looked on so kindly now. She reshaped the entire ground floor of her sixteenth-century palace in central Seville to fit her finds – she really must have been extremely well off – and filled the upper floor with more recent treasures. It is hard to escape the notion that she must have been compulsive in her collecting – there is so very much here. But as a visual evocation of the city's layers of history it's brilliant.

From a hot street we walk into darkness, and a stern man demanding payment. The walls are coated in eighteenth-century tiles: five elegant, blue and gold robed young ladies surrounded by lutes and birds, leaves and glowing fruit, represent the five senses. Gusto (taste) proffers what looks like a decanter, although she can't be enjoying its contents much: the only missing tile seems to be the one that should feature her head. The floors are laid with complete mosaics, some patterned, some with figures; the walls decorated with fragments. The open courtyard, with its Moorish arches, has a 2,000-year-old floor of medallions in which gods fight, recline, or simply stare out at the modern mortal. Other rooms contain coins, statues and marble columns, a depiction of Bacchus in a chariot drawn by two tigers – twin symbols of alcohol's dangers and freedoms, seeming to bound across the centuries towards Gusto's frivolous decanter. Upstairs, the marquetry and paintings, the Limoges porcelain and Baccarat crystal are carefully arranged out of tourists' reach, their splendid isolation far less satisfying than the earthy immediacy of the ancient stones downstairs.

Just a street away there's an even more startling example of modernity layered over the past: the Antiquarium. While excavating for a car park in 2003, the remains of several Roman villas and a fish-salting plant were found. The mosaics are lovely, including a drinking vessel in the Caso de Baco (House of Bacchus), two lovebirds kissing and a Medusa, still with a couple of blue locks. Why would anyone decorate their floor with a ghastly creature best known for a coiffure of poisonous snakes and the habit of turning observers to stone? Because, it turns out, Medusa is also an icon of protection: her awful head, given by her slayer Perseus to Athena, goddess of wisdom, was placed on the latter's shield, and her evil power thus turned to beneficial use. She protected homes all over the Iberian peninsula and Hadrian, the Iberian Emperor who at one point offered to rebuild the Jerusalem Temple, on condition that a statue of himself as Jupiter was placed inside, unwisely laid claim to another divine prerogative by placing Medusa on the centre of his own shield.

The Antiquarium is now in the foundations of an 'urban centre', the former salting factory lurking beneath restaurants whose condiments the Romans could not have imagined. And an extraordinary structure rears above both centre and road, like a parody of a Roman monument. The Metropol Parasol is a latticed timber monstrosity that resembles an alien invasion – the kind of oozing horror that could turn a Medusa to stone. The locals call it *las Setas de Sevilla* (the Seville mushrooms) but to me, despite its wooden frame and sunken roots, it feels untethered from the city's history. What resonates in my imagination are the Antiquarium's mosaics, the damaged oil lamps in a format that remained unchanged between the first century and the eighteenth, and the belief – the certainty – embedded in that snake-wreathed head that their ancients had used the same forms of protection as they did. It doesn't matter, I reflect, as I head for Santa Cruz, whether you actually believe these stories: as with the phantom vines on Kentish hills, their existence tells us something about what we long for. Perhaps the giant mushrooms' existence does, too, although for the life of me I can't work out what.

Santa Cruz, which means Holy Cross, was once the Jewish quarter in a city with the biggest Jewish community in Spain. It is delightful, this tourist hub with its tiny winding streets and pretty squares, but the willed invisibility of its former residents is disconcertingly apparent in much more than that dogmatic name. A high wall in an appealing patchwork of styles bears a sign reminding us that this was the eleventh-century city boundary, built by the Moors and still featuring the embedded pipes that brought water to the royal palace and the city during the Christian era, but there's nothing to tell me that this is one of only two remaining segments of the wall of the Jewish ghetto. I see no *mezzuzim*, the little oblong symbol, containing a prayer scroll, which every Jewish doorway displays, some evidence of which often survives the inhabitants' departure. Santa Cruz itself is no longer the church it once was: the French, in a bitter case of poetic justice, razed it during the Napoleonic Wars, and now it houses the French consulate, a more amusing example of historical amnesia. Of that vanished church's previous life as a synagogue, the only evidence is the central garden's tiny plaque. In the little Jewish Interpretation Centre, which has no interesting relics but many stories of persecution, I am guided towards another example of disappearance: the Jewish cemetery near the Jardines de Murillo, which became a car park. There is a single remaining tomb: go to basement level, pretend you are searching for your car, and there, in bay 9, it is.

This elision and erosion may be a result of expulsion – what else does an expelling force aim for, but to wipe out all memory of whatever, or whoever, is being expelled? – but it is not anti-Semitism. It is the inevitable layer of sediment that accrues over bulky outcrops of truth on which later generations might otherwise trip. Causing pain, like experiencing it, is too uncomfortable to hold in mind. Standing in that ludicrous parking bay, I am overwhelmed by the feeling that the past is, essentially, unrecoverable in its original form, no matter how deeply we inhale, or how far down we dig. Even drinking, I say gloomily to C, is simultaneously an act of remembrance and a consignment of this particular moment to oblivion, an encroaching amnesia at least as powerful as any percentage proof.

As I walk back through the Alcázar gardens, the lush grounds of a Moorish palace between Santa Maria la Blanca and the Tobacco Factory, I pass a giant column dedicated to Christopher Columbus, with its bald date of 1492. It looks terribly out of place, this monument to conquest, planted like a spear amid the orderly gardens, their heady flowers chosen to remind the Moorish incumbents at every inhalation of their distant Arabic home. As if in phantom echo of that long-ago yearning, I catch sight and scent of an enormous eucalyptus tree, and the distinctive stripped bark and cool menthol breath offers a sudden, insistent reminder of Australia, provoking a nostalgia of my own, so sharp it is almost painful. It is time to move on.

The wines of Bodegas Forlong in Puerto de la Santa Maria aim to take me simultaneously back to the past and into the future, which is a little ambitious. Alejandro Narvaez, who used to work for a Grand Cru Classé, Château Smith Haut Lafitte, has swapped the gravelly soil of Graves in Bordeaux for the *albariza* (chalk) of Andalusia. He has planted a local grape, Tintilla de Rota, as well as the sherry grapes Palomino and Pedro Ximénez and, further towards Jerez, the international varieties Syrah, Merlot and Cabernet Sauvignon. His wines are organic, and fermented using indigenous yeasts, those that have chosen to make their home in his winery, rather than commercial ones. His tiny winery has barrels – but also man-sized *dolia* in which he is trying to bring back the ancient techniques. He even ferments some of his wine with herbs or cinnamon. 'My wines have a flavour very similar to the Romans' wines because they are very mineral,' Alejandro says seriously, and I have too much respect for his dedication and for his wines, which are pleasant if a bit lacking in length or memorability, to raise my eyebrows.

He fines (that is, softens the wines and clears them of sediment) using egg whites, which a lot of people do: the gunk adheres to the egg and sinks to the bottom. But it's the enormous variety in vintages that really shows how unmodern these wines are. Assemblage 2014, which is 60 per cent Merlot, 30 per cent Tintilla and 10 per cent Syrah is aromatic but light, tasty but without much staying power, while the 2013 feels much richer, headier and more structured. Few modern wines fluctuate to quite this extent, so advanced have we become in the field and the winery. Although most winemakers understand that the fantasy of human control of nature is just that. And we still cannot control the weather.

The Tintilla 2014 has a lovely blackberry and cinnamon mouth and great freshness but, again, no length. It's odd, because Alejandro supplements those impressive *dolia* with time in oak, but the idea of these lasting years like the Romans' legendary Falernian is impossible to credit. I prefer his whites, and they are fermented in stainless steel, with built-in temperature-controlling equipment – that is, about as far from ancient methods as you can get.

Columella, first-century AD author of the 12-volume *De Re Rustica*, one of the most important works on Roman agriculture we have, would have appreciated this tasting. He was very clear on the importance of paying attention to the ancients, while simultaneously weighing their knowledge against modern gains. A little down the coast is Cadiz, and the narrow Strait of Gibraltar that serves as gateway to the Mediterranean, the sea the Romans called their own: Mare Nostrum. Cadiz, like Empúries, was a great Greek and Roman city – once given preferential treatment, and indeed

Roman citizenship, by Julius Caesar himself – that has faded away, if not quite to the same extent as its northern counterpart. 'Nobody even knows who this is,' says Manuel gloomily, gesturing at the marble statue of what looks like a young man holding a sickle aloft, his other hand resting on a yoke for oxen. Here he is, Lucius Junius Moderatus Columella – a native of Gades, as Cadiz was called then, and a man after my own heart. 'This, with very good reason, we prefer to all other stems whatsoever,' he wrote of the vine, waxing lyrical about its wondrous adaptability while warning that place nonetheless played a vital role: 'For its cultivation is not the same in every climate and in every soil … and which kind is best of all is not easy to say, since experience teaches that to every region its own variety is more or less suited.'

How should we define this 'own variety': as the most native, or as the most congenial? There are ancient echoes here of a very modern argument: who is best suited to this soil, he (or she) who was born to it, or the person best placed to extract nourishment from it? This was not, in human terms, a Roman argument. The whole world could be Roman, and without giving up its own ethnic identity, because that was not a concept the Romans understood, according to Mary Beard. She has said they were the first to come up with this dual idea of nationality, one that does not seem to have thrived since, although it exists just fine in the world of wine, where so-called international varieties – Cabernet Sauvignon, Sauvignon Blanc, Shiraz – can be simultaneously as local as the ground they grow in. A California Cab, a New Zealand Sauv or an Aussie Shiraz is a well-settled immigrant, one that can often coexist happily, in the same soil or even the same bottle, with grapes so local that nobody else has heard of them.

Manuel is not so preoccupied with grape varieties as with ways of turning those grapes into wine. He is an archaeologist with a consuming interest in consumables. He and his friends, like the Durands at Mas des Tourelles, are trying to make wine that is supposedly Roman in style. Once again, I do not share with him my suspicion that Roman wine – white and sweet and probably oxidised, pitchy from the resin used to seal the amphorae, awash with honey or herbs or even chalk dust, and diluted with water – would have been disgusting to modern palates, although this, while certainly strange, is not.

I can see why this weird project has ensnared him. It is not so different from my own, although Manuel is very focused on Cadiz. It is one of the oldest cities in Western Europe; this whole patch of coast has been washed by tides of wanderers. The Phoenicians arrived after being thrown out of their original homeland, Canaan, by Moses's followers, claiming their Promised Land. (They can't have held on to their resentment, since according to the Bible they later gave King Solomon wood to help build the First Temple in Jerusalem.) They gouged Spain's northern hills for lead for their anchors, as we have seen, and in the south they dug out precious metals, but they also planted vines. Their heirs include Columella, who followed his own logic by planting a vineyard here, on his home patch, that Manuel and his friends reckon they have found, around 40km south of Jerez, then called Ceret, near San Fernando on the Arillo river. The poet Martial, born further north in Iberia, praised Ceretanum, the local wine, in an epigram that announced it good enough to keep for close friends. (He was clearly a nicer man than Voltaire, that craven Burgundy-lover whose measure of quality was wine you hid from friends.) And later beneficiaries of that Phoenician and Roman toil were the winemakers, some of them English, who would make Jerez famous for a strangely wonderful wine, the descendant of Martial's Ceretanum: sherry.

'This place was very important for a long, long time,' says Manuel. 'There was a Temple of Hercules here and everyone came with offerings.' He gestures out, across the hot, white square, with its flower stalls and prettily pastel buildings, towards the Gibraltar Straits. Many of those offerings would have been liquid: clearly, you wanted as much divine help as was available to sail through those fearsome rocks unscathed. Amphorae have been found all over the region, and equipment for making them was uncovered at Barrio Jarana, in 2004, along with a Roman villa; the surviving mosaic is almost certainly of Bacchus.

Baetica gave Rome wine, writers and emperors; some of this was repaid in wealth and influence. There should also be a statue to Cornelius Lucius Balbus, the Phoenician banker from Cadiz who was friends with General Pompey and the poet Cicero, and became banker to Pompey's friend and eventual nemesis, Julius Caesar. This earned him honour (he was Rome's first ever foreign-born Consul, and probably won Latin rights, one step below Roman citizenship, for his native city) and immense wealth. Much of the booty from the Gallic Wars went through his hands, and some of it evidently stayed there: it is said that when he died he left 20 denarii to every Roman citizen. He is supposed to have dined with Caesar the night after the latter crossed the Rubicon. This was a fateful move – bringing an army into Rome's domain, a treasonable act that would lead to civil war and ultimately, the fall of the Republic – and as usual, I find myself wondering what they might have drunk. Sangiovese, or an early equivalent, from the hilly east coast of Romagna, perhaps. That is where the Rubicon lies, even if nobody can agree on precisely which river it was. Still, some of the best Sangiovese clones in Tuscany come from here, although it is Chianti and Brunello di Montalcino, both a couple of hundred kilometres west, that now produce the greatest Sangiovese wines.

In the Bodeguilla del Bar Jamón restaurant in Puerto de la Santa Maria, we try out some of Manuel's Roman wines, which he bottles under the label Baetica, on some carefully researched Roman-style dishes. *Mulsum* was the honey-sweetened wine that was distributed, along with *crustulum* (pastry) to the people of Rome in exchange for political support; the young chef, Borja Fernández Serrano, pairs it with Cadiz bay anchovies with citrus and garum, the Romans' fish sauce. The wine smells but doesn't taste sweet, and the match works surprisingly well.

Later, after pig shoulder carpaccio with plankton oil and anchovy pâté, meatball covered with almonds and served with almond sauce, and a fried bread dessert soaked in wine and drenched in melted chocolate, I get Manuel to acknowledge that the base of all these wines is Cabernet Sauvignon, hardly an ancient variety. Still, so what? Even the violet wine Antinoo is savoury and drinkable, and Mesalina, which is cinnamon flavoured, works with both the meatball and the dessert. Stronger than the spice, I can taste the longing to roll the past around one's mouth. Louis Barruol's dismissive description of wines such as Baetica and Domaine des Tourelles as 'business', while not entirely wrong, misses this desire to reach across the abyss that separates us from the ancients and really taste history. Manuel holds Roman-style feasts in suitably venerable locations, including the grounds of Italica. They sound convivial, in the Roman sense, although I can't imagine they cut their wine with water. I can imagine Martial, who wrote mouth-wateringly of preparing for a banquet, thoroughly approving. 'All shall be seasoned with pleasantry free from bitterness,' he wrote, at the end of a menu that included lettuces and leeks, mint for flatulence, sow's teats in tunny sauce, chicken, and 'a ham which has already appeared at table three times'. He goes on: 'there shall be no licence of speech that brings repentance on the morrow, and nothing said that we should wish unsaid. But my guests may speak of the rival factions in the circus, and my cups shall make no man guilty.' Now, really, who can argue with that?

When we get home to our own oak table, C will Google the recipes of the Roman gourmet Apicius (from a book which was more likely a compendium of others' dishes published under his name) and try making his distinctive Roman sweet-sour dishes using Baetica's flor de garum, a light version of the fermented fish sauce which every culture seems to have in some form or another. (Ours would be Worcestershire sauce, which contains anchovies.) We will both rapidly become addicted to its slightly fishy tang; it's a marvellous flavour-enhancer and must have been more so for a culture with a far smaller range of available foodstuffs, none of them artificial. For the last drops of the bottle, he makes lamb chops with cavolo nero and potatoes with garlic and flor de garum and a multi-coloured tomato and shallot salad with sherry vinegar and basil, and I open two of my father's wines from Bandol in Provence, a Lafran-Veyrolles Bandol 2000 and a Domaine de Terrebrune 1990. Neither is remotely drinkable. They are old and irredeemably faded; the Terrebrune is a little corked. There is, I point out, something glumly appropriate about this. Try to taste the past and you risk drinking vinegar. So we drink the Wine Society's Exhibition Shiraz 2010, made by Mount Langi Ghiran a couple of hours west of Melbourne, and toast the Old World with a wine from the New.

I'm going next to Sanlúcar de Barrameda, I tell Manuel, and he nods: 'You'll eat good fish there – *estupendo!*' And, he has no need to add, you will drink sherry.

Nobody knows how the strange method of making sherry came about, but I am very glad it did. The new-fermented wine, made within the triangle of Jerez, Sanlúcar and Puerto de Santa Maria, is aged in a *solera* system, which means that it is poured into the first of successive layers of butts (barrels), usually stacked, then is transferred to the next, topping up the year before and being topped up in its turn, and so on until the final row, when it is bottled and the space created by that bottling allows the topping-up cycle to continue. This means that sherry, like soil, is never just the product of a single year, but an aggregate. It means that the barrels in which it ages are so old that Javier Hidalgo tells me that some in his bodega (winery) are from Napoleon's time. The dirt on them is so layered it is like a visible equivalent of the wine within: time powdered, instead of liquefied. And Hidalgo, who says his grandmother told him never to sell the bodega – 'It is a terrible way to make a living but a nice way to live' – is an accrual of generations of sherry-makers, rather like his wine, in style if not in substance. The Hidalgos have documents back to 1792 but were here for at least a couple of generations before that, so Javier is a man who works every day of his life among his ancestors and their sloughed-off cells, which must surely make up some of this dark barrel-coating. He has inherited, and must live with, their decisions on grapes and wine, their name on bottles (and on the enormous bodega), and their medals in the little tiled office. And he is also stuck with their Manzanilla brand La Gitana, whose name comes from the nineteenth-century gypsy who used to deliver the casks from the tavern to the fish-ermen in Malaga harbour; they called it 'El Vino de la Gitana' – the gypsy lady's wine. Although putting up with La Gitana's phenomenal success is probably not much of a hardship.

There is another powdered layer crucial to the drier styles of sherry – flor, a yeast that lives in this part of the world and that naturally accumulates on the sherry after fermentation, quilting the young wine and protecting it from oxygen, as well as imparting a specific, Marmitey flavour. Flor changes between Jerez and Sanlúcar de Barrameda, which is why the driest sherry, called Fino in the former, is Manzanilla in the latter. 'Flor is very choosy, it likes a very moderate, humid climate, here more than elsewhere,' says Hidalgo. In other words, it likes the seaside: no wonder the inhabitants have such a healthy respect for salt that they even have a church dedicated to the Madonna of the Perspiration! I tell him that those with a scientific cast of mind point out that there is no reason for sherry aged in Sanlúcar to taste salty. Hidalgo shrugs: 'I cannot explain it but it is true' – and we touch glasses in a swift toast to the inexplicable: the murky layers of human ignorance, too infrequently acknowledged.

Hidalgo has wines named for the Napoleonic Wars, including a Palo Cortado for private consumption called Wellington and an Amontillado called Napoleon. That seems very, er, diplomatic, I say, as he dips a *venencia*, an ancient instrument that resembles a shot glass on a long stem, into each barrel for me to taste. Again, that shrug: 'My family supplied both sides. Business is business.' I am reminded of Xavier, in Barcelona, drawing distinctions between the warmongers and the traders. Wine purveyors are necessarily the latter, viewing the sea as a trade route rather than a path to glory and conquest. This Javier (the spelling is Spanish as opposed to Catalan) is a peaceable fellow, who likes bird-watching in the marshes with another scion of an ancient sherry family, Beltran Domecq, now head of the sherry regulatory board. ('Estevez, Domecq – every family has these names,' another sherry-maker tells me.) When I met Beltran for lunch in London, he told me all about *albariza*, the white chalk of this country that opens up to allow moisture in the autumn, then closes tight in spring to keep it safe for the vine roots in summer. Champagne's sunny southern sister, I think, picturing an undulating wave of chalk beneath Europe, humping up here, to the north of the continent and then beyond Dover. Beltran seemed like a human equivalent – one of those families who surfaced in Jerez to make sherry generations ago, yet have stayed English in a way that few residents of our rainy island have. 'We were forbidden to speak Spanish at home', he explained in his cut-glass accent: 'our mother and nanny wouldn't allow it'.

This is Jerez's own *solera*, these men with generations of sherry percolating through their blood. One Spanish, the other – well, what is he? If you ask how long a family can stay in one place yet continue to be foreign, through sheer bloody-mindedness, the Jew in me will answer: a long time.

The Napoleon is lovely and bready with a touch of bitter orange. Age Fino or Manzanilla after the flor has died off, so that oxygen seeps in and enriches the wine, and it will become Amontillado, a deeper, lusher style; administer a judicious dose of alcohol to kill the yeast, preventing it from maturing under flor at all, and it will be Oloroso. This is the next move up the sherry scale towards sweetness – still dry, but round and full and more alcoholic. Hidalgo and Domecq don't understand why more Oloroso isn't sold, given that it is perfect with nuts or Manchego cheese or oxtail or beef cheek … I was once told to drizzle it over steak as I griddled it, then drink it as an accompaniment to the meat, and that was good advice. Hidalgo's is old, orange again but the fruit is candied now, the scent of Christmas pudding.

All these wines are made from the Palomino grape and, with the exception of the relatively rare and much-beloved Palo Cortado, where the flor dies inexplicably in the middle of the process, all are created by human influence. Those humans have come here from many places. Domecq's family are originally French: they were aristocrats, accorded the privilege of presenting each successive monarch with a pair of white gloves, until the Revolution called time on such telling oddities. But there are also names like Williams & Humbert or Osborne that signal the Britishness of some wanderers who ended up here – merchants intending to profit from their countrymen's thirst for heady Spanish wine. The fourteenth-century English poet Chaucer (whose father was a wine merchant) wrote of sherry's dangerous but alluring 'fumositee' – still, surely, the best word to describe a wine so pungent that you can, as Jan Pettersen of Bodega Fernando de Castilla pointed out to me, just wave your hand over your stationary glass and wonderful scents will curl into your nostrils. There is no need to bend over and sniff.

Do writers find that many-storied sense of history particularly appealing? Or perhaps, like me, they simply love the wine. Shakespeare put some of the most resounding praise of sherry (known, then, as sack or sherris-sack) into the mouth of his bon viveur Falstaff, who has, as he himself admits, 'a whole school of tongues in this belly of mine': sack makes the wit nimble and the blood warm, which in turn renders the heart courageous, 'So that skill in the weapon is nothing without sack, for that sets it a-work; and learning a mere hoard of gold kept by a devil, till sack commences it and sets it in act and use.' Prince Harry, he says, is valiant because 'the cold blood he did naturally inherit of his father, he hath, like lean, sterile and bare land,

manured, husbanded and tilled with excellent endeav-
our of drinking good and good store of fertile sherris,
that he is become very hot and valiant'. And he ends
with the resounding call that has echoed down the
centuries: 'If I had a thousand sons, the first humane
principle I would teach them should be, to forswear
thin potations and to addict themselves to sack.'

Shakespeare was writing less than a century after the
English sea captain and buccaneer Sir Francis Drake
had plundered Cadiz, destroyed part of the Spanish
Armada and carried off, along with his treasure, a fair
portion of sherry. The wine's popularity in England
barely wavered until the twentieth century although
its centre, Jerez de la Frontera (the frontier in question
being between Christian and Moorish Spain), now has
the dilapidated beauty – the peeling buildings, grandiose Gothic or Mudéjar churches and smelly drains – of
a place whose time has been. The wanderers' wine still
travels the world, although too many associate sherry
with the caramel sweetness of Harvey's Bristol Cream.
True sherry lovers prefer Pettersen's wines, or those of
others who, like him, say they would not make a wine
they themselves aren't happy to drink.

In Bodegas Tradición, the barrels are stacked in high,
cavernous rooms that look like churches and are called
cathedrals, which puts me in mind of the Catalonian
wine cathedrals of César Martinell: how easily wine and
religion blend! Here, the bready, slightly sweet smell of
sherry rises in an intoxicating miasma, lighting the brain
with gastronomic promise like the olfactory equivalent of
a stained-glass window. Some of the walls, smeared above
with black fungus like a child's finger painting, are four
metres thick and date from the eleventh century, when

they enclosed the city. They keep the place cool, which is essential in this climate: the *merma*, or angels' share – the part that evaporates through the wood as the wine ages – is 4 or 5 per cent here, which is a pretty hefty votive offering.

Bodegas Tradición is, appropriately enough, a layering of old and new. Joaquin Rivero's family have been sherry-makers since about 1650 but this company began in the 1990s, with the purchase of barrels of fine old sherries with which to begin the topping-up process. This means that all their sherries are old, an obeisance to history that may make marketing sense (and may say something about Rivero's feeling for his venerable family name) but is entirely contrary to the current vogue for *en rama* sherries. These are young, almost unfiltered wines that need drinking early, so standing as a gentle corrective (should one be needed) to the long-opened sherry bottle, going cloudy and faintly rancid on a drinks cabinet shelf. Still, there's nothing fusty about the wines I'm trying – the Amontillado is what cellar-master Pepe Blandino calls a '*rompe copa*' – that is, bright enough to break the glass.

And when I have viewed the cathedral and the sacristy (another churchy name, this time for the private store of precious old sherries), a miracle awaits. In a small art gallery within those ancient walls, a different type of Spanish treasure, some of it not much younger: art. The owners love their native painters, and here I find Goya and Velázquez, close enough to stroke. (Are the paintings covered in an infinitesimal, invisible layer of sherry via the fumes from the bodega and the ecstatic sighs of post-tasting visitors? I like to think so.) I admire the gold leaf and lurid, fairy-tale figures of a late fourteenth-century altarpiece by Juan de Levi, even as his name sets a familiar bell dinging in my brain – and, sure enough, this painter of the Passion is from a family of Jewish converts. He would have witnessed the massacre of 1391, a decade before painting this celebration of Christ's martyrdom; a century later, his great-grandchildren would have been exiled or murdered when the Jews were forced out of Spanish territories.

But here in this room I can move painlessly on through Spain's past: the gloomy but graceful Saint Francis of Assisi by El Greco, the luminous grapes of El Labrador, so accurate that scientists are using them to learn about seventeenth-century viticulture, or the gap-toothed, cigar-puffing bullfighter in the Napoleonic hat by the nineteenth-century painter José Jiménez Aranda. How, I wonder, did the wine they drank taste? It can have resembled ours very little, what with the pre-phylloxera grapes and the early vinifying methods. Those who have tasted pre-phylloxera wines (and they are mainly millionaires) claim they far outpace even the finest modern wines, but I think of the first-century AD Romans praising 200-year-old Falernian, and I wonder. I suspect rarity has a flavour all its own.

I stare until Daniel, the kind employee acting as my guide, shows signs of despairing of ever again seeing his wife and family, and then remember I am supposed to taste his wines. A two-year-old Fino from a very old bodega resembles an infant crown prince from a venerable line; another, 12 years in bottle, is appley with a touch of walnut, and buttery (*untuoso*, says Daniel, nodding). There's a lovely Palo Cortado, redolent of oranges; and an *añada* – a rare vintage sherry – from

1975, soft and creamy with a buzz of acidity and a squirt of bitter orange right at the back of the mouth, a very unserious wine but terrific.

Up a glass-walled staircase is an office full of ancient books and mementos – the undrinkable detritus of winemakers' pasts, including a certificate for relics from Admiral Nelson's ship, bought at a charity benefit for sailors in 1805. The list is interesting but the treasures itemised, including a scrap of the HMS *Victory*'s flag, are long evaporated – the archivist's equivalent of the angels' share.

What with the range of wines and the range of paintings, I feel like a pianist executing a glissando on a chronological keyboard; I slip back into the dusty streets beyond the towered wall dizzy, and slightly dislodged from my place in time.

So the ring road around Jerez is a shock – as is the gargantuan set of buildings behind it. Bodegas Marqués del Real Tesoro is nearly three centuries old but its sprawling home is not: when Grupo Estevez bought the company in the 1980s, they moved it here from a beautiful but impractical old building in central Jerez. I wait in an enormous courtyard, surrounded by windows but covered with a canvas roof to fend off the heat. Even these slightly cooler temperatures must be hard on the antiques with which that room is stuffed. There are beautiful *bargueños* – two-tiered wooden portable writing desks, popular in Renaissance Spain and particularly appealing to a wandering writer – and I have never seen so many grandfather clocks in one place. These tall oblongs of gracious history, some 400 years old, require the weekly services of a professional clock winder to align them with the minutes they defy.

The man responsible for all this collecting, José Estévez de los Reyes, was a self-made, Jerez-born entrepreneur who loved sherry, art and horses, and the silica mine he developed and then sold freed him to indulge those passions to an extraordinary degree. As we trot upstairs to see the labelling room and then a mezzanine over the enormous 'cathedral', or sherry store, we pass collections of silver and of elephants, more grandfather clocks, and art that ranges from fascinating (early Salvador Dalí and Antoni Tàpies, both from Catalonia) to, frankly, not very good: there are several enormous paintings by a friend of the family that incorporate Señor Estevez's beloved horses, their trainer and various employees of the company.

In the bar I taste through a selection of their sherries, including La Guita, the crisp, almond-flower wine that is one of my favourite Manzanillas, and an *en rama* version (this one entirely unfiltered, since it isn't travelling anywhere), which has a bit of oxidation and a touch of cellar nose but also honey and sea air – all, surely, attributes that ancient wines might well have displayed. They are a big company with many sherries, but some stand out. Don Gonzalo Oloroso, a VOS (*Vinum Optimum Signatum*, or sherry aged over 20 years) named for the thirteenth-century knight Don Gonzalo Valdespino who, they say, was given vineyards as thanks for helping to drum the Moors out of Jerez, has a nose like fresh wood, a mouth of caramel, coffee, citrus peel and a bit of tar, and a valedictory sweetness, like an airborne parting kiss. The VOS designation and its older brother, *Vinum Optimum Rarum Signatum*, which signals 30-plus years ageing, are controversial, because, really, how can you tell the age of a wine blended with other wines over years? And isn't 20 or 30 years a fairly random number anyway? To me what's more important is that this wine is delicious, and that some version of it – wine from the same vineyards, at least – would have been drunk by the Romans, by the Jews who followed them here and by others of various nationalities and persuasions, all the way down to my father, who always had a bottle of good dry sherry in the fridge door, to divert his sharpening appetite as he cooked – never a swift process, although the results, when they finally arrived, were superb.

In a room of the giant winery that is as carefully climate-controlled as the cathedral where the wine butts age, there is a collection of the modern equivalent of holy relics: more than a hundred drawings by Andalusia's most famous son, Pablo Picasso, disruptor of worlds and devotee of bacchanals. One sketch even has a bearded man reclining behind an amphora – smiling slyly as he watches us watching the three naked dancing girls beside him, as if daring us to acknowledge that our prurience is at least as great as his. Picasso was perhaps more interested in Greeks, given his obsession with the Minotaur, but I am the spectator, queen of all I survey, and this fellow looks Roman to me.

En route to Córdoba, as the vines become whiter and the land beneath them so dry that Jerez seems lush by comparison, I stop at a rather extraordinary winery in Alguilar de la Frontera. The wine of Montilla-Moriles is much less famous than sherry (and a couple of locals bristle, intolerantly, when I accidently refer to their wines as sherries) but there are similarities. Instead of Palomino grapes to make the dry wines, Pedro Ximénez – the grape responsible for the black, incredibly sweet dessert wine of Jerez – goes into the *solera* system. The result is lighter, less complicated, but still very delicious, all hazelnuts and orange. The winemakers of Toro Albalá assert their primacy via a 'pure' – that is, vintage – wine, and they let me taste a 1931 and an extraordinary 1945, redolent of mandarin jam and dark chocolate (100 Parker points, I am told, proudly, although the numerical awards of the American wine writer and inadvertent wine tyrant Robert Parker are not what set me salivating). The scents of both are beautiful – in fact, one of the women who work there tells me she uses the wine as perfume: 'two drops on the wrist before I go out'. Then they show me the museum.

Albalá's owner, Antonio Sanchez, is nearly 80 now, and comes down from his next-door house each day at 1 p.m. to drink Fino with his friends, although he still oversees every major decision. His wife is a woman after Queen Isabella's own heart: while I was there, she yelled down to the young Italian showing me round that she should go home and stop taking jobs from the Señora's sons. (Her sons do, in fact, work in the bodega.) Señor Sanchez is responsible for the 'museum': a supremely bizarre collection of oddities and rarities. There is a stone funeral urn from the Roman era and lots of oil lamps, just like those in the Seville Antiquarium – and in the Barruols' little museum at Château de Saint Cosme, although this collection is on a very different scale. There is a Soviet record player and some Nazi guns. Most of a multi-volume 1772 edition of the *Encyclopédie* – that great attempt by Diderot, Voltaire and other luminaries of the French Enlightenment to explain the world – is shelved next to a circular second-century mosaic, still on its hunk of mortar and earth, so that it resembles a decorated stone wheel. There's a miniature bodega from 1846, Albalá's founding year, which apparently contains some of the original Fino. And, laid out like a languorous guest who has tired of reading the Diderot, there's an entire slave skeleton from the Roman era, grubbed up along with phylloxera-infected vines, long before it was obligatory to turn such finds over to the authorities.

I heft a tome of the *Encyclopédie* on to that usefully placed Roman mosaic. I open to Voyage (Education): 'The great men of antiquity did not believe there to be any greater schooling for life than travel …' The writer, le Chevalier de Jaucourt (himself no mean traveller), ends his meditation by recounting Caesar's crossing of the Rubicon. The decision to bring his army into Roman territory – tantamount to a declaration of war on the Republic – led, as Jaucourt says, to tragedy both for Caesar and for Rome, but there seems something poignant about the fact that the victorious general was on his way home: his actions made a battleground of the one place that should have remained a sanctuary.

We turn briefly south to Lucena where, for a few hundred years, the Jews lived in peace, listening to great local scholars and poets such as Maimonides and Judah Halevi, and cultivating both the traditions of Judaism and those that still divide Iberia's Sephardim from the Ashkenazim, Eastern European Jews. Tolerance built the glory of Sepharad, and after expulsion, that much-loved place was burnished into a glamorous myth, just as the Temple had been 1,400 years before. Like the Garden of Eden, these are the emblems of perfection, places we can no longer reach, their inaccessibility a vital part of their importance, like the gods whose absence is such an essential aspect of their power.

We stop for lunch in a dark but elegant restaurant called Las Tres Culturas. The menu and decor celebrate the benign cohabitation of Moors, Jews and Christians under Moorish rule – an atmosphere of mutually bene-ficial tolerance, known as the *convivencia*, that didn't sur-vive the Reconquest of Spain by the Christian monarchs. I wander round, admiring menorahs, urns and drawings, musing on the limits of tolerance, and the rumours that King Ferdinand, co-architect of the Jews' eviction, had a grandmother who was actually a *conversa*. Solid wall gives way to glass, and I am so distracted by the enticing contents of the cellar revealed there that I accidentally sit down at the wrong table – much to the startlement of a young man, eating alone. Were my Spanish good enough I could have made a joke about *convivencia*; instead I apol-ogise and scuttle back to my own place.

The three cultures certainly mingle happily here, judging from the unlikely food combinations – red tuna with walnuts, lamb with raisins and a Jewish spe-ciality, aubergine with honey. A fresh, cheap *en rama* Fino, unlabelled, washes it all down: when I ask where it came from, the waitress points to the next street.

The other main indication of the three cultures in Lucena is the Church of San Matteo, which was once the mosque and before that, when Lucena was the site of a renowned *yeshiva* (a Jewish school for Bible scholars), a synagogue. Some of the synagogue may also have been used to construct the parish church of Santiago, which clearly echoes the shape of the Toledo and Segovia synagogues. Perhaps they bought the grapes for their sacramental wine from the Montilla-Moriles vineyards that were then redeployed, after the Islamic hiatus, to provide wine for the Eucharist. My favourite beverage may have played a sinister role for the Jews once the Inquisition began in 1480, given the prohibition against drinking wine made by non-Jews. A supposed *converso* buying wine from Jews would have been suspected of 'Judaising': secretly retaining his old faith. And once the Jews had been expelled or forcibly converted, did those *conversos* buying wine from one another come under suspicion, too? Cohabitation without tolerance is viciously complicated.

In 1958, during the rebuilding of a house in town, the tombstone of Rabbi Amicos, from the tenth or eleventh century, was uncovered. A half-century later came a find more important still: the Jewish cemetery, outside the walls as such cemeteries must be according to biblical law. Discovered in 2006, it apparently dates from the eleventh century, the heyday of Jewish Lucena, or earlier. On the chalk-pale hillside, elongated metal circles filled with dark gravel mark the graves. The contrasts of colour and density are poignant, the delineated patches as ghostly as the chalked outline of a murder victim. Beside us, the cars whizz oblivious along the new southern road that was responsible for this rediscovery. Our worship of speed, our need to save time, led to a dig that peeled back the hillside – where the remains of people with different habits of worship lie in mute testament to the pointlessness of time-saving. But there is no shelter here, and it is too hot to stay long.

Some say the *convivencia* is a beautiful myth, testament to our desire for happy coexistence, rather than to any actual friendly cohabitation. But the urge to share ideas, food and drink, to tolerate and understand one another, is surely as old as war. The word *convivencia* shares an etymological root with the Romans' banquet, the *convivium*, and, if the meanings are somewhat different, the impetus is surely similar. Certainly, there were purges and cruelties in Moorish Spain, as in every other place and time. Still: the vineyards were not grubbed up, although Caliph al-Hakam II may, in 966, have ordered that they should be: the locals argued that the grapes were for holy Crusaders to eat. Generally, Jews and Christians could continue their worship, with its wine, unhindered, although not untaxed. And there is beautiful Moorish poetry that indicates a fair few Muslim wine enthusiasts, too.

Sherry is a living testament to the *convivencia*. To arrest the flor's growth, distilled alcohol must be added. It was the Arabs who discovered distillation and brought the process to the West. Without them, we would have neither brandy nor sherry. Yet the *convivencia* is much disputed, in a way that the *Pax Romana*, another display of conquerors' forbearance, is not. As if there were something far stranger in agreeing to disagree than in forcing conversion or departure at sword point.

Tolerance is not affection. 'What do we tolerate? What we do not like,' points out Federico, my Andalusia guide. Still, for a brief moment in the bloody history of the world, three major religions managed to live with each other's alien practices in a style more akin to the calm Roman absorption of foreign gods than to the fiercely partisan monotheism characteristic of all three Peoples of the Book. And, as always, when people talk instead of fighting, culture flourished.

'Oh, beguiling Córdoba!' wrote Ibn Zaidun, eleventh-century minister to the Caliph, or ruler: 'Can a heart parched by separation from you ever quench its thirst?' Córdoba, first Moorish capital and for 300 years an 'ornament of the world' (as a tenth-century Saxon canoness memorably put it), is the city where the three cultures still visibly meet – four, if you include the Romans, as the bust of first-century AD philosopher-statesman Seneca at Almodóvar Gate indicates you should. We arrive from the south, crossing the Guadalquivir river once again, and briefly rejoining the ugly if resonant Via Augusta. We wander around in the orange-scented park outside the old city walls, trying to get our bearings, admiring the wonderful perfume as well as the fidelity to the city's ancient tradition of tolerance that has impelled someone, on spotting graffiti announcing *'refugiados no bienvenidos'* (refugees not welcome) to cross out the *'no'*. 'Sometimes even to live is an act of courage,' wrote Seneca.

Past him, through the walls and I'm in Calle de los Judios, the Street of the Jews. In a side street I find the old synagogue, with its double-height walls and its plaque commemorating twelfth-century native son Moses Maimonides, a Jewish physician, as well as a great scholar and sage: 'We possess nothing more appropriate than wine for strengthening one who is weak and enfeebled,' he wrote. I have a feeling he and my father, also a doctor, would have got on wonderfully.

What is amazing about this little synagogue, apart from its survival more than five hundred years after the Jews were expelled from Spain, is how Arab it is, with its keyhole arches, tessellated designs and curlicued plasterwork. It is an architectural style called Mudéjar, after the Moors who stayed on in Christian Spain and did not convert: a difficult life, but evidently not too difficult to obstruct the creation of beauty. The remains of Hebrew script borders the decoration, *convivencia* writ large: three cultures, with different if intersecting beliefs (and very different drinking habits), learning and borrowing from one another for the spaces most important to the worship that was central to their lives. The script is from the Song of Songs, a biblical passage of eroticism and wine worship that has always enthralled me: 'Let him kiss me with the kisses of his mouth – for your love is more delightful than wine.'

After the Expulsion of 1492, the building became a hospital for hydrophobes – surely a rare complaint in this dry country – then a home for the guild of shoemakers, finally a school. Its origins were forgotten until the nineteenth century, and the preservation of those delicate curls of plaster seems like a miracle of biblical proportions.

The Arabised nature of this decor is just a faint if pretty echo of the extraordinary place of worship a couple of streets away. I have been to Hagia Sophia, a cathedral that became a mosque, in Istanbul, and I have been to more churches built atop others' places of worship than I can count – more, almost certainly, than I know. But I have never seen anything like the Mosque-Cathedral of Córdoba, with its seemingly endless repeating red and white arches, so uniform in comparison to the riotous variation of colour, shape and pattern on the walls. There are vaulted ceilings and fringed archways, 56 chapels, according to my count, and clusters of Visigothic fragments from the early church – even a display of stone-masons' squiggled identifying marks on their work, which do not show whether an individual is Christian or Muslim, although both would have been involved in shaping this syncretic building. The Umayyad Caliphs, chased out of Syria in the eighth century, gradually bought out the church of San Vicente (itself, as so often, built over a Roman temple), and reimagined it as a great mosque, in the image of the one they had been forced to leave. I walk beneath those replicating arches, thinking about other replications. As María Rosa Menocal, the late scholar and historian of medieval culture, has pointed out, 'the *qibla* of this mosque – the orientation that in all mosques points the faithful toward Mecca when they pray – is not in the direction of Mecca but something more like due south, as it would be if the mosque were indeed in Damascus' – a whole building, tilted towards longing.

Eventually, after much wandering and gazing, I reach the building's centre and find an entire cathedral, the choir of carved mahogany, the ceiling gilt and the altar adorned with a painting of the Last Supper. *Gustate et Videte Quam Suavis Est Dominus*, declaims the carved inscription below: Taste and See How Sweet is the Lord. This is Psalm 34, an Old Testament song of praise converted into an exhortation to drink the wine that is Jesus's blood, in the middle of a building dedicated to Allah. And it is more, because the Last Supper is a Seder, the Passover supper that celebrates God's sparing of Jewish firstborns in His savage campaign to persuade Pharaoh to release the Jews from slavery and send them on their way to the Promised Land – the land of milk and honey, or of wine. This was the Jews' great journey, or their first one, anyway. There are all sorts of vinous rituals during the Passover Seder, including the dipping of one's finger ten times into one's wine glass and then tapping the blood-coloured liquid on the plate, to signify the ten plagues. Bugs and boils and blood, to say nothing of all those dead children, but what about exile? It is at the end of the Seder that Jews repeat the wistful entreaty: next year in Jerusalem – although that Jerusalem is no more the twenty-first-century city than Damascus was the true Mecca.

After hours in this beautiful gargantua even the orange trees in the courtyard feel immeasurably far away, and I stumble out into bright sunlight and walk aimlessly. Córdoba old town is a pleasure to wander, from the Roman bridge across the Guadalquivir to the Alcázar de los Reyes Cristianos, the Palace of the Christian Kings, with its display of Roman mosaics and the beautiful gardens where Ferdinand and Isabella discussed with Columbus his impending trip west. I'm working up a thirst, waiting to duck into one of the many little bars for crispy fried squid and good Fino. I order ham, too. It seems important, here, to eat pig – a gesture of solidarity with those long-ago *conversos*, swallowing this tasty abomination and washing it down with what was, I hope, good wine, perhaps sneakily bought from a fellow *converso*, so that the prohibition against buying from Gentiles (intended, oh the irony, to prevent the use of wine that might have been meant for idolatrous libations) was in a sense circumvented.

We take the scenic Route of the Caliphate towards the Alhambra, which is slower than the motorway but still faster than those ancient rulers would have believed possible. It really is incredibly beautiful here, in this valley between the Sierra Nevada mountains and those of the Sierra Morena: dark foliage and tousled silvery-green olive trees emerge from misty hills, while, further back, the snow-capped mountains wear a string of little tufty clouds draped stylishly around their shoulders like a feather boa. We stop at Luque, a defunct station on the edge of the Sierras Subbéticas, which still has its old olive presses, little different from those the Romans would have used for the vast quantities of oil from these, the world's most prestigious olive groves. The old station is now a restaurant.

I have been looking for what is lost in the ground and in my glass; in Andalusia it rears up before me in marble and brick. The Alhambra is no triumphalist assertion of domination, like a Roman arch or amphitheatre, but yet another longing for home, in three dimensions and at two removes, built less as a boast than as a sigh. In the early eleventh century, the Caliphate of Córdoba, riven by civil war, was falling apart, the Moors founding smaller kingdoms called *taifas* – including one near Granada, the town sometimes known as Gharnata al-Yahud, 'Granada of the Jews', for the community that already thrived there. Hilltop Granada soon became an important city, and the beautiful palace, built over a Roman structure of coloured clay the Arabs named Hisn al-Hamra, the Red Fort, was laid out with memory gardens that evoked both paradises: the heavenly one and the gardens of lost Córdoba.

In a strange way, this teetotallers' palace, as far west on the Mediterranean as Jerusalem is east, feels like the closest I can come to gazing on the Temple. This isn't quite as whimsical as it appears. The Alhambra was founded by a Jew, Samuel ibn Naghrela, or Shmuel Hanagid, like my grandfather a man with more than one name, and like the biblical King David a soldier, poet and politician, who rose during the *convivencia* to become Granada's Grand Vizier.

'Even the mourner whose tears fall with his heart's blood, disperses his grief in retreat with wine,' he wrote, and he, like his master, had plenty to grieve. Once more, they had been made to move on. 'Wars will cease ...' it promises in the Old Testament, 'Nation will not take up sword against nation ... They shall all sit under their own vines and under their own fig trees, and no one shall make them afraid.' The yearning enfolded in those words, for a life of peace and plenty, rooted and secure! And yet: how few of us can settle for the paradise we find. We glance wistfully backwards or yearningly forwards, make plans to see what's over the next hill or who is at the next table. We refuse to stay still, saying instead, each in our own words: next year in Jerusalem.

My heart is in the East
But I dwell in the West.
I eat without taste,
Live without joy or rest.
How easy in my eyes to leave
This Spanish life of mine,
Just to see with those same eyes
The dust of the ruined Shrine.

This from Judah Halevi, in the early twelfth century. He did, too, sailing the width of the Mediterranean to die in Jerusalem: a wanderer returned, if only to a Kingdom wrested from Islam by the Christian Crusaders. To my mind, exchanging this building of surpassing beauty for holy dust was not much of a swap. Everything about the Alhambra announces the mastery of a desert people over parched land and unceasing sunlight, from the cool of the fretted marble enclosures to the water that sits tranquil or trickles enticingly through each courtyard. Hanagid, as befits a good royal servant, has not left his mark, although some say the famous marble lions in the Courtyard of the Lions – 12 of them, water dribbling from their lips, supporting a gigantic basin – were placed here by his son. To a desert people like the Moors, water was wealth. In the Islamic paradise, Federico tells me, there are four rivers, of which the first is water; the others are milk, honey – and wine, the blessed nectar of the righteous, who have successfully avoided it on earth. How I would like to think of my father lounging in Paradise, eyes closed to better appreciate the divine music – and the wonderful wine. No use pointing out that this Jewish atheist would have no place in a Muslim heaven; like Shmuel Hanagid, I am constructing the palace I need. Dreamily, I gaze at the delicate fretted arches that edge the Courtyard of the Lions. They attest to the importance not of heavenly wine but of earthly water: the giant marble basin could never have squeezed through them, so the palace must have been built around the fountain.

Later, the hilltop castle ('a day's ride from the coast,' says Federico; why so far? I ask, and he grins: 'Pirates!')

will become the treasure of Spain's first rulers of a united Christian Spain, Ferdinand and Isabella. Federico points out a wall decorated with the dollar sign, the S-shaped symbol that originally signified paper backed by Spanish gold.

Convivencia, which had risen with the Umayyad Caliphs and fallen with them, was already long dead when Boabdil, last Emir of Granada and the end of a line of Moorish rulers stretching back 700 years, quit the Alhambra and went into exile. That was in 1492, the year Columbus sailed for what turned out to be America. The fiercely Christian monarchs may have kept the palace because it had no association with Islam; did they know of its Jewish founder when, later that same eventful year, they signed the order for the expulsion of their territory's Jews – right here, in Hanagid's building? The palace built by exiles became the home of the perpetrators of the next great wave of disastrous departures. After over a thousand years, the Jews would have felt this to be their home; for the Moors, too, being sent back where they came from, after so long, would have meant little. We dream of a mythic elsewhere – a lost paradise or a Promised Land, an Underworld or a Heaven – and perhaps we need that dream to live, but it is right here that we cling to. 'Where are the people who once lived here? Where are the many builders and vandals, the rulers and paupers, the slaves and masters?' wrote Hanagid, presciently, in the poem 'In a Ruined Citadel': 'They passed from their palaces to the grave, from pleasant courts to dust.' And yet they left so much: their palaces and their words survive them. And their dust, let us not forget, has become our wine.

Anna Maria, one of the Planeta 'aunties', at La Forestaria
in Sicily

7

SICILY:
Memory

*The life of the dead is entrusted to the memory of
the living*

CICERO (Author's Translation)

Before the Italian mainland, almost opposite ancient
Carthage, is an island so fertile, and so strategically
placed, that it has been visited by virtually everyone. Poets, heroes, soldiers and slaves sailed to Italy
when Rome was the centre of the world, and if
they arrived from the west they found Sicily in their
way. Aeneas, founder of Rome, paused here. The
Phoenicians, the Greeks, Normans, Arabs and even,
briefly, the Spanish have laid claim, so it's hardly surprising that the Romans, just barely across the water,
did the same.

And the wines are amazing ...

Sicily has had geological shocks to match the cultural
ones. This enormous island – 25,000sq. km, a tenth the
size of Great Britain – has suffered volcanic eruptions
and earthquakes. It is easy to see why the inhabitants

believe that a giant is trapped under their island, writhing in his bonds and shooting flames through his mouth.
The north has Etna, the volcano that disgorged molten
rock just months before my visit; in the south, the earth
quakes. If towns such as Scicli and Ragusa are gorgeously decked with curlicues and monsters in elegant
pale stone, if their innumerable churches rise in flowing
scrolls, their innards white and gold in gorgeous celebration of God's glory and man's, it is because a tremor
in 1693 brought these buildings' predecessors crashing
down. A sad postscript: in 1968, a series of quakes in
the western Belice Valley did similar damage but the
rebuilding was much more pragmatic, and to this day
some inhabitants will leave their new, relocated homes
on a Sunday afternoon for a picnic on the land where
their families once lived – their *terroir*.

The land remembers, too. There is sand in the southern vineyards and ancient lava in the north. Local grape
varieties cling timorously to the soil they know – and
that soil seems to change every few miles. 'We have
fifty-five grape varieties and twelve different soils: it's
Disneyland for winemakers!' Patricia, who is one of
them, tells me. There are international varieties, too, but
fewer than there were, as the ever-shrinking world starts
to realise the value of difference.'For in fact,' wrote Pliny
of the Eugenia vine, which had been imported from
the hills of Taormina, below Mount Etna, to Alba in
northern Italy, and thrived there as nowhere else, 'some
vines have so strong an affection for certain localities
that they leave all their reputation behind there and
cannot be transplanted elsewhere in their full vigour.'

There is evidence of early winemaking all over, from
the Phoenician, or possibly earlier, *pigiatoia* (outdoor

press) carved into a hilltop above Planeta's Ullmo winery, on the west coast between Palermo and Sciacca, to the writings of Strabo, who tells us that the district around Messina 'abounds in wine' called Mamertine which 'vies with the best produced in Italy'.

Caesar drank Mamertine, claims Alessio Planeta, a loquacious man with kindly, bespectacled eyes who is principal winemaker of the family business – one of the biggest producers of quality wine on the island. Planeta have five wineries dotted around Sicily on different kinds of soil, including one on northern Etna, where they are trying to revive the Mamertine. These were, according to Alessio, the only vines permitted at one point in Roman Sicily, the Mammettini having helped Rome beat Carthage (their name comes from Mars, god of war). Other varieties were forbidden, in an attempt to repress Sicilian culture: the Romans, says Alessio, were a little bit Fascist – not a casual term when used by a man whose parents were for a time subjects of Mussolini.

We are at dinner at Alessio's house. He lives just by the coast, surrounded by olives but with no vines in sight – presumably, the winemaker equivalent of leaving the office. The jasmine and frangipani in his garden are so strong it is hard to smell the wines … but they, in particular a 2007 Merlot, with its balsamic piquancy, green pepperiness and depth, are lovely.

Alessio is a man at ease with history. 'Baroque?' he snorts, of the southern Sicilian towns beautifully rebuilt after the 1693 earthquake: 'Baroque is new. Palermo and Syracuse are Sicily's most beautiful towns, and Palermo is a disaster.' We eat a soup of zucchini leaves and drink a Chardonnay that will, by the end of the

warm evening, taste like the salty liquor in an oyster.
We talk of the *Odyssey*. The Sicilians might, according
to Homer, have lacked culture – a word that originally
referred to having the skills to cultivate the soil – but
then their earth was so abundant it barely needed any
assistance:

> Surely the earth, giver of grain, provides
> The Cyclops with fine wine, and rain from Zeus
> Does swell our clustered vines. But this is better –
> A wine as fragrant as ambrosia and nectar.

That's Polyphemus the Sicilian Cyclops, given Greek
wine by his captive, Odysseus. The implication is
clear: the Greeks use skill to craft great wine while
the lazy Sicilians take advantage of nature's generosity,
with satisfactory but never ambrosial results. They are,
in every sense, uncultivated.

It's a nice parable of the introduction of wine culture: the Greeks getting the Cyclops drunk on civilisation. (They would then take advantage of his inebriation
to spear him in his single eye, and escape.) The Cyclops,
says Alessio, were actually native Sicilians, who wore ele-
phant skulls as helmets: the single eye was the trunk hole.
There is no way to know if this is true, but, drunk on
heady jasmine and good wine, I am prepared to believe it.

In Palermo, wrote D. H. Lawrence, the locals call the
roof gutters 'dogs' umbrellas', although neither dogs nor
masters were in any danger of a soaking when I was
there, except perhaps from sweat. What a place to make

wine! But Sicily defies both relentless sun and unstable foundations. The island is so marvellously fertile it even helped sustain Rome's mythical founder: according to Virgil, the Sicilians gave wine to Aeneas, which the shipwrecked hero and his companions drank to comfort themselves as they waited for permission to enter Carthage. Later Dido, Carthage's Queen, famously enamoured of Aeneas, would make a grimmer use of *her* country's vines, pouring purple wine on an altar in an attempt to discover whether her lover planned to stay with her. The wine turned to blood, Aeneas duly sailed back to Sicily en route to Italy and destiny – and Dido committed suicide.

This is the kind of history that Palermo understands, perhaps because the city was founded by the Carthaginians, sometime between the eighth and the fifth centuries BC. Carthage, as we saw in Spain, was destroyed by Rome, and the erstwhile inhabitants would probably be pleased to know that their historical enemies are hard to find here, in the capital of an island that has seen so many conquerors. The Romans made Sicily a province in 241 BC, all except Syracuse, whose canny ruler Hieron II struck a deal with the conquerors, but here as nowhere else they must tussle for prominence and it feels to this outsider, at least, that the retrospective splendour that still bolsters Italian confidence all across the mainland, based on the triple glories of the Renaissance, the Holy See and the everlasting renown of the Roman Empire, does not apply in Sicily.

I walk quiet alleys (it is Sunday, Sabbath for some) past walls so uneven their surfaces look like flaking paint, to a pair of churches perched on a stone platform above the street. One is Chiesa San Cataldo, which looks blockish from the outside, with three odd red domes, but has a restful simplicity decorated only with floor mosaics within (if you can get in – a custodian needs to provide the key). The other is Chiesa dell'Ammiraglio, aka La Martorana. Both are Norman, from the twelfth century, although La Martorana was later given a fancy Baroque front; otherwise they couldn't be more different. La Martorana's lovely, lacy campanile hints at the wonders within: golden, Byzantine-style mosaics, including one of King Roger crowned by Jesus. Ibn Jubayr, our Moorish friend whose travels through the Mediterranean were funded by repentance money for the wine he was forced to drink, came here only a few years after the church was built and marvelled, calling it the most beautiful monument in the world. He loved Palermo: 'This is the metropolis of these islands, offering a life of both ease and splendour: everything one could desire of greatness both real and apparent; all one needs to live. It is an ancient and elegant city, magnificent and pleasing, and seductive to look upon.'

So seductive, in fact, that you can miss fragments of the more distant past as you gaze in dazzlement at medieval glories. In front of that stone platform, at street level, there is a chunk of Roman fortification wall that is now ignored by tourists admiring the wonders of the churches above. It is clearly the bedding place of a homeless person and there is rubbish everywhere, a token wire at ankle height its only protection from heedless modernity. Only 25 years have passed since judges were being murdered by the Mafia in this city; with 2,000 years of adventurers, most of them violently disposed, perhaps Palermo has developed an indifference verging on amnesia towards the long-departed. This is certainly a city comfortable with the untoward. The night before, sitting in a nice little bar, where the men at the next table puff on cigars (I'm sorry for the disturbance, the man in charge says to us earnestly, as if he has no say in who lights what inside his restaurant, and maybe he doesn't), we hear the cacophony of a motorbike crash just outside; everyone smokes on, unconcerned. On our way back to our hotel, we spot stairs, a gap in the buildings, statuary, and turn almost involuntarily, from a street that is splendid enough, in its tawdry way: a crablike move off the sensible path. At the top of the stairs we find a fabulous fountain, a building beyond with plaques to Garibaldi, Umberto I and John Paul II (who passed this way, apparently), and we stand there like the tourists we are, photographing, as a car creeps towards me. I can see the driver, close-trimmed beard and black-rimmed glasses, entirely expressionless and forgettable, but he keeps edging closer, and I keep shuffling, until I figure he must have the right to park at the top of these steps, so I move completely out of the way and he goes over, front wheels grinding air, the noise horrible, the car balanced like a seesaw between reason and insanity. Out of craven instinct, we start to walk, slowly and silently, away, herded by the fear of the abnormal, *we just can't understand what he is doing* ...

By the time we leave the square, ten minutes later, he still hasn't moved, despite a flurry of interested (I wouldn't say concerned) onlookers, and we go down to the port where the boats of the fortunate bob, and watch confetti outside the imposing Gothic church of Santa Maria della Catena flutter away and drown.

I skirt that same piazza next day, rendered ordinary by sunlight save for its fantastic statuary, and wander further along Via Maqueda, stopping at the church of San Nicolò da Tolentino and its dilapidated convent. The church is silent even on a Sunday morning, but you can walk the centuries along its chapels, with their peculiar mixture of suffering and glory. Past triumphant Mary with a solid halo, affixed with shiny pointed stars, that looks like nothing so much as a levitated crown of thorns (maybe that's deliberate?), then Jesus toting his cross, with evocative art everywhere, just everywhere, and a full-size coffin in which a figure of Christ lies dead, which reminds me of the slave skeleton found in the vineyard at Toro Albalá.

Further along Via Maqueda I spot an oddity: a street sign in three languages, Italian, Arabic and Hebrew. I have found the Giudecca, the home of Palermo's ancient community of Jews, who may have been part of the original slave cohort brought back to Rome from Judea, after the Jewish Wars, or may have been older still – some say Caecilius of Calacte, a Sicilian rhetorician in the time of Augustus, was a Jew. The Jews were thrown out (or forced to convert) by Ferdinand and Isabella, who owned this island at the time of the Inquisition. (One richly deserved consequence of the expulsion was huge loss of revenue from the many taxes on Jews – including one on wine gone bad.) San Nicolò da Tolentino is, in fact, on the site of the old synagogue – oddly known as the Meschita (mosque) by non-believers, but, then, in a city that in tolerant early medieval times had 300 mosques, perhaps that was the comfortable designation for a non-Christian house of worship. This is an island where perceptions seem to shift like tectonic plates, and the language adapts accordingly. (And sometimes, more than the language. Six months after I leave, it is announced that part of San Nicolò will be given back to Palermo's renascent Jewish community, to create this city's first synagogue in over 500 years.) I look at this solid church with its prominent crosses, the statues of the Virgin recessed in so many outer walls, and contrast it with the misnamed, invisible old synagogue barely marked by a couple of street signs. Triumphant Catholicism, shouting its primacy from the rooftops. Of the three religions of the Book, only Christians (and not all of those) blazon their iconography everywhere. How well that must have worked when most people were illiterate! It works now: there are far more Catholic than Jewish images in my head, thanks partly to the art of the Renaissance, and to cathedrals such as Reims.

I drive out of Palermo, winding up past gum trees and olive groves into the parched, patchwork hills, their drastic red-tinged outcrops startling against a sky of powdered blue. My driver pulls a seatbelt across his portly stomach only when the *carabinieri* wave us over: the Sicilians are, in general, as dismissive of car safety as of other drivers on the road, which is a worrying combination. My first view of Sicilian vines after all that sparse shrubby green hillside feels like a glass of cool water at the end of a long, hot hike: they look so rich and juicily green compared to the dusty surrounding shrubbery – although wilder and more wilted than many I saw earlier on my travels.

In the gracious Spanish-style villa of Tasca d'Almerita winery, on the family's Regaleali estate, a marketing manager called Bogata starts talking about aristocrats and Mussolini. (On the wall of Planeta's winery in Vittoria there is still an inscription from the dictator: 'He who drinks nothing is a lamb; who drinks justly is a lion; and he who drinks too much is a pig.') Sicily's reputation as a great vineyard faded after Visigoths and Ostrogoths overran the Romans' territory, although the callous treatment of the province under the Empire was partly to blame. Sicily was Rome's breadbasket, and the sun that ripened wheat and grapes would have crisped the backs of naked slaves, working for distant masters who were rarely obliged to witness their suffering. Here is a pattern that will repeat through history: absentee landlords sucking dry the source of their wealth, which they spend in the glittering metropolis, oblivious to those who work for their gain. The owners of the *latifundia*, the great Sicilian estates, had grown rich on bread, much of which doubtless went to appease the Roman plebians, and there is a brutal justice in the idea that late Rome's increasing reliance on *panem et circenses* (bread and circuses), to render the masses docile, may have contributed to the Empire's fall.

Sicily, if not her wine, remained great under the Arabs and the Normans; it was under those most Christian monarchs Ferdinand and Isabella that the island fell into centuries of disrepute, and I like to think their hounding of the Jewish and Muslim communities was partly responsible. By the time phylloxera swept mainland Europe, Sicily was a producer of rotgut wines, at the mercy of another rapacious aristocracy, this time local, and one of the most backward places in Europe. Lack of assiduous cultivation had rendered her uncultivated. For a while, she deftly filled the gaps in wine production that the louse left, until phylloxera arrived here, too, and then it was the usual story: two world wars and a rickety aftermath, followed by slow regeneration.

But the wines that cheered exiled Aeneas have as much potential now, and the sheer variety of soils and grapes – and temperatures, from those baking lowlands to mountain cool – is fabulous. Volcanic Etna is black; down south, the pulverised remains of the denizens of an ancient sea make the soil glow white. It can be red with iron or brown with clay, and the names of the grapes read like poetry: Carricante and Catarratto, Nero d'Avola and Nerello Mascalese, Grillo and Inzolia and Frappato and Perricone ...

Bogata drives us into the vineyards and tells us about Giuseppe, the count whose obsession revived the estate's wines. It was after the war, Palermo had been bombed and the aristocracy who had lived so well off Sicily's bounty were, largely, poor. But Giuseppe, a well-travelled aficionado of Châteauneuf-du-Pape, looked at his arid land and saw the possibility of fine wine. He must have had resources: it took him over 20 years to make a wine that lived up to his ideals. But he was not a quitter, even if he was occasionally a pragmatist, producing wheat for Mussolini as his ancestors would have done for Rome's elite. (Il Duce gave him a prize, and obliged him to go to Palermo to collect it. This is the first and last time I put on a black shirt, he growled to his diary.) In 1943, he decided to plant more vineyards. 'He suffered for years, tried and failed, couldn't arrive from great grapes to great wines,' says Bogata, a company employee from Hungary who nonetheless refers to the long-dead count as Grandpa. In the 1960s, he brought in oenologists from the north and the knowledge gap narrowed. They began controlling the fermentation temperature. The wines stopped being alcoholic swill, good only for selling on to France and Tuscany to bolster the density of their blends.

We stand on parched earth looking out at a panorama of deep green vineyards and trees ('the vineyards' lungs') and marvel at his effrontery. 'You have to be crazy to make wine here,' says Bogata. 'All the other wineries are near the coast.' How grandiose we can be, we humans, and to what wonders and horrors that overweening faith in our own perfectibility can lead! Grandpa was a romantic, in every sense: we are shown the Nozze d'Oro vineyard, with Inzolia planted in the clay at the foot of the slope and a form of Sauvignon Blanc (a mutation, as the grape adapted to the Mediterranean climate, now known as Sauvignon Tasca) at the top. The count blended these two grapes into a celebration of 50 years of marriage to his countess, Franca, a golden combination for a golden anniversary. 'We call these two vineyards the lovers,' says Bogata, and the musky golden wine we try over lunch is a fittingly lovely commemoration of a whole range of joint achievements, half a century of cohabitation being far from the least of them. Giuseppe was a fierce advocate of local grapes, unlike his son, Count Lucio, who planted Cabernet Sauvignon on the sly. When his father tried and liked the results, he came clean – brave man, to make a fool of formidable Grandpa. Lucio's interest was timely: Cabernet and Chardonnay were

Sicily's passport out of obscurity, in the late 1980s, showing the world what the island could do with familiar, pronounceable grapes. Lucio even, sacrilegiously, put a little Cabernet in Rosso del Conte, a blend of Nero d'Avola and Perricone that Grandpa considered his first real success. He pronounced himself happy with it, at last, in 1970 – 27 years into his project. Bogata pours the 2012, made two years before the wine became a pure blend of indigenous varieties once again. It is glorious, full of mint and liquorice, and I raise my glass to Grandpa's persistence.

Nero d'Avola is pretty well known now, and I will taste it all over the island. It is an exception: many indigenous grapes are happiest in their own corner and do not, like Pliny's Eugenia vine, much like to travel. Perricone is something else. 'This is the grape forgotten twice,' says Bogata. At the end of the eighteenth century, an English merchant named John Woodhouse noted the similarity of the local wines, which were fortified and aged in wooden casks, to port and sherry, and begun tinkering with them. The popularity of his fortified Marsala wines was assured by Admiral Nelson's enthusiasm during the Napoleonic Wars, and so Perricone was rendered unrecognisable as Marsala Ruby; later, phylloxera consigned it to oblivion again. The 2014 is soft and truffly, 15 per cent alcohol but very balanced, good with grilled lamb.

Marco Sferlazzo of Porta del Vento, a quiet-spoken former pharmacist with close-clipped greying beard and navy linen shirt, believes fervently in Perricone. 'All the world plants international grapes; there are fewer than ten Perricone producers and they are only in this area and Trapani, a little further south.' Marco, like the old Tasca count, has vision and stubbornness: he spent ten years working as a pharmacist and making wine in a garage with a friend before he could afford to start his own vineyard. Still, Porta del Vento is as different from the grandeur of Tasca d'Almerita as could be: a tiny winery on a breeze-cooled hilltop (Porta del Vento means Gate of the Wind) with a tasting room of wooden frames against a bare stone wall. It's lovely now, at summer's height, but the large stove testifies to how cold it must become in winter.

It's quiet up here and you see eagles; my urban soul is soothed. One aspect of winery visits I love is this glimpse of different lives: I'm the product of generations of city-dwellers, people who were periodically forbidden to own land so invested their love in books instead. There is something particularly wonderful about sitting down at a table while a winemaker, who lives such a different life from me and thinks in another language, lines up a series of his wines that try, as he is trying, to express their native particularity. When Bogata, resident in Italy for seven years now, brings up the intricacies of language – how she can talk eloquently about wine in Italian but not in her native tongue, for example – I am on familiar ground: when we wrap our minds around a different linguistic structure, those minds change shape – and sometimes, as my grandpa found, it's not just the minds that change. Our languages, born of voyagers and conquerors and interpersonal complications, have much that we do not even recognise. I think again of the etymological root that host and guest and hospitality share with enemy or stranger. Which you are may come down to whether you can find a language in common. As a winemaker once said to me, political difference discussed around a table, with a bottle of wine, is diplomacy; take away the table and the bottle and you have a war.

Marco's vines grow deep into 11-million-year-old sandstone and his wines are delicate and mysterious: Saray and Ishac are clearly named for the biblical characters ('they are the two most interesting names in the Bible'), but he will not tell me why, even when I recount the story of my grandfather Isaac/Jack. The Saray, made from Catarratto, is an extraordinary wine: marzipan but without the almond bitterness, savoury and aromatic with lovely acidity. Ishac is made from Nero d'Avola. 'It makes a really interesting wine up here in the hills,' he says, and he's right. It has a lovely woodiness and lots of dark fruit and seems to deepen in the mouth: clean, long, very aromatic and a beautiful ruby colour, too.

On the way back into the city, I'm still pondering the significance of naming Sicilian wines for Sarah and her son Isaac. Wine in the Bible is, after all, a symbol of fruitfulness and fertility, from Israel as the Lord's vineyard ('for the vineyard of the Lord of hosts is the house of Israel, and the people of Judah are his pleasant planting ...') to Jesus's word like new wine. In Genesis, Sarah becomes fertile late, bearing Isaac in old age, so maybe Marco's names are a reference to the time it took him to become a winemaker. Is there a connection, I wonder, between our waning interest in religion (in the West, at any rate), and the declining importance of symbolism in wine? This is not an argument in favour of religion, but of remembrance. These stories are so important – we lose part of ourselves if we forget them.

Here, at least, the wine stories are hard to ignore. 'There is so much archaeology in Sicily that if you look under the table you will find a story,' Bogata had said, and later that night I pretty much do. We are eating in Gagini, a terrific restaurant where delicately crisped local prawns are strewn with breadcrumbs and orange petals, and the pillowy, herb-scented home-made pasta is some of the best I'll ever try. The sommelier has recommended a wine from Marsala that is not, however, a traditional Marsala wine; Nino Barraco has planted his Grillo vines practically on the seashore ('the trunk of the vines is in the sand,' the sommelier explains enthusiastically) and so we are drinking Sicily's western coastline, all sea salt and lemon. *Grillo* means cricket, which the Sicilians think is lucky: 'it is the horse of the fairies,' the sommelier tells me, and so it proves. In a rest between courses, I nip across the road to photograph the excellent wine I'd drunk the night of our arrival, when I'd been too travel-addled to snap the essential aide-mémoire. The bartender remembers me, and tells me that I tasted, not the Grillo listed on the menu, but one from the Whitaker vineyard, named for Joseph Whitaker, scion of a Yorkshire merchant family who made a fortune in Marsala in the nineteenth century. Joseph was an orni-thologist and self-taught archaeologist who bought the tiny island of Mozia, off the Sicilian coast, for its plenteous Phoenician remains, and had the sense to ask Tasca d'Almerita to work the tiny vineyard there. Now they own it, and this was a wine I had badly wanted to try; it turned out I already had. The wine tastes of pears and sea breeze, and comes from grapes that have, I like to think, been nourished as much by all that Phoenician pottery as by the soil. It is one of my favourite Sicilian wines and I am grateful both for the wine and for its unlikely appearance, like a dug-up treasure, on my journey.

We drive out of Palermo, down the west coast to La Forestaria, a gorgeous resort owned by Planeta winery, with an infinity pool overlooking vines. Like the Tascas, the Planetas are old Sicilian aristocracy, although even they were once immigrants, if very privileged ones: from Spain, in the sixteenth century, when this island was still a Spanish territory.

One of the wines we taste at lunch will become a request every time we eat seafood over the next few days, which is often: Alastro 2015. This is 70 per cent Grecanico (yet another local grape, its name indicative of Greek origins), 15 per cent Grillo and 15 per cent Sauvignon Blanc. It has a softness backed by citrus and a juiciness that means it works like a squeeze of lemon on fish and shellfish.

We eat meatballs and salad with Plumbago, a gorse- and thyme-flavoured Nero d'Avola that feels very Mediterranean — and very different from that Porto del Vento. How complicated Sicily's wine map is! But I like complications. I suspect the fear of insufficient knowledge is partly responsible for the difficulties many people now have with wine: they are busy worrying that they aren't sufficiently 'expert', while the so-called experts are cheerfully trying yet another utterly obscure wine, constantly exploring, learning, never staying still. An expert, I think, is simply someone with a fuller understanding of what they don't know.

The Planeta aunts, Anna Maria and Carolina, are in their eighties and can still remember the days when a gently brought-up girl did not take a job, but lived in idle luxury that may have been a euphemism for stultifying boredom. This all changed with the war when, instead of exchanging recipes with other well-born women to pass to their Montsù (a corruption of Monsieur: all the best chefs were French), the ladies' pampered mother had to invent ways to feed her large family – and with nothing, because Palermo was destitute. Both girls learned to cook. They do not agree on anything, certainly not on recipes.

Over dinner, Anna Maria produces a fragile scrap of paper called a *pizzino*, on which those bygone ladies would write the Montsù's instructions. These *pizzini* were also used by the Mafia, their very ephemerality a virtue for those who didn't wish to leave a paper trail, although in the end they were not quite ephemeral enough: the Mafia boss Bernardo Provenzano was caught with the help of incriminating *pizzini*, written in a code he'd borrowed from the wartime communications of Julius Caesar.

The Sicilian ladies were, oddly, more cautious still: only ingredients were written down, no method. Nobody seems to know why – perhaps to allow the Montsù his artistic freedom, although I prefer to conjecture that the oral transfer of information was both an acknowledgement of the ephemerality of a dish of food and an obeisance to the mouth, that vital culinary accoutrement. Anna Maria almost drops her fragment of history in the soup, and her niece Francesca shrieks with alarm.

The aunties, two portly ladies in flowered dresses and frameless glasses, are even better champions of the health benefits of wine than the Jewish sage Maimonides was: they drink as heartily as they argue. They bring out their century-old moulds, inherited from that long-suffering mother, and show us how to make *cotognata*, the Sicilian membrillo. Before the 1960s and the advent of refrigerators, food could only be preserved using sugar or salt, and with this long-lasting quince paste you were guaranteed something to offer visitors. The Sicilian aristocracy love sugar with the kind of passion Don José felt for Carmen, but quince, which must be cooked before eating, is not fancy, although it does take time – 'that's why the young don't like it,' snorts Angelo, our chef, himself decidedly young: 'Today's young people don't 'ave time for nothing.'

He shows us how to make home-style tomato sauce, while the aunts look on, their identical giant pearl earrings bobbing. 'No real Sicilian buys tomato sauce at the supermarket,' he says. 'We cannot. For us it is like mother's milk – we can always recognise our own mama's.' Angelo gestures to the two aunts: 'There were four sisters and they had four ways to make tomato sauce!'

Carolina uses a garlic clove, even though the Planetas apparently hate garlic: bad for tasting wine. Our Montsù adds basil, explaining that the classic Sicilian pot for basil has an Arab face, because of the long-ago seduction of a Sicilian princess by a faithless Arab. Rather than go into a decline, or kill herself like Carthage's Dido, she went straight to the sultan's court, cut off her sometime lover's head and planted it in a basil pot. The story puts me in mind of the Palermo women whose fierce opposition helped to end the Mafia wars in the

1990s, after 40 years of male failure. Angelo is dwelling less on feminism than on vengeance: 'We are beautiful people but don't touch us or you'll be sorry!' This has something in common with the feisty stories of Josephus, who described the giant golden vine above the Temple doors. His Jews are stubborn and bellicose, proud in defeat but never victims, rather like Angelo's princess, but both versions leave out a great deal. After all, plenty of people have touched the Sicilians: this is an island that has been abused by occupiers, absentee landlords, corrupt governments and murderous criminals. Sometimes, the first step is to admit that you are oppressed. And, sometimes, the next step may be to plant your oppressor's head in a basil pot.

Anna Maria, the younger sister (but not by much), is the family pastry chef. 'I fight always with my husband so I get very hungry,' she says, and whenever she gets hungry she prepares a cake. ('Prepare it yes,' mutters Carolina, 'just don't eat it!') Later, we will all eat her cake – in fact a tart, with sour cherries and *crema pasticcera*, France's *crème patissière*, so powerfully flavourful I think there is cinnamon in it, when actually there is nothing but fruit and sweet cream and that precious import: sugar.

You can skirt the fourth-century AD Villa Romana del Casale, with its famous mosaics of dancing girls in what look like bikinis, without difficulty: on a giant, sunny island the interior is easily overlooked, particularly by me, given that almost all the wineries are near the water. Instead, I pop in to see a less famous remnant from the same era, the Villa del Tellaro, south of Noto, where the vibrant if damaged mosaics include Bacchus surrounded by gambolling satyrs and maenads. It only requires a quick stop – much of it remains beneath the next-door lemon orchard – but I like the idea that you can scrape away the topsoil anywhere here and find a message from the past, like a buried *pizzino*. Sometimes, however, no scraping is required. As we drive south towards Noto, we pass Agrigento, an extraordinary temple complex, still thrusting its battered columns skyward in seeming defiance of weather, seismic activity and foreign conquerors. Some temples are Greek, others Roman, but it was wealth from wine and olives that paid for them.

Two hours' drive south-east along the coast is the region where Cerasuolo di Vittoria is made: the only DOCG (*Denominazione di Origine Controllata e Garantita*), or top-quality wine designation, in Sicily. To assume that this signifies the finest wine in Sicily would be to make a grave error, not just about the wines but about the Italian modus operandi. Here, the winemakers have managed to work together; elsewhere, history and personality have prevented the kind of unity that Italian bureaucracy rewards. On Etna, for instance, many of the best vineyards are above the arbitrary line drawn in the DOC classification of 1968, so most of the area's best wines cannot so much as depict the mountain on their labels, much less use the word Etna. (Maybe they should refer to the Pillar of Heaven, which was the Greeks' name for the volcano.) They are battling this, of course, but there are those within the DOC (the country's second-highest classification) who are happy with things as they are. The result is the kind of complication that seems to gather around wine like mist in a spring vineyard: the best Etna wines frequently can't mention Etna, and the wines that do mention Etna are not always the best Etna wines. As more than one winemaker tells me resignedly, Sicily has no problems except the Sicilians ...

Just north of Vittoria and south of the beautiful Bosco di Santo Pietro nature reserve, where the sand glows red-brown beneath the vines, Arianna Occhipinti also declassifies several of her wines, because the DOCG rules decree that she must use at least 50 per cent of Nero d'Avola in any wine labelled Cerasuolo di Vittoria, and she is in love with the Frappato grape. Sometimes these quality designations seem more trouble than they are worth, at least to the confused drinker. Italy has over 70 DOCGs and some are no more illuminating than that Etna DOC, viticultural legislation having, perhaps inevitably, as much to do with politics as with wine. By the time you have learned the grapes and percentages – to say nothing of the pronunciation – of Cerasuolo di Vittoria, you could have memorised the names of a handful of good winemakers. There were wine labels, or at least recognised names, in Pliny's time – one Mamertine was called Poitian after its original owner – and this still, frequently, seems the best way to make one's choice.

Certainly, any wine with Occhipinti's name on the label is worth drinking. She is an extraordinary woman, who grew frustrated studying conventional oenology, which was skewed towards mass production and industrialisation ('wine is not something to be "constructed" from a distance by hands that aren't paying much attention,' she wrote in a plaintive letter to a prominent journalist), and planted her first vines on a rented hectare when she was 21. Now in her mid-thirties, she owns 25ha and a beautiful winery, its barrel room lined with the limestone and tufa soil that feed her vines, a nineteenth-century *palmento* (wine press) decorating the entertaining area. Every wine she makes is terrific, from the entry-level SP68, named for the road that runs past her farm, to her Siccagno, an elegant, lightly eucalyptus Nero d'Avola. Her uncle Giusto co-owns a very successful winery down the road called Cos, where they age wines in giant buried amphorae that the Greeks (and Giusto) call *pithos* and the Romans (and I) *dolia*. Their wines are much fêted, their use of ancient Greek glamour canny without being cynical. Still, they are not as good as Arianna's, and the atmosphere of her winery, somewhere between a home, a playground and an office where everyone loves their job, is closest, in my experience, to Ridgeview in Sussex.

Arianna's boyfriend, Eduardo Torres Acosta, works for Passopisciaro on Etna, which I also visit, and there could scarcely be two more different places, even if both do make very impressive wine. Passopisciaro is the property of Andrea Franchetti, whose Tuscan wines are world-famous; he bought this place deserted save for shepherds using it as pasture. The owner had fled in terror after the Etna eruption of 1947, and ash on the vines is still frequently a problem; more of a problem were the shepherds, who refused to leave, and a delicate negotiation had to take place. But that's the most antiquated story attached to this winery: the wines are so-called icons, with the three-figure prices to prove it, and while the selection of individual parcels makes for a nice comparison of different volcanic *terroir*, I was a lot happier at Arianna's, where I tried wines I could actually afford in a friendly, informal atmosphere with an owner who is about as far from absentee as it's possible to be.

'I don't like life to be easy,' shrugs Arianna, when I ask why she bothers growing almonds and an ancient strain of wheat as well as vines. Her struggle is our pleasure, just like that of her vines: the wheat makes a superb pasta she serves us with local aubergines, lemon zest from her trees and capers from the Bosco di Santo Pietro mountains we see from the kitchen. And it matches her Frappato, which is fantastically aromatic and has a delightful almond-skin bitterness. This, she tells me, is the wine that represents her vineyard. She likes to vinify in unlined concrete because 'it lets the wine breathe'. I cannot imagine her working with anything that isn't fully alive.

I have been describing a Sicily-shaped arc from north-west to north-east, warily stalking Etna. Last stop before I pounce is in Syracuse, just south of the volcano. This was once a city to rival Athens; in fact, in 415 BC, when the Athenians declared war on Syracuse, they lost. Fittingly for a coastal city, the most interesting elements are on the fringes, inland in the Archaeological Park or on the island outcrop (now bridged) known as Ortygia.

Once their native ally Hieron II had died, between 216 and 214 BC, the Romans did conquer Syracuse, despite the efforts of the great Syracuse-born scientist Archimedes. He invented the lens and mirror combination that set fire to the Roman fleet, and became so absorbed in the workings of his invention that when the enemy did succeed in breaking into the city, he failed to feel the Roman sword fatally entering his flesh until too late. Before crossing on to Ortygia, which is mentioned by Virgil in the *Aeneid* ('stretched in front of a Sicanian bay lies an island … men of old called it Ortygia'), we stop at a waterside restaurant for superb seafood – squid salad, breadcrumbed anchovies, dinky garlicky mussels that must be tweaked from their shells – and forgettable rosé, which is not an insult. Rosé consumed in lunch-time sunshine, between one thing and another, is part of the flow of the day. It is not meant to be remembered.

On the island I want to see the Duomo, a cathedral whose pre-Christian antecedents are more visible than most. The impressive, impassive Baroque front is a post-1693 earthquake addition, but the grape-laden vines, symbolising the Passion of Christ, that curl up the columns framing the doorway find an older echo inside, where a marble *krater*, an ancient Greek wine vessel, sits guarded by seven thirteenth-century bronze lions. The mosaics behind are Norman, the next chapel, beneath vaulting ceilings painted with saints, is eighteenth-century and there are columns from the fifth century BC, when this was the Temple of Athena, embedded in the walls. Do important houses of worship come to resemble the places they represent? Reims Cathedral was a war-damaged survivor, Córdoba Mosque-Cathedral seemed to reach plaintively back to a multi-layered past. The Duomo, crowded and fascinating, is like a timeline in three dimensions.

This great church announces itself, those embedded columns visible from the street, before you even
reach the flamboyant entrance. Other fragments of the
past are more obscure. In the tiny streets behind the
Duomo, where even the names of the lanes recall biblical rivalries – four Vicoli alla Giudecca, a pointed Via
del Crocifisso and a wistful Vicolo dell'Olivo – a hotel
owner found a basement full of water, with limestone
steps leading down: 18m below, workmen discovered
a *mikveh*, the ritual bath where observant Jews go to
purify themselves before marriage or after menstruation.
Painstakingly hollowed out of the stone, like a *palmento*
for humans, it is from the sixth century – eight centuries older than the deep green *mikveh* in Carpentras.
I am thrilled: at last, a rare remnant of the community
that lived on this island for over a thousand years, until
the 1492 expulsion, and one a lot more substantial than
anything I'd found in Palermo. Access is only via the
hotel's hourly guided tours, so with a cluster of others
I carefully descend those ancient steps into a little room
carved out of the grey stone, with three small pools, a
hollow for private bathing either side and a wonderful vaulted ceiling that is, they think, Byzantine. There
are no inscriptions, no insights into the lives of those
ancient Jews: the only other evidence is the cluster
of ancient Greek water tanks that probably indicated
to the Jewish community that a spring, essential since
mikveh water must be continually purified, existed here.
The later construction of the fortifying walls round the
island cut the spring off from its exit, so now a pump
is needed to remove the constantly bubbling water. It's
amazing that it didn't bring the building down at some
point during the hidden centuries. But it is a magical

little place, and a reminder to the wine-obsessed among us that, for all that the blood of the grape is essential to Judaism, another liquid takes primacy – one without which there is no wine.

The guide mentions in passing that the nearby church of Giovanni Battista was once the synagogue to which this *mikveh* was attached. This seems a useful contrast with the Duomo, so I walk across the Giudecca to see, and in fact the large church, still in use despite its rooflessness, is rather lovely, at least until you spot the handwritten sign on the door, in two languages: THIS CATHOLIC CHURCH NEVER BEEN SYNAGOGUE [sic].

I had not hoped, coming here, for a waft of sour prejudice, and I retreat, with relief, to a place where more ancient bias has blown or seeped away. At Neapolis Archaeological Park, Greek and Roman remains coexist peaceably. The Roman amphitheatre can be viewed only from a distance, although its arches, giving on to a white stone stage, are impressive even from afar, and I can see the gouged-out central pit, where beasts would have awaited their turn to die. Perhaps those bloodied animal ghosts jostle for prominence with others who perished on the gargantuan Greek altar to Zeus, nearby, but the Greeks surely win through weight of numbers. Built by Rome's friend Hieron II, who was, despite his evident negotiating skills, one of several rulers of ancient Syracuse so brutal that Tyrant became a designation rather than a judgement, it was able to accommodate 450 oxen for sacrifice at the same time – which must have been a sight to behold, whatever your views on wanton animal destruction. The Greek theatre, however, has been covered with modern temporary seating for plays – ancient Greek ones, naturally – which take place here each July. You still get a sense of the enormous, intact stadium, glowing white under the relentless sun, but those seats ruin the atmosphere, so we turn aside, into the Latomia del Paradiso – the Paradise quarry – where ropemakers used to work, cool among the limestone and flowers. Here the mischievous or tuneful can create echoes in a giant slit named (by the artist Caravaggio) the Ear of Dionysius, possibly after a judge in the Bible who was converted to Christianity by hearing Saint Paul preach, or else after an early Tyrant of Syracuse who, it was believed, used it to eavesdrop on the slaves working in his quarries. You can walk in, between chill, dark, sloping walls, and certainly this is the closest any of us will come to a journey down the ear canal. It is a light – and cool! – moment between the sizzling pale limestone carved by long-dead hands for the bloodthirsty pleasures of long-dead citizens, and the black volcanic sand of a living volcano: Etna.

What better place to trace history than these vineyards nourished by the earth's hot and roiling core? Etna spits menacing streams of lava and rock, and clouds of ash, with disconcerting frequency. Nonetheless, there are grapes here – Carricante, Nerello Mascalese – that grow almost nowhere else, and in those and in better-known varieties (Planeta make a very good Riesling up here) you can taste the minerals that seem like the land's apology for the destruction it periodically causes. Mineral content here is around 4 per cent, which is very high, but then there is very little here but minerals.

We visit a secret garden where some of the vines are
140 years old: phylloxera cannot survive here. As always,
the gaps in our knowledge nag at me. We know that
volcanic land takes about 300 years to regenerate fully
and regain its exceptional fertility after an eruption, but
we don't know if that enormous upheaval changes the
taste of the wine. We are able to make wine from pre-
phylloxera grapes in places like this, but what would
the wine world be like if that plague had never come?
How would the wines, and the map of vineyards, differ? They are not beneficial, these questions. We cannot
taste the distant past. We can only learn the myths and
rituals by which its drinkers lived and send our imag-
inations, inspired by our senses, travelling across that
great divide. Or perhaps, like Burgundian monks, we
should just lick the soil. I know that loving wine is
partly about embracing your own ignorance, learning
more while making peace with the enormous amount
you will never know. Still, among this ancient tangle of
bush vines, I feel wine's simultaneous pull and push: the
generosity in sending us travelling, and the parsimony
in providing an itinerary.

But Etna is no place to complain about any aspect of
travel. 'I keep trying to leave but the volcano is mag-
netic ... I get here and I can relax,' the bartender at
Monaci de Terre Nere tells me, serving an appropriately
effervescent cocktail he calls an Etna Spritz: Campari,
Amara (a local variant on Cointreau), Murgo's sparkling
Nerello Mascalese and soda. Odd to find a place where
the very earth tenses and shivers relaxing, although
there is something comforting about a danger that
is both very visible and entirely beyond my control.
And this beautiful former monastery, with its lava walls

and infinity pool with view down towards the sea, was designed for contemplation.

The monks made wines – there is another old *palmento* to prove it – and so do their replacements, but they also champion other, more eclectic Etna winemakers, including Frank Cornelissen, a Belgian natural wine fanatic whose output ranges, as natural wines tend to, from fantastic to faulty. Natural wine, the creed of minimal intervention, including refusal to add anything at all to the fermented juice except a tiny amount of sulphites (and even that is controversial), seems to bring out the worst in people, I complain to C over dinner. Otherwise pleasant human beings turn into snarling horrors in its defence, but I maintain my right to weather their condescension and keep faith with my own tastebuds. We are eating sea urchin with Alice Bonaccorsi's Val Cerasa Etna Bianco 2013, which is organic rather than natural – that is, there are no pesticides or chemicals used in the vineyard, but intervention is permitted in the winery. It is an odd wine, funky but dry, made from 100 per cent Carricante grapes grown, as is usual for Etna but unusual elsewhere in this hemisphere, on north-facing slopes. Wine is not a natural product, I point out; nobody walks though the garden and says, Look, there's a wine! Fermentation is stopped according to whim; fining or racking or oak-ageing are all at the discretion of the winemaker … It is an odd fantasy of omnipotence, the notion that one can do nothing and yet create a wine that is simultaneously the perfect expression of its location and of its creator's will. It puts me in mind of those biblical tales of heavenly punishment for overreaching, and I cast my eyes fearfully towards Etna's smoking peak. As for sulphites – as

Bogata at Tasca d'Almerita pointed out, 'there are more in your morning juice than in most wines'.

Not all natural wines taste nasty; while I've had very peculiar (and expensive!) wines of Cornelissen's, the rosé Susucaru 2014 that accompanies our roast beef carpaccio and home-grown spinach is perfectly pleasant. C points out that there is also an element of historical blindness in wanting to go back to the way our forefathers did things – all naturally, apparently – without looking properly at how those things were done. We hanker after purity, in our E-additive, sugar-coated age, but we are wrong to ascribe precisely the same fears to our predecessors. As we have seen, chalk dust, seawater and all kinds of herbal oddities were added to ancient wines, and they were aged in clay coated in resin or even lead. Columella advised a careful consideration of ancestral methods but in our time that respect often seems to give way to a fantasy of how things once were. I remember Sara Pérez in Catalonia talking about what we lose when we lose the past: she looks for forgotten winemaking methods and old vineyards and documentation on the people who owned them, while I wander around ancient synagogues or monuments. We all invent stories, about the history of the vines and the taste of the wines. We cannot help ourselves. We reach out, with fingertips and tongues, and create coherence and connections where we cannot bear to believe that none exist. The search for a binding narrative is a comfort for those things we will never see or hear or touch again. I had not seen my quest for knowledge as a way to assuage my grief, but talking to the Planeta aunties – that rare, precious opportunity to hear the stories of people in their eighties with an entirely different life experience – has brought that possibility home to me. 'It is the colours I miss when I leave the countryside,' Carolina had told me, as the sky turned hazy mauve beyond the vineyards and tomatoes glowed on the dinner table, and her powerful sense of the beauty of here and now made me think of Reims Cathedral, and all the bleached Roman monuments: the colours of the past that we will never see. We must not forget, in our age of click and swipe, how to stop and look while we can. *Carpe diem*, as Horace wrote: pluck the day. Here I am, right now, with deep green leaves drooping over our tree-shrouded balcony, a full moon, a full glass of pretty pink wine, and C to gaze upon. I am a wanderer at rest, briefly aware of all the joys of this particular present. I leave the past suspended, like the sediment at the bottom of my bottle, and am, momentarily, perfectly content.

'We do not inherit land from our ancestors,' Arianna had said to me, quoting Antoine de Saint-Exupéry, the explorer, aviator and author of wondrous children's story *The Little Prince*: 'we hold it for our descendants.' A winemaker, immersed in the cycle of the seasons and the vagaries of the weather, drinking aged wines, knowing that 40 or 50 vintages is the most even the long-lived can hope for, can't avoid an understanding of time's fluidity. It trickles away in both directions; we try our inadequate best to catch it as it flows. But sometimes, it's important just to cup and hold the present.

A convivial Roman mosaic at the Villa del Tellaro, near Noto
in Sicily

Soccorso Romano of Il Cancelliere winery in Campania

8

CAMPANIA:
Resurrection

This is Vesuvius, lately green with shady vines;
here the noble grape had pressed the dripping vats.
These are the heights which Bacchus loved more than the
hills of Nysa;
on this mountain the Satyrs recently danced;
this was the abode of Venus, more beloved by her than
Lacedaemon;
this was the place made glorious by the fame of Hercules.
All now lies buried in flames and melancholy embers;
even the gods might wish that this had not been
permitted them

MARTIAL, *EPIGRAMS* (Author's Translation)

From the living volcano I move on to the dead one,
except it isn't as dead as all that. 'The Etna is always quiet
and slow: it is advising you of its plans,' says Gaetano.
'The Vesuvio will not do that, for sure.' Gaetano is a one-
man embassy for Irpinia, the neglected inland segment
of the region called by the Romans Campania Felix,
the Lucky Country. They loved Naples, Pompeii and

the Amalfi coast, and not much has changed: mountainous Irpinia, 50km from that incredible coastline, may have hazelnuts, mozzarella and pecorino cheeses, chestnuts, black truffle, great meat and wheat and spectacular views through the Apennines but the tourists largely ignore it, and when they do want to visit they find doing so less than straightforward. The vines here were probably planted by the ancient Greeks, using an Etruscan method called *vite maritata* (married vines) that involves training the vines up trees instead of stakes. This was the method we heard of back in Burgundy, the shining example of harmonious cohabitation that Vertumnus used to seduce Pomona. It is apparently effective, and a few winemakers still use it, although it may have drawbacks. As we saw, free workers demanded contracts that took into account the dangers of picking treetop grapes, obliging vineyard owners to pay, should it become necessary, for a funeral.

Campania has much in common with Sicily across the water: not just dominating volcanoes and often, although not always, the same domineering ruler, but also an ancient past as part of Magna Graecia and a recent history marred by organised crime. This is the impoverished south: there is no active tourism or wine body to offer assistance, and very little infrastructure. This is particularly annoying as Irpinia is one of only a very few areas to contain three DOCGs, the top designation of wine quality: Taurasi, made from red Aglianico grapes grown in a cluster of 17 villages, and the whites Fiano di Avellino and Greco di Tufo.

The latter is the Greco grape grown in a particular soft, well-drained volcanic rock called tuff or tufa, with which the Romans liked to build. This was the Romans' favourite wine-growing region, home to Falernian and other legendary crus: some speculate that the *aminean* grape praised by Pliny and Columella might have been an early form of Greco. The wines here are still great. Perhaps Campania Felix should actually be translated as the Merry Country.

Fortunately, the people here are as dynamic as their official bodies are dormant. 'I will come pick up you at 8.30 a.m. at Naples train station,' says Gaetano in his delightfully idiosyncratic English, and he does. A plump, voluble man in his late thirties, he was working as a wine importer for one of the bigger Campania wineries a decade ago when an American guest in a smart Positano hotel rang and asked for a wine tour, with transport from the coast. Neither he nor his colleagues were able to help, and the lady didn't visit. Gaetano was, he says, so upset he didn't sleep that night – 'is very important people visit my area because I'm very proud' – and the upshot was The Wine Bus: a bespoke guided tour to whichever edible part of his much-loved region you wish to see. Of around 150 wineries in the region, 65 or 70 are, he says, his partners, and his blazing energy and pride extend to Perugia, where he wants to set up a Wine Bus, and 'maybe Orvieto too because I love Orvieto too much!' But Irpinia has his heart. He wants it to be the next Chianti: 'When you go to Tuscany all is perfect,' he says, in a tone that from anyone less kindly would be disdainful. 'For the money you spend there in one week you can stay here one month!' If the reputation of this overlooked region is restored, Gaetano, whose family has lived here for at least 300 years and probably much longer, will deserve his neighbours' gratitude.

Gaetano wants to show me a big and a small winery, to understand 'how we make wine in Italy: the contrasts between the industrial and the artisan, the big commerce and the family business'. But first, in the Mediterranean tradition, some ham. Prosciutto makers Ciarcia weathered the Second World War and the doldrums that followed, but now they are thriving, with a smart shop that also sells local products from small producers and a large, modern facility that smells richly of curing meat. These pigs' legs are beautiful, salted and larded, with a protective coating of rice flour and fat carefully smeared, by hand, near the bone, and months in ever less chilly, less humid refrigerated rooms. At the end, they get a final three months at room temperature, during which the salt squeezes out of the meat in tufts that resemble crystals of frost. (It is a mountain product for this reason, since before refrigeration they would have needed chilly spaces to cure the meat. It is always around five degrees cooler here than in Naples, and Irpinia is the first place, in Italy in midsummer, that I see rain.) The ham, which will hang for 16 or 18 months altogether, tastes wonderful. With the exception of a headily intense, melting capocollo, it's lighter than the ham the Spaniards make, and it has a gentler history: there was an Inquisition here but it was concerned principally with repressing so-called Christian heresies such as Protestantism, and I find no reference to the practice of forcing Jews or Muslims to prove their newfound Christianity by eating a meat their forefathers regarded as an abomination. In England, C explains, a ham is a bad actor; here, Gaetano replies, to call someone a prosciutto is to call them an idiot. Poor pig, I think: poor clever, tasty animal that has come to carry so much more allegorical weight, in religious and colloquial terms, than its coarse pink back should have to bear.

Bambinuto is a titchy winery with seven hectares, named for the mispronunciation, by Marilena Aufiero's Venezuelan family, of *benvenuto*, welcome: a story of recent arrivals and linguistic confusion I like very much. A former lawyer ('but I wasn't interested') she has laid out zucchini pizza, *al taglio* (that is, in oblong slices, Roman rather than Neapolitan style) and her 11-year-old daughter helps serve, while her 15-year-old son joins us later with an ease that very few teenagers I know display among strange adults. Maybe a business run from home – she deals with the wine, he is a *carabiniere*, and I kick C to forestall any drunken policeman jokes – is conducive to this fluidity between social visits and professional ones. And after all, winemaking is one of the most sociable professions in existence.

Marilena's wines are good, particularly the whites: she is, says her husband, the 'queen of white wines' and unafraid to wait until a wine is ready: a single-vineyard Greco di Tufo called Picoli, from 2013, is delicious, rich and full of fennel. They didn't make the wine in 2014, which was a dreadful vintage all over mainland Italy – much to the annoyance of the Sicilians, whose perfectly good wines get tarred with the same brush. The 2015 is clearly not ready. 'It is hard to sell a three-year-old wine here, they think last year is too old!' says Marilena, but it is one of the tasks of winemakers, their eyes fixed on the unpredictable sky, their work channelled through seasons, their oak barrels smoothing out the angularity of youth, to teach us how to wait. And how to rejoice when the waiting is done: *Dove non è vino non è amore e null'altro diletto havvi ai mortali*, announces Euripides on the back of the Picoli label – translated by Gaetano as 'no martini no party!' There is a taste of clay in the wine, too, and, sure enough, Marilena says there is clay in the soil as well as limestone, and the vineyard is so subject to landslides that they have to replace 150 vines every year.

We try a 2015 Falanghina named Insania ('Marilena she love Falanghina too much!') that is completely different from the Grecos: a bit woody and hazelnutty with something green (parsley, I say; celery, maintains C) and excellent structure, with a nice hit of caramel right at the end. In Italy they think Falanghina is the *aperitivo* but Marilena says it's great with fish – 'the Picoli is very strong, it's not good with clam pasta or seafood, but this is!' Gaetano tells me that the name of the grape comes from the Latin, signifying a Roman phalanx, or close array of troops – nearby Montemiletto, or Soldiers' Hill, was used by the Romans as a watchtower in their many battles with the local Samnites. This was the third century BC, but the locals have forgotten nothing; when I visit Il Cancelliere winery, just a little further south on the slopes of Montemarano, their mountain will be described to me as 'the place the Romans couldn't conquer'.

Marilena brings out her *passito*, the sweet wine made from grapes sundried for concentration in a method not dissimilar to that described by Columella (and old even then), and sponge cake dabbed with jam. This *passito*, Proditio 2011, is made from Greco and tastes to me of halva, the Middle Eastern sesame and honey sweet that my sister and I were mad for as children. It takes me back to a delicatessen in Streatham in an era when treats were rarities, breathlessly anticipated, and happiness hung threadlike from a parent's whim. We try her excellent brandy, too; in fact the only variety we don't taste is her Aglianico, an ancient local variety said to derive its name, and its origins, from Greece. On the way to our B&B, Gaetano mentions that his parents make some Aglianico, too, which he dislikes.

'Is like grape juice,' he snorts. 'My father thinks his is real and others are not real because they add sulphites.' Which is certainly a new angle, for me, on the naturalistas' debate over using sulphites. Some say it causes headaches, but it certainly helps to stabilise wines that can otherwise taste terrible. And sulphites are naturally occurring: the Romans, who probably didn't know about sulphur's stabilising properties (or, at least, didn't leave us written evidence of their knowledge), would still have had inadvertent help from sulphur in their *dolia*.

In between showing tourists his country, and entertaining them while he does so, Gaetano fills other gaps in people's knowledge: he traces family members for foreigners of Italian descent, usually Americans, to re-establish contact. This does not seem to me so different from reintroducing them to the descendants of ancient wines. He has tracked his own family back to the 1670s: they were here, with their chickens, olive and hazelnut trees, their little vegetable garden, all just as Gaetano's parents are now. His mother cooks fresh and local, he says, 'so when I go outside I prefer the fancy restaurant'. Odd for a city-dweller to hear, in an era when even fancy restaurants are keen to shout about their artisanal and local ingredients.

So he takes us to a fancy restaurant: Marennà, at the disconcertingly large and modern Feudi di San Gregorio winery, has a Michelin star. The chef, Paolo Barrale, is Sicilian, just as the best Italian chefs were in Roman times, and he has been here since the restaurant opened 12 years ago. I don't know who frequents its cool, industrial-chic rooms, but I know why they do. The *tubetti* pasta with beans, mussels and coffee is one of the finest dishes I eat in Italy, and Pietracalda, San Gregorio's top Fiano di Avellino, which is floral and mineral, like a chamomile plant growing out of a rock, makes a lovely match.

Feudi began around 30 years ago, when Avellino-born Enzo Ercolino and his two brothers decided to return and try to help mitigate the aftermath of the devastating 1980 earthquake. They succeeded: the winery now sells 3.5 million bottles a year. It has vineyards on the slopes of Vesuvius, making a wine whose name, Lacryma Christi, is said by some to come from the tears of delight Jesus shed, on his ascent to heaven, when he beheld the beauty of Mount Vesuvius and the Bay of Naples. Others, more prosaic, suggest that medieval monks filtered the wine through cloth, and the drops squeezed out looked like tears (although surely they made mainly red wine, in which case those drops would have resembled blood). In any case, the name seems appropriate for wine from vines grown on a volcano. The most famous biblical instance of weeping by Jesus is when he hears Lazarus has died, and resurrects him, a miracle that both helps ensure his own crucifixion and foreshadows the Second Coming. And the richness of the soil here, as on Etna, is another kind of resurrection: a belated reward for volcanic destruction.

'O happy beyond measure the tillers of the soil …' Virgil had written in his collection of poems the *Georgics*, a century before Vesuvius erupted. This was partly an encomium for the natural life under Emperor Augustus – *georgos* means one who works the soil – but only partly. The Emperor had rewarded the troops who won him the civil war with land in Campania, and – in a story as old as husbandry – the incumbents had been dispossessed to make room for the new owners. That bucolic life had acquired a tinge of exile. 'Tityrus, here you loll, your slim reed-pipe serenading the Muse beneath the canopy of a spreading beech,' Virgil had written in an earlier series of poems, the *Eclogues*, 'while we must leave our home and the fields we love: we must flee our homeland.' And what a homeland: Pliny claimed that the greatest wines in existence in his time were three Falernians from Campania.

Feudi di San Gregorio, named for the sixth-century Pope Gregory the Great, has 300ha of vineyards in around 700 plots, which sounds almost Burgundian, in distribution if not in size. The San Gregorio owners (Capaldos now, rather than Ercolinos), like the Guigals, buy in grapes from local producers. (These little patches are separately vinified, then blended before bottling.) The interiors of the winery are constructed from cement coated in tufa, which conducts humidity well, while the walls of their cellar are cork. It all looks, and sounds, very smart; Gregorian chants, also named for that early pope, play as you tour. I am startled to see a nativity scene, even one made entirely of cork: it's midsummer. Still, the Campanians love nativity scenes, whatever the season – in Naples, where we see several, we are told there is a tradition that Jesus was, in fact, born there.

Certainly, this is a place that, despite its ultra-modern winery, is absorbed in the past. The Capaldos have also experimented with *vite maritata*; they claim to make one wine, Serpico, from 200-year-old ungrafted Aglianico vines, which means that, however many attempts at Roman winemaking I try, this beautiful blackcurrant wine, with its strong but pleasant taste of iron, may be the closest I'll ever come to tasting the vines of my forefathers – particularly as southern Italy had Jewish communities from at least the first century AD.

We drive through splendid scenery, pink and yellow houses bright counterpoints to the varying dark foliage of tree-coated hills. We are supposed to visit a Roman mausoleum – this area is, of course, thickly seeded with Roman remains – but it is closed, opening days being so eclectic here that even the locals cannot work them out, with the plethora of saints' days and other holidays fluctuating wildly from one village to the next. At Il Cancelliere, over 550m up Montemarano, there are pretty white decorations in the shape of gates at the end of several rows of vines: a festival, recently finished, says Claudio Panetta.

As with Bambinuto, this is a tiny, family enterprise: they have just seven hectares of clay, limestone ... and volcanic dust, from Vesuvius. It's not yet fully a paying concern – every family member has another job – but the Romanos (Claudio is a son-in-law) have had vineyards here for over a hundred years. In the hard times after the Second World War they simply sold their grapes; only in 2005 did they start making wine again. The whole set-up feels ancient, from the vineyards (and vegetables) outside the front door to the small cousins running round, scooped up by whichever adult is passing, and the men proudly patting their barrels – Slavonian oak, plus a century-old chestnut barrel and a new one, the latter made by the original maker's great-grandson. Claudio thinks Aglianico (the only grape they grow), while 'never easy drinking', has everything: aroma, fruit, flavour, power. 'We want the oak to touch it as little as possible.' They are, however, hoping oak can help the 2014s. In that year, there was so much rain that the volcanic dust ended up in the wine – and it's true, you can taste it. The following vintage, tasted in barrel and clearly immature, is already much more accessible. 'The 2015 likes the spotlight; 2014 will spend all its life behind a curtain,' says Claudio, sadly.

They bring out meat and cheese for the tasting, under a canopy of vegetation overlooking a hillside of vines, and when C remarks on the quality of the Parmesan they insist, to our sheepish delight, that he take an enormous slice home. They have not used sulphites since 2013; they harvest entirely by hand and also follow the phases of the moon, a biodynamic practice that Columella recommended and which was sneered at, 1,900 years later, by the otherwise great early twentieth-century historian of ancient vines, Raymond Billiard. Roman beliefs, in planting and grafting while the moon is waxing and pruning by the full moon, are now treated with more respect. It is not just the vine – or the moon – that works in cycles. At any rate, 'here in Montemarano it is tradition!' says Claudio.

How much of our grandfathers' – and grandmothers' – wisdom we lose, and must work to recover. Here they seem to have safeguarded a whole endangered way of living that any Roman citizen would recognise, and when I look at the lettuce and potatoes, the hazelnuts, kiwis and olives growing beside the vines, I think of Horace: 'Blessed the man who, like the first mortals, ploughs his ancestral acres with his own oxen, far from wheeling and dealing and free from all usury.' Sentimental, perhaps, but emotion comes easily on a scenic hilltop, with friendly hosts and excellent, strong red wine called Nero Né, in tribute both to the colour (*nero* means 'black', *né* is local dialect for 'very') and to the Emperor, whose dark reputation feels very out of place here. 'In Irpinia, red wine doesn't exist,' says Claudio: 'there is just white and black', and certainly the Nero Né Taurasi 2010 is a red so deep it resembles mahogany, while the Nero Né Riserva 2008 glows in an unholy fashion that its imperial namesake might have approved. The former in particular is just beautiful, the fruit so far back there's just a reminder of raspberry, winding round tannins strong as stakes; and it's heartening to see these kind and hardworking people doing, in their modest and generous way, well.

On the terrace of the house, several elderly people sit quietly; they wave as we leave. They are waiting, it turns out, for a family lunch: mortified, we mutter apologies. They had invited us to share their meal, Gaetano says; I am English enough to be glad he refused. Before we leave, we enter a hut that turns out to be a kitchen, separated from the main house, as in ancient times, in case of fire. In a huge shallow frying pan, the women are crisping battered courgette flowers, which they insist we try. They are hot, light, delicious.

I am still thinking about lost knowledge – the temptation to think we know better until what our grandparents knew vanishes, as irretrievable as the wine knowledge my father tried to share with me, or the taste of Pliny's Falernian. A vast amount of wisdom was saved only by the Moors translating the Greeks and Romans into Arabic, during Córdoba's heyday, when the city contained 300 libraries; generations later, they were able to pass those lost books back into languages threaded with the descendants of classical vocabulary. Why do we so often reject what we are bequeathed, or is a certain level of ignorance and insouciance essential to accomplishments that wiser heads would deem impossible?

I had wanted to visit Mastroberardino, where the latest of ten generations of winemakers are making wine in the shadow of Vesuvius. Within the circumference of the Pompeii ruins, they experiment with different training methods as described by Pliny the Elder, including *albarello*, the stick on a hillside I saw in the Rhône, and *arbustum*, sustained by a tree: *vite maritata*. Antonio Dente, Mastroberardino's agronomist, tells me that one reason pruning became common is that by keeping the vines at human height they prevented *pericula arbusti*: the dangers of climbing trees to pick grapes.

Time forbids: I need to go west. Manuela Piancastelli of Terre del Principe and her husband Peppe Mancini are reviving various forgotten indigenous grapes in Caserta province. When I contacted her about visiting the vineyards, an hour's drive towards the coast from Irpinia, her answer to my logistical queries was simple: we would stay with them. They would be moving soon, to be closer to their vineyards and their tenth-century cellar, dug into the tufa stone in the tiny village of Squille, but for now their spacious house, atop a basement winery, had a whole apartment for guests.

Peppe is not someone to disregard a grandfather's wisdom; it was largely his childhood trips around the vineyard with his grandpa Guiseppe that inspired him to rootle through his uncle's oldest vineyards and rediscover two almost extinct Campania grapes: Pallagrello Bianco and Pallagrello Nero, which, despite their names, are distinct varieties. He was a lawyer, Manuela a journalist, but as happens, wine obsession took over. Now they have 11ha of Pallagrello and Casavecchia, another obscure variety. I am delighted to see that even the wine writer Jancis Robinson and the ampelographer and grape DNA expert José Vouillamoz, in their rigorous and comprehensive book *Wine Grapes*, write that Casavecchia, which has a DNA profile that 'does not match that of any other variety in Campania or anywhere else', might be the *trebulanum* grape mentioned by Pliny the Elder, and, once again, I feel the compelling tug of old stories and the drive, strong as hunger or lust, to construct a narrative that makes sense of the world.

We wash away the travel dirt, such as it is, with a cool, refreshing Le Sèrole Pallegrello Bianco 2014, which has a pleasant touch of honey, and glints gold in the beautiful evening light. From the couple's large, vine-canopied terrace we can watch the surrounding mountains turn black, backlit by apricot. It is very peaceful.

Whether or not Pliny drank any of them, these are extremely old varieties, and ungrafted: the underlying uncertainty of life beside a sleeping volcano does have some advantages. 'Vesuvio is quiet since 1944,' says Manuela, 'but the next eruption will be like '79 again ... They don't know when. We stay here and what 'appens 'appens.' There is no DOC designation that incorporates her grapes so all the wines are labelled with the less specific IGT – *Indicazione Geografica Tipica* – in this case, Terre del Volturno. The Volturno is the river where Hannibal camped, plundering the surrounding fields and villages, while he tried to tempt the Romans into battle during the Second Punic War.

Manuela, a calm, beautiful woman with short white hair and kind blue eyes, fires up when she talks about her grapes – 'Pallagrello means small ball: the white is small and delicate, very feminine, very sexy, with what looks like a nipple! The Nero is less delicate and matures later. We feel like the father and mother of these wines,' she adds, and certainly they nurture them like parents. Their plan is to reduce their holdings to just seven hectares so they can concentrate even more on the quality of what they produce. 'We are always trying new things,' says Manuela, reminding me once again that good winemakers, unlike most of us, know how much they don't know, and see that as a challenge rather than a failure.

Peppe, balding, mustachioed, a courtly and gentle man, bustles in with a simple dinner of roast meats and potatoes, and we try two vintages of their Ambruco, which is entirely Pallagrello Nero. The 2012 works with well-cooked beef and gravy; 2008 with a type of simple local cheese called Caciotta. The unfamiliar grape turns out to taste of blueberry and blackberry, dark chocolate and a touch of pepper. These are not unusual flavours for wines – and yet in a blind tasting I think I would realise that I did not know this grape. We talk of Naples, and of the *castrati* – the young boys castrated so that their voices didn't change and they were able to make beautiful, unearthly music for the decadent pleasure of the Neapolitan rich. This had a certain gruesome aptness given that Naples was originally named Parthenope, for the ancient Greek siren whose beauteous singing failed to win her Ulysses, and whose name means maidenvoiced. Her grave may have been here or, if you prefer the Roman legend, Jupiter may have turned her into the city in a fit of jealous rage over her love affair with a centaur called Vesuvio – whom he transformed, of course, into the volcano. Sicily has its chained, submerged giant, Campania these creatures writhing from frustrated desire. These stories serve as explanation and comfort for the inhabitants of restless lands.

Manuela, the native, has offered to show us round Naples. She and Peppe met when she went to interview him about the grapes he had discovered. 'They changed our lives, these grapes,' she laughs, 'but we have changed their lives, too!' They are a delightful couple, gracious, generous, intelligent and clearly firm in their commitment to their shared project and to one another. Where did the winery name come from, I ask later, and Manuela replies that Terre del Principe – the Prince's Land – is her tribute to Peppe, 'because he is my prince'.

She takes us to the oldest, Greco-Roman part of the city. Here, ancient Egyptian merchants, who arrived from Alexandria once Cleopatra's Empire was subsumed into Rome's, erected a statue to the god of the Nile. It's still there, after various travels, thefts, a new head and even the miraculous rediscovery of the original presiding sphinx, looted during the Second World War, in an art shop in Austria. The nearby church, which has a floridly lovely marble tomb by Donatello, is called Sant'Angelo a Nilo. The city's memory, it seems, was better than that of its citizens, since for centuries the statue and the story were lost – but the name of Piazzetta Nilo remained.

The road we walk down bustles with small shops hollowed out of venerable buildings, wares bunched busily on outer walls, upper storeys crowding towards their opposite number until just a sliver of hot sun hits ancient paving stones pocked and polished with use. This fantastic street has several names, including Via Benedetto Croce and Via San Biagio dei Librai, but it's known as Spaccanapoli (literally, 'Naples-splitter') and it is also one of three surviving Decumani – the principal east–west roads every Roman city possesses. The Decumanus Maximus would cross with a Cardo Maximus going north–south, and I will find one here, but, meanwhile, I turn off to walk past the ancient Cathedral to Via Sapienza: Knowledge Street.

I turn into the church of San Gregorio, an extraordinary Baroque riot of painting and carving and statuary: even the ceiling is entirely decorated, and how one is supposed to concentrate on the glory of God rather than gilt here is a mystery to me. This, says C, craning upwards, was the Counter-Reformation: Catholicism, always the Western religion most interested in spectacle, going overboard in its attempts to announce its primacy over Protestantism and win back those who had strayed. A better counter-attack than the Inquisition, I think as I stumble around, almost too blinded by curlicues and cupids to notice the carved Book of Generations in a side chapel. Here, in an echo of Chagall's Tree of Jesse in Reims Cathedral, Jesus is announced as the son of David who is the son of Abraham, in Greek, Latin and Hebrew, and the whole is decorated with that other reminder of the continuation of the generations: grapes.

There is quiet, and a rest for the eyes, in the courtyard. Here, it is easy to recall that this is a convent (there are still nuns selling devotional items and taking donations), and that the church was built atop a temple to Ceres, Roman goddess of grain and fertility. There are columns carved from volcanic rock and someone, somewhere, is playing the piano.

We do briefly peep inside the very different – French Gothic – Naples Cathedral, where a vial of dried blood belonging to St Januarius, the patron saint of Naples who was martyred in the early fourth century, is said to liquefy miraculously several times a year. This really is a much stranger place than I'd realised, I think, as we walk back west down the second Decumanus, Via Tribunali. Mostly, tourists hear about pizza or crime (even from Campanians: 'Naples people very crazy for Rolex,' Gaetano told me), yet nobody mentions how charming the city is, unruly and friendly and almost entirely lacking in twenty-first-century gloss. Its vestiges feel very close to the surface, what with the houses and belltowers made from plundered Roman bricks, the archway supporting ordinary apartments that was an ancient gate to the city, the plaques announcing the generosity of Emperors ... And then we turn into the church of San Lorenzo Maggiore, and head down some steps, and find that ancient Neapolis is, in fact, just a few feet down. Here is the covered market, even cooler than it would have been 2,000 years ago. Arches rear behind one another in diminishing echoes and the flagstones of the ancient pavement accommodate my slingbacks as readily as they once did leather sandals.

Actually, there is both crime and pizza down here, in this third-century relic preserved by a medieval mudslide and rediscovered via Allied bombing. At least one empty window has holes where bars once protected the contents from thieves; and there's a bakery, with an oven almost identical to a modern pizza oven, although this one, like its more famous sibling down the road in Pompeii, will have been used for bread. I love Pompeii, its wine bars and its excellent graffiti ('Curses on you, landlord, you sell water and drink unmixed wine yourself'), but Naples, so close by, seems so much less discovered. There are Roman, and probably Greek, remains under the whole city. View it from the air and you see a strange curve where the building of later houses followed the line of the Roman amphitheatre. Nero sang on its stage, apparently, obliging his subjects to stay and listen on pain of death. There are so many buried antiquities, and so much tufa was quarried here to build, that the locals say that Naples is a city that is 60 per cent built on nothing. I see that differently. Like a vineyard, only the modern sprouting is visible, but it is imprudent, even dangerous, to dismiss what lies beneath. No wonder the inhabitants are superstitious.

Ovens two millennia cold are all very well, but the living require pizza. Manuela takes us to Sorbillo, a noisy, cheerfully madcap restaurant with fabulous food; all 20 of the founder's siblings are apparently pizza-makers. Twenty-one kids, really? I ask Gino, who is something of an international star: he has guested on *MasterChef Australia*. He shrugs: he is number 19. 'In the past, there was not the television ...'

There's one more stop before we leave: the Monastery of Santa Chiara. Built in the fourteenth century, it was fiercely bombed during the Second World War, badly damaging frescoes which were probably biblical scenes (possibly, appropriately enough, the Apocalypse) and may have been by the great Giotto. The restoration effort was incredibly swift, given the chaos and pen-ury of the post-war period, and there was one benefit to the destruction: the discovery of Roman thermal baths beneath the church. Now, there's an open archae-ological site tacked on one side, a harsh contrast to the gardens, carefully coaxed into artful loveliness, on the other. The latter are as ordered and tended as a vineyard, with restored eighteenth-century majolica tile pillars shining yellow and blue among the greenery; the for-mer orderly, too, but crude and bleached: gaping squares of raw bricks and white tufa. Among the treasures dis-played inside is a full-size pillar in the helical style called Solomonic, because it was the shape of the columns framing the First Temple, built by King Solomon, and destroyed in 587 BC. This is a plaster cast of what was once marble, and it is delightful: covered in vines, with putti clambering among them and standing on each other's fat shoulders to reach the succulent grapes of the 'vineyard of the Lord' mentioned in Isaiah. There was a theory that the originals here were plundered from the Second Temple after its destruction in AD 70, but that strikes me as an attempt to claim a sturdier foundation for this church than already existed – perhaps sensible, given that it turned out to be resting on hollowed-out bathing quarters.

We walk from reverent shade back into the sunshine, and see a poignant little plaque, which says, in translation:

> After centuries of glory
> this temple
> destroyed by war
> rises as an altar of peace
> in the heart of ancient Naples
> and welcomes the names and memory
> of those who shed blood
> in the hope of love among nations
> August 4, 1943 – August 4, 1953

It is time to go.

So we drive back up into the hills, away from all those churches, to an alternative place of worship: Manuela's vineyards. She uses pergola trellising – like a canopy, and very like the shady vines over her terrace, although here the point is to keep sun off the grapes, as well as hoisting them above the reach of wild boar. They are beautiful, these ancient, be-nippled grapes, pendant clusters of living jewels backed by mountains that are, for now, benign. As Manuela glides towards them I am struck by the fact that this really is her home: never mind that she is Neapolitan, this is the hearth that she has chosen, the place she nurtures and would defend. Watching her, I realise that finding the soil that suits you best is important – more important, perhaps, than knowing where you came from.

Maybe finding a place to belong is open to chance –
as arbitrary a good fortune as planting grapes in a spot
where they turn out to thrive, or encountering combinations of words, in prose or poetry, that make the heart
sing. If we are lucky enough to happen on the right soil
and left to inhabit it peacefully, we can root ourselves
and flourish, to the benefit of all.

We try more Terre del Principe wines that night, in
a local restaurant: a dense, blackcurrant–jam Cento-
moggia 2013 Casavecchia with crispy-skinned pork
belly and small fried fish, and Piancastelli 2012, a tenser,
more restrained but still rich blend of Casavecchia and
Pallagrello Nero with ribbony pasta and mushrooms.
The food is fine, forgettable; the wines and the conversation far more worthwhile. We talk of Casavecchia,
which means 'old house' – the vine was found near a
Roman villa – and must be particularly carefully harvested, says Manuela, because 'the tip is delicate like
glass'. And she and Peppe tell us about Luigi Vanvitelli,
the eighteenth-century architect whose palace at nearby
Caserta (still there, and still spectacular) included in its
capacious grounds a Vigna del Ventaglio, or fan-shaped
vineyard, with each of ten segments planted to a different grape. Two of them were Manuela's Pallagrellos: it
was only when phylloxera came that they, along with so
many others, were lost. 'It is because they like poor soil,
and don't produce many bunches,' says Manuela fondly.
'The water is the enemy of the vineyard. The vines
must suffer to give their best.' Balance, she adds, is the
most important thing in life ... 'And the most difficult!'

I am going next to the Campi Flegrei, the Romans' Flaming Fields – volcanic land where they built natural thermal baths and where sulphurous steam still snakes from the ground in mute reminder that this land is far from dormant. But there is one more thing Manuela wants to show me, and she's prepared to drive me an hour and a half round the edge of the Gulf of Naples to do so.

Cumae was the first Greek colony on the Italian mainland. The Greeks came in the eighth century BC bringing grapes (and some say Falanghina, Greco and Aglianico are all here because they did) and also an alphabet. Much later, after the Romans came, Martial would write of Trifoline, the wine they made here: 'I, Trifoline wine, am not, I confess, of the first order but I hold, at least, the seventh place.'

The Greeks founded Parthenope, later Neapolis, a century or so after their arrival. In the *Aeneid*, Parthenope's greatest son, Virgil, described the arrival of his wandering hero, Aeneas, to ask the prophesying Sibyl when the Trojans would be able to rest:

Grant what I ask (no more in the end than my fate
Has assigned): home ground for my people
In Latium, refuge for our wandering gods
And all Troy ever held sacred.

The Sibyl's grotto is still here, a mysterious tunnel carved from yellow tufa, the upper reaches tapering in a way liable to provoke a pang of panic in a claustrophobe. The confined space might even have bothered the Sibyl herself, if she looked anything like Michelangelo's depiction on the ceiling of the Sistine

Chapel: a muscular, sturdy woman, prosaically hatted and unshod, her book of predictions open beside her. Legend says she lived a thousand years, getting smaller and smaller until she was just a voice kept in a jar, but here she looks broad enough to bang her head on those sloping walls, and fierce enough to bang the wall right back. She was part of the founding myth of Rome, having given three books of prophecies to the young city's king, back in the mists of time. Actually, she sold them, and at a fantastic price; originally there were nine books, and when King Tarquin tried to bargain, the ruthless vendor kept throwing books into the fire, until with three remaining he relented and paid up. Those three books burned in their turn in a fire that preceded Virgil's birth by only a few years, which may have been part of his impetus to preserve her power in *his* book, at least.

In the tunnel, metal rods now bolster the ancients' handiwork; openings in the rock let the bright summer sunlight in, if only to offer a contrast with the soupy darkness between. It is exciting, and daunting, to walk in Aeneas's steps, through 'the cave of wondrous size/ The Sibyl's dread retreat' – a tunnel old when Rome was young, opening into a curved cave, sea-green with lichen. But Virgil also describes a second, more striking part of Aeneas's encounter with the Sibyl. Dissatisfied, like a modern reader of newspaper astrology pages, with her somewhat vague response, he asks another favour, a big one: to be guided down into the Underworld to see the shade of his beloved father, Anchises. With the Sibyl as guide, he bridges the worlds of the living and the dead, descending at nearby Lake Avernus – which is still there, its name (which means 'birdless') still recalling the infernal depths. Nobody who misses someone beloved could fail to be moved by Aeneas's plaintive cry: 'But reach your hand, O parent shade, nor shun/The dear embraces of your longing son!'

It isn't possible. Even for a hero, still breathing in the land of the dead, touch is no use: he can see his father, and hear him, and that is already far more than the rest of us will ever have. As Orpheus, another mortal who crossed the Styx, discovered, we can look backwards – in fact, we cannot help ourselves – but we can never reverse time. In the land of the imagination touch has no place: the past is ungraspable. So Orpheus cannot restore his beloved Eurydice to life, and the shadow of Anchises, too, flits away, 'Like winds, or empty dreams that fly the day.' He shows his weeping son the future, when Rome will be ruled by his descendants, and leaves him with what seem to me very clear instructions. He must go forward. Looking longingly backwards is no way to live.

I climb through the shimmering heat to the tumbled stones of Apollo's temple: the views here are spectacular, cliché-inducing, the turquoise sea spread out beyond the tree-tufted coast, the mountains of Ischia pushing up the horizon, but this is, according to Virgil, the sea into which Icarus plunged, when his triumphant flight from captivity took him too near the sun and the wax on his man-made wings melted. I look at the dilapidated home of Apollo, the sun god, which may or may not have been founded by Daedalus, the grieving father whose invention those wings were, and up at skies that are, like all in Europe now, etched with the soft white traces of passing aeroplanes. What we receive from our fathers is never less than complicated. Apollo was claimed by Emperor

Augustus as an ally of his family – a statement that also seems, in its hubris, to fly a little close to the sun. Standing atop layers of ancient belief and desire, in the breathless heat, thinking about fathers, mortal or otherwise, I recall Auden's poem about Bruegel's wonderfully witty painting *Landscape With The Fall of Icarus*: 'About suffering they were never wrong, the Old Masters ...' How I would love the chance to see my father smile, feel him tweak my cheek and cry '*Ziskeyt!*' – a Yiddish endearment that means, literally, 'Sweetness'. There is nothing sweet about grief. When home is a person and that person is gone, then nostalgia really is a sickness, impossible to assuage or requite ...

Heart aching, I pad slowly back down the hill and get back on the road. Which swiftly narrows to a car's width to pass beneath a high, man-made curve: the Arco Felice, or Lucky Arch, built by Domitian in AD 95 to take his Via Domitiana through Mount Grillo. 'It is very strange to travel on so old a road,' says Manuela softly, 'but in Italy everything is possible.'

We drive past vines, apricot trees, and the remains of the forum built when the city was already a few centuries old, on our way to visit another kind of Sibyl. At La Sibilla winery we must say goodbye to Manuela. These inevitable farewells are surely the worst part of travelling, but she has her home and her prince to return to, and I must travel a little further before I rest.

Luigi di Meo's family have farmed this land for at least five generations, and while he is very young – 27, getting married in a couple of weeks – there's no disdain for older wisdom here. Luigi actually makes a wine in an old-fashioned style that's a tribute to his grand-father, despite the old man having pooh-poohed the idea ('He said, "it will taste like vinegar!"'). I admire his clear-sightedness, but you don't live on land called the Flaming Fields and forget that everything is fragile, and I think of the Sibyl, sending a succession of prophesying books up in flames, and the impenetrable difficulty of resurrecting knowledge that has been lost, whether wilfully or by misfortune.

Actually, Luigi lives squeezed between the past and present, which can have its complications. Next to the family house is a cellar hollowed out of the rock by the Romans. 'We built our house on their aqueduct,' he says wryly. Walk up through the vineyards outside the house, however, and you quickly hit the motorway that runs right through them. Usually, vines aren't permitted so close to major thoroughfares, but unfortunately the reverse doesn't apply, and 'here was born vineyards first'. By quite some way: we climb up past his Piedirosso and Falanghina vines to a hilltop with spectacular views. We are on a strip of soil jutting into the sea, the Gulfs of Gaeta and Naples reaching round either side to embrace the sharp pure blue of the Mediterranean. Down there is Baiae, holiday resort of Rome's emperors; up here are old Falanghina vines and parched grass that barely conceals oregano, rocket, fennel and bright tomatoes. They don't need chemicals, what with the sandy ash-filled soil, and they don't need to graft their vines, either: phylloxera cannot survive on sand. Nonetheless, they are giving grafted Falanghina a 'small try': ungrafted vines put out too many leaves. 'We want a kind of bonsai version for fewer problems in the cultivation,' he says, which makes me wonder what kind of unexpected favour the forced grafting of

European vines might not have bestowed. Most suffering has some benefit, and vice versa.

Much of Baiae has endured but is now underwater. The volcanic activity that fed the prized hot springs proved untameable, even by Emperors, and the water levels rose and submerged the baths and pleasure palaces, preserving them and rendering them inaccessible – unless you know where to look.

Where to look and how to interpret what you see is a theme on this hilltop, too. 'We are not allowed to plant more than fifty centimetres deep because there are Roman ruins everywhere. The roots can go down naturally but you can't make a hole,' Luigi explains. What is obvious is the tell-tale broken white wall of a Roman villa; I'm not surprised that some dignitary chose this gorgeous spot with the hills giving gently on to the blue bay, and say so. Luigi smiles: this was not, he claims, just any dignitary, but Julius Caesar himself. It was said of Caesar's house that he chose its location because, from there, he could see three ports: Baiae, the old military base (Cumae) and the new military base (Miseno), and that triangulated viewpoint is available from here – and from nowhere else, says Luigi firmly. Just as that angry, lust-possessed giant Vesuvio inadvertently guarded the remains of Baiae, so that divers or sojourners in glass-bottomed boats can look into drowned antiquity, so Bacchus has performed the same service on land, because all the finds on this slope, including Caesar's villa, were unharmed thanks to the vines that grew over their roofs.

Luigi, one of three brothers, is only recently back from working in Argentina, 'because everyone thinks if your family has a winery your life is all sorted out, but in fact it is very hard to do something new. They just say, "We have always done it this way."' Poor boy, caught between his grandpa's scorn for the past and his parents' mistrust of a different future, although he seems ready for the challenge. His Domus Giulii 2010 Falanghina boasts on the back that it is 'an expression of time … A perfect synthesis between the ancient and the new.'

Beneath another canopy of vines we eat sliced meat and cheese and try three excellent wines, two very different Falanghinas and a Piedirosso, the 'red foot' grape which takes its name from its red stalk's resemblance to the claws of the wood pigeon, *Columba palumbus*, and which may, or may not, be Pliny the Elder's *columbina* grape. I go back to the Domus Giulii, its vivid lemon and green pepper seeming to paint the pale walls and bright foliage of its namesake on my tongue. Beside those staunch ancient walls, I was able to squint down on Bacoli, on the edge of Lake Miseno: Naples' best beach, these days, but it was Rome's most important military port before Ostia, which is just outside the Roman *urbs*. I sip, and let my mind flow over the gallons of Italian wine that must have accompanied those departing soldiers, as well as the foreign wine that would have washed back on to these shores, particularly after Vesuvius's eruption. Cause and consequence, humans at the mercy of nature – however much they might wish to deny their vulnerability. Had it not been for the eruption, Pliny the Elder would not have died – of inhaling poisonous fumes or a heart attack, accounts differ – on the ash-blanketed beach to which his scientific curiosity had lured him. Farmers would not have planted vast swathes of replacements for Vesuvius's lost vines, impelling Emperor Domitian to pass the vine-restricting edict that undid him. And we would not have Pompeii, miraculously preserved beneath the debris.

Luigi, nice boy though he is, is angry. On our way down the hillside, near the road, he discovers a dismembered moped. 'What is in the mind?' he barks in exasperation, dialling the local police. 'Aren't you worried they'll steal grapes?' I ask, but he clearly doesn't credit them with that much discernment. 'They just steal *motorinos.*' There are broken beer bottles nearby. It is a very modern desecration.

Next I must go further up the Via Domitiana – the road we took from Cumae, one of many that led and still lead to Rome. I cross Hannibal's Volturno river and head through the Falernian fields, which the Consul and poet Silius Italicus claimed were sown with vines by Bacchus himself, past spectacular mountainous country to Villa Matilde, where Salvatore Avallone also juggles city and country, the ancient and the modern. Along with his ten-year-old son, he is waiting to show me the vines of Monte Massico, in a natural depression so fertile that if Sicily was Rome's breadbasket, this could be called its fruit bowl. Salvatore is also CEO of his family's Naples hotel, the Grand Hotel Parker's, a place as grand and as eccentric as its name suggests, out on Corso Vittorio Emanuele with gorgeous views of Vesuvius: luxury and destruction in one frame. But his first love is these vineyards, and his little boy's patience with Papa's passion makes a charming antidote to all the unhappy fathers and sons I've met, in spirit or flesh, so far on my travels.

Salvatore's father Francesco was a renowned Neapolitan lawyer obsessed with the grapes that made the Romans' Falernian; his research uncovered pre-phylloxera grapes that were, he and a group of learned friends claimed, the very varieties once used to make that legendary wine. Eventually, logically enough, he planted his own vineyard here. ('He named it for my mother as repentance for having spent thirty years out looking for vines rather than at home with her'; a confession accompanied by wry laughter.) Still, Avallone senior was highly aggravated when his son, after also training as a lawyer, gave it all up to live and work in the vineyard. His sister also works for the company, and they now have vineyards in three areas of Campania, including Avellino and Benevento, but it is here beside Monte Massico that the most interesting vines grow.

Both Pliny and Strabo maintained that the most exquisite nectars in existence came from Campania. And of all those nectars it is Falernian, 'indomitable' (Persius), 'immortal' (Martial) and 'fiery' (Horace), the 'wine that Caesar served on the occasion of his triumph [in the civil wars]' (Pliny the Elder) that was the most renowned.

'What decency does Venus observe when she is drunken?' ranted Juvenal, in his *Satires*, deploring the luxury and idleness the *Pax Romana* had engendered and the consequent effect on women's morals. 'When she knows not one member from another, eats giant oysters at midnight, pours foaming unguents into her unmixed Falernian, and drinks out of perfume-bowls, while the roof spins dizzily round, the table dances, and every light shows double!' Here is excess unrestrained: a mythical drink to rival Eden's fruit in its delicious flavour and terrible consequences.

'If you look around, you see mountain, mountain, mountain and sea. The area of Falerno is like a cup. The fresh breeze comes down from the mountains, the salty breeze up from the sea.' You can grow anything here. 'Not my problem!' says Salvatore, waving at the peach trees next to his vineyards, but they don't look like they are anyone's problem. So fertile is the soil that every spring, each vine's roots must be painstakingly uncovered and the supplementary shoots growing underground stripped away, or they will sap the strength of stem and fruit.

There have been vines here 'since the Romans times,' says Salvatore in his 'bloody English' (his words, not mine; my Italian should be so good). But after phylloxera, they were replaced with fruit and vegetables. You have to wait at least five years before a vine can make decent wine, 'and people cannot wait five years before eating!' It was his father's obsession that led to the local resurgence of the grapes – Aglianico, Piedirosso, Primitivo – that are now those legally permitted in wine labelled Falerno del Massico. Francesco Avallone, unsurprisingly, helped write those rules.

But, I say, those are red grapes, and most of what I've read indicates that Falernian was white; Falanghina is also known locally as *uva falerno*. 'What type of vine you plant is not so important,' maintains Salvatore: 'it is the soil and the weather that matters. You can produce Merlot, Cabernet Sauvignon, Cabernet Franc and Petit Verdot everywhere but in only one place will those grapes taste like Bordeaux. Pinot Noir is totally different in Burgundy and in Oregon, in the US. It is *terroir* that we have to protect. You can plant vines any place you like.' You could, he suggests, plant Aglianico in Burgundy, and maybe it would be good. 'Heresy!' yelps C.

The sky is very blue, the lines of vines very straight: they funnel the eye down the slope to a chunky, dirty looking building nestled in front of the foothills. That is Masseria San Giuseppe, a twelfth-century castle built on the ruins of a Roman cellar. A couple of kilometres away are more ruins, in the village that was once the loading point for amphorae of the legendary wine, destined for Rome's ports or further afield. The former port is now 600m from the sea. I think of Richborough, and the closed-in Wantsum Channel. No matter how many ruins I clamber over, how many relics I eye, nothing gives me a real sense of the enclosing years like the picture of earth silting up waterways, reshaping coastlines and forming new outcroppings of land. We think of soil as entirely stationary, belonging only to one place – as fixed, certain, able to hold and nurture ambitious structures from vines to victory arches. What is *terroir*, if not a taste of this one place? But soil moves, too. It quakes and slides, mingles with the dead, breaks down and builds up. It is the earth's memory, but like memory it is mutable.

In the winery restaurant, a little stark but warmed by its huge open grill, we taste Falanghinas and Aglianicos from across the Villa Matilde properties. The Falanghina from Benevento, Rocca dei Leoni 2015, is much more immediate and floral than the Falerno del Massico Bianco from the same vintage; the former, made from cooler-climate, mountain-grown vines, is also lower in alcohol. The Massico is fruitier, lots of pear, a bit of stone, and tastes as well structured as that ancient castle. I actually prefer it to the posher white Falerno, Caracci 2014, a single vineyard wine which 'have to sleep in bottle another year', according to Salvatore, but then it is his favourite match for pumpkin soup with lobster, which sounds like something I need to try. When we tour his cellars, we see that he is actually trying to mature some wine in amphorae; like most winemakers, he loves to experiment, and the destination – no matter how satisfying, in terms of quality – won't excite him half as much as the journey. He seals the amphorae with beeswax, he explains animatedly: 'the Romans used pitch but I don't want my wine to taste like retsina [Greek wine made with pine resin]. Beeswax is still natural, but it is very hard to get off afterwards!' For Salvatore, as for Columella, we have history in one hand and modern advances in the other, and to jettison either would be like throwing gold into the sea for Neptune to swallow. 'I want to create modern wine with an ancient story,' he says, seriously: no journeys back into the Underworld for him. 'Roman wine will have been a form of balsamic vinegar!' he exclaims. 'Why would I want to make that?'

The Aglianicos range from the unashamedly commercial to the incandescent. Rocca dei Leoni 2012 tastes like a quaffer for people who don't want to spend much; nothing wrong with that, but it can't stand up to its brethren and I forget it almost instantly. The Falerno 2011, which has 20 per cent Piedirosso, is earthy, with a touch of marzipan, while the Camarato 2010, which has the same proportions but better-quality grapes, each kind from a single vineyard, is lovely (it is only made in good years) but far too young. I want to wait until its sour cherry sweetens and its structure softens slightly. It's a baby I'd like to meet as a young adult. The Taurasi, too, from that strictly regulated part of Campania I liked so much, is immature with a 2010 birthdate, but it is still terrific, earthy and gutsy and full of life. We also try a 100 per cent Aglianico sparkling rosé, which I find too strawberry (although it's a very pretty candy-floss colour) until a dish of zucchini Parmigiana arrives, and then the acidity and bubbles slice efficiently through oil and cheese, while the strawberry softens to a complementary soft orange. The Camarato is an excellent match for entrecôte cooked in Falerno Rosso, while that Falerno is surprisingly good with the accompanying salty apple salad. As in Priorat, we are indulging in our favourite game of mixing wines and dishes and seeing which work most happily together: our own form of *vite maritata*, perhaps. We taste two dessert wines, an Éleusi 2009, made in the *passito* style from Falanghina grapes, and the rare Deira 2005, an Aglianico *passito* made in a very similar manner but tasting entirely different – the former viscous and beguilingly honeyed, the latter rich, full of sweet red fruit, a little chocolatey.

Falanghina, Salvatore tells me, comes from the Latin for a finger, which then became *falanga*, a long (so, finger-shaped) stake used to support vines. I think of Gaetano telling me about Roman phalanxes, and about Juvenal's *Satires*, where he makes reference to Falernian vines trained up elm trees. Then I think of my grandpa's birth certificate, and decide to stay quiet.

In the West, whatever our religion, we grow up with an image of resurrection that involves a man tortured to death then revived, as he revived Lazarus, to much rejoicing. The treatment of the grape – crushed, then revived as wine – has been likened to the treatment of Jesus (who did, after all, say that he was the true vine) but in fact, everything to do with wine involves a cycle of death and revival. I would like to see that revival include the reintegration of wine into the life of our culture, including our conversation. I think of Salvatore spreading beeswax on his amphorae, to bring back to life the ancient methods without spoiling the wine for modern drinkers, and I recall Virgil's advice to would-be beekeepers in the *Georgics*: 'First find your bees a settled sure abode.' Even bees, according to that poet of exile and homecoming, must have a place of their own! In the fourth and final *Georgic*, Virgil recommends slaughtering cattle to propitiate the shades of Orpheus and Eurydice, and then ends with a startling vision of resurrection: the honey bees issuing forth from the dead animals' bellies, like a living assurance that life remains sweet and will triumph, and that death, for all its power, has no dominion.

Manuela Piancastelli with her beloved Pallagrello grapes

The author at Titus's Arch in Rome

9

ROME:
Power

Arms and the man I sing, who, forced by fate
And haughty Juno's unrelenting hate,
Expelled and exiled, left the Trojan shore.
Long labours, both by sea and land, he bore;
And in the doubtful war, before he won
The Latin realm and built the destined town,
His banished gods restored to rights divine,
And settled sure succession in his line;
From whence the race of Alban fathers come,
And the long glories of majestic Rome.

VIRGIL, *Aeneid* (Trans. John Dryden)

The past is never dead. It's not even past.

WILLIAM FAULKNER

In Rome, the past assumes all kinds of formidable shapes, like a powerful magician. It has the jagged curve of the Colosseum and the symmetrical arc of the Pantheon, the tumultuous magnificence of the Trevi Fountain (supplied by the only Roman aqueduct still working, the Aqua Virgo), and the looming, gigantesque mass of the Vittorio Emanuele monument. All this history juts from the ground, the man-made equivalent of the fossils poking from the cave walls in Champagne. Perhaps ambition roots better here than elsewhere, just as Pinot Noir does in Burgundy or Aglianico in Irpinia. This was the city to which the world came, involuntarily or otherwise; and to this city, where the greatest generals once rode in triumph with the saddest humans following in their wake, I have come like Aeneas to the Sibyl, to seek an end to my quest.

As usual, I didn't quite get here in a straight line. Ostia Antica, Rome's great port, now a slightly inland offshoot of Rome's favourite beach, was the city's only working harbour until it outgrew its capacities, and first Claudius then Trajan supplemented this port with others. (The latter is beside Fiumicino, Rome's main airport, and you can see its traces from the air, if you fly in daylight.) Soldiers and merchants, slaves and subjects, flowed in and out like the tide, and so did wine: there is proof, still, within Rome proper.

We drive up from Campania, along the soulless motorway; the hills look pretty from our concrete funnel, but there is no time to pull off and explore. We pass Sperlonga, where Emperor Tiberius's villa was found to contain a natural grotto with statues describing scenes from the *Odyssey* and the *Aeneid*, and Setia, now Sezze, once famous for Setinum, the favoured wine of Tiberius's predecessor and adopted father, Augustus. Still – the modern world doesn't welcome meandering, and so we power straight, at very modern speed, towards the Eternal City. C is driving and I peer fretfully out, trying and failing to picture what I'm missing. The unquiet soil of Italy is so filled with interesting remains it makes the Rhône look barren by comparison, and I find myself imagining a giant even larger and more irritable than the one beneath Sicily, trying to shake off innumerable itchy buried relics ...

Ostia brings together my three interests: the wine that was shipped and drunk; the Romans doing the shipping and the drinking; and the Jews, whose ancient community is still visible in the roofless remains of the oldest extant synagogue in Europe. From southern England to Rashi's Champagne, Carpentras and Barcelona and Alhambra in what was once 'Granada of the Jews', I have been looking for traces of a people who were both economically and religiously important in Western culture, and I have been depressed by how efficiently they seem, in the main, to have been effaced. All those vineyards; all those centuries of raised Kiddush cups, of Passover prayers that next year, the wandering shall be over and this supper shall be held in Jerusalem ... I don't want to go to Jerusalem, but I am ready to stop wandering.

The powerlessness aggravates me. Yes, the Romans won the Jewish Wars and yes, they became Christian, with good reason to efface their theological rivals, but it rankles that they are still, two millennia later, in charge of the narrative. Their might is incontrovertible in Ostia, where there is nothing modern to obstruct our view of the past. Or, rather, the several pasts, layered one on top of the other: no Ostian would ever have seen the city as we do, with earlier structures protruding and jostling their successors, all crowded into one walkable modern terrain.

First there's the necropolis or burial ground, which must always sit beyond the *pomerium*, the city's legal and religious boundary. Once, part of this was the approach to the river; now, thanks to the creeping, silting soil of thousands of years, the water is four kilometres away. Beyond the ghostly gate, the Porta Romana, begun by the great first-century BC orator (and Consul) Cicero and finished, five years later, by his sworn enemy Publius Clodius Pulcher, there is the Decumanus Maximus, the main street, still the broad thoroughfare, paved in basalt blocks, of a powerful conurbation. (How many of our roads will last so long?) Past the rows of shops, past the baths with their mosaics, including a gigantic mono-chrome Neptune in a four-horse chariot, accompa-nied by various sea creatures and Eros riding a dolphin; past the Caupona Fortunata, with its floor mosaic that translates as 'Fortunatus says: If you are thirsty drink from the cup' – and then, presumably, pay Fortunatus, the tavern-keeper. Further on, there are more drinking mosaics, aimed at third-century AD soldiers. I climb the outer stairs of the theatre, built in the first century BC, and, as I crest the ramparts, a spectacular view of ancient Rome unfurls before me. Steep curving steps, the semicircle of stage below, and beyond, like sentinels or bit players, the pillars of what was once an enormous portico surrounding the Piazzale delle Corporazioni, or Square of the Guilds. Here, the most successful trad-ers of the Empire are marked for eternity, or pretty close, in monochrome morsels, mosaic after mosaic of ships or goods from Narbonne or Sardinia or Tunisia. How glorious this city was, how it must have bustled and thrived, with the river, key to wealth, beside it! Now the watercourse of the Tiber has turned and only the *Fiume Morto*, the Dead River, remains, along with the relics of the city, mute, still and deserted save for sentimental tourists.

Where the Decumanus splits, I fork left; down to the sepulchre of Cartilius Poplicola and the Porta Marina baths, with their poignant broken arch framing trees, near the city's western limits, facing the retreated sea. The synagogue is practically the most inaccessible building in the entire complex, which may have been deliberate: those ancient Jews will not have wanted their holy house defiled by proximity to idol-worshippers. At first this, the oldest Jewish building I will ever enter, seems to me to have a sad, vestigial beauty: I can't visualise the *mikveh*, the ritual bath, mentioned on signs near the entrance, and the phantom, roofless rooms feel lonely and abandoned. But the *bimah*, the raised platform where the Scroll would have been kept, is still there, and standing guard before it, two columns. Carved into the underside of the top of each is a menorah, the seven-branched candlestick that once stood in the Temple, and still serves as an instantly recognisable symbol of Judaism. Among the floor mosaics I spot a Solomon's knot, with its message of eternity. And I recall that when this place was first built the Second Temple still stood, and the Jews were a warlike and powerful people who managed to cause the Romans more trouble than Gaul, Hispania or Britannia – even if they were a people also adept, from biblical times, at bringing trouble on themselves. Ostia Synagogue, like much of Ostia, is layers accrued over centuries, a large fourth-century AD building that contains echoes of a smaller, first-century AD one. When this building was begun, I think, the Jews would still have had land of their own, and deep-rooted vines of their own, and I take this comforting thought with me into Rome.

There are no vineyards in the city now, although there were: Vigna Clara and Vigna Stelluti are northern suburbs whose names bear witness to their former function, and there is still at least one monastery (Santa Croce of Jerusalem) growing farm produce within its walls – in a garden that contains Rome's only ancient amphitheatre excepting the Colosseum. Or there was: when I enquire, I find that Pope Benedict closed Santa Croce in 2011: 'too much of sex, drugs and rock 'n' roll,' says my informant, cheerfully. Some things change; others never do.

Where to start with the Eternal City? Just as Italy, with its hundreds of native grapes and seemingly countless wine regions, is dizzying for a wine-lover, so Rome is daunting for a student of antiquity. I contact Fabio, a former archaeologist who is now a professional guide, and ask him to take us to Santa Costanza, the mausoleum of Emperor Constantine's daughter. There used to be Bacchic scenes in mosaic all over the dome, but they were destroyed during a seventeenth-century restoration. Later, eighteenth-century visitors mistook the giant circular building for a temple to Bacchus, and used this as an excuse to drink to excess within its walls. But I am interested in that earlier moment, on the cusp, when the vines of Israel and of Bacchus curled their tendrils around Christianity. Constantine was the first Christian Emperor; his daughters Constantina (Costanza) and Helena were both baptised, probably in this very place. His mother Helena was, too, and travelled to Judea at an impressively advanced age to found churches, point out the 14 Stations of the Cross and discover the relics of that very cross; and if anyone was foolhardy enough to question her divinely inspired knowledge of such things, their fate has not come down to posterity.

Helena we have met before: it was her stolen relics that made Dom Pérignon's abbey at Hautvillers a thriving and wealthy place of pilgrimage, so we have her to thank, tangentially, for Champagne. She is also responsible for founding Santa Croce of Jerusalem, for pilgrims who could not get to the Holy Land, and perhaps installing a fragment of the True Cross within its walls. She would surely have disapproved of its ignominious end. Her granddaughter Constantina – a 'cruel and aspiring woman ... tormented with an insatiate thirst of human blood' according to Edward Gibbon, author of *The History of the Decline and Fall of the Roman Empire*, but nonetheless canonised in the thirteenth century – may have been buried in Santa Costanza with her sister, or alone, or somewhere else entirely. Nobody can agree, and her life, at the crossroads between Imperial paganism and Christianity, makes for still more confusion. Her second husband Gallus was a Christian, apparently, but his brother – married to her sister – was Emperor Julian the Apostate, who in his short reign tried to take the Empire back to the old beliefs, so it seems quite possible that what we have is a pagan crypt built for a Christian, covered with decoration later taken to be pagan by the descendants of Christians. (Julian had abortively attempted to rebuild the Temple in Jerusalem. Gallus put down a revolt by Palestine's Jews, and established a permanent garrison in Galilee. The fourth century was a confusing time.) Many of the surviving mosaics are wreathed in vines and show workers cheerfully pressing

and plucking grapes, and Constantina's impressive por-
phyry sarcophagus, once here but now on display in the
Vatican Museum, is covered in reliefs of putti harvesting the vines. Were the missing mosaics Old and New
Testament scenes suitable for a Christian burial place,
as some have maintained, or were they Bacchic rev-
els? Fabio, who is fiercely well read, maintains the former: 'The harvest, sowing and then reaping, recalls the
will and effort needed to be a good Christian or Jew,' he
points out. 'We can only flourish if we take care of the
land.' True, but pagan practices of sacrifice and worship
were simply the same thing in reverse; the gods must
be propitiated if we, and the land, are to flourish. And
wouldn't a new faith try to demonstrate its difference? It
is the fact that we can't tell that particularly interests me.

Fabio points out that from Judaism to Christianity was
a fairly short step: one deity, all the same origin myths,
and so on. Whereas for the Romans, worshipping multiple gods and easefully absorbing new arrivals into the
pantheon, the jump was a big one. There is definitely a
pagan burial place over there, he says, waving casually in
the direction of the Church of St Agnes; he too knows
that the Christians often built burial places atop older
ones, and he cites St Peter's Basilica, which had been a
pagan burial ground before it became a Christian one.
Nero blamed the Christians for the Great Fire of Rome
and crucified Peter (and Paul, among many others) in
AD 64; his burial there made St Peter's a coveted spot
for Christians to be interred, until Constantine piously
built the predecessor to what is now one of the world's
most important churches.

It is power I'm interested in, I say, as we walk back up the Via Nomentana, past Mussolini's house. The power of wine. So we get on the underground – surely the smallest buried train network of any great city, thanks to the packed ruins beneath the surface – and come out at Piramide. Down an unexceptional street, by a black iron railing, a man with a briefcase stands; he has agreed to unlock Monte Testaccio for me. The path circles up the hill and our shoes crunch on dead leaves and pottery. We are walking on between 50 and 200 million amphorae, the disposable carriers of the Roman Empire. This is power of a particular kind – not the power that built Rome's monuments but the power of the masses, the power that the emperors tried to propitiate by spending fortunes on *panem et circenses*: blood sports and free food. Those amphorae filled with oil or wine could not be reused – 'and anyway, they were so cheap, why would you send them back for refilling?' remarks Fabio, and they were dumped here, outside the *pomerium*, naturally, and then lime was shovelled over them to help with the smell. When it rained, that lime became like liquid concrete, and the result is a tall, artificially made hill that seems to announce the lasting importance of trade at the centre of an empire now in fragments. Somewhere beneath my feet will be infinitesimal traces of all the wines I have been seeking, from every place that I have stopped along this journey. Here is wealth and power piled high, still vying with Rome's seven hills after two millennia.

'We've learned so much from this hill,' says Fabio, picking up a curved slab of amphora, visibly grooved from an ancient potter's wheel. 'We know who sent what where ... so for example, in the fourth century, the Empire is starting to disintegrate, the barbarians are encroaching, politics is a mess, but we know traders were still shipping in wines from Morocco; the lines of communication were still open.'

When Rome still had a Carnival, farmers would roll pigs down this hill then chase them, in the crazed, lawless spirit of the Roman winter festival, Saturnalia; when that was stopped, this became, as so many pagan places did, a religious site, bordered with the Stations of the Cross. It's amazing, I think, that wine really did flow across the divisions of ancient society, solidifying like this limey hill into the monolith we moderns think we see. I look out across Rome, to the Colli Albani, the hills where Frascati wine is made; it's a grand expanse, if you ignore the 1920s slaughterhouse the size of a city in Testaccio, just below. Fascism never worked there, says Fabio: too working class. In the middle-class areas Mussolini slid in on velvet. He adds, startlingly, that Il Duce wanted to destroy the city's Roman remains, except the Colosseum. 'Ancient Rome is abstract, people don't want to deal with the reality, they just want the idea of its glory. That's why the Vatican was built on top of all those pagan remains – you lose the inconvenient truths and keep what pleases you.' That way, the legend survives, unmarked by reality – or almost.

Fabio is talking about wine. Frascati comes from *fraschetta*, a hut made of branches where workers could have lunch in the shade. 'You can still go into one and eat roast pork and drink the wine of Castelli Romani,' he says, although the castles (*castelli*) themselves were destroyed by bombing during the Second World War. The soil, he says, is tufa: 'these were volcanoes'. And still are; the Albani woke up 20 years ago – a particularly sinister kind of resurrection – and now another eruption threatens. Unquiet land, all the way up the Italian land-mass: did that help shake the Romans loose, to wander as far as they did? But they were, in a sense, untethered already, the descendants of immigrants, whether Trojan Aeneas or orphaned, savage Romulus.

Fabio moves on to religion – but he is still talking about wine. The tradition that says the soldiers gave Jesus vinegar to drink, on the way to his crucifixion, sounds odd ('Why were they carrying vinegar? Were they making Caesar salad?') until you think that sol-diers would have been given wine substandard enough to resemble vinegar – and that's assuming that Salvatore of Villa Matilde is wrong and all Roman wine was not in some sense curdled. So, in fact, their gift would have been an act of kindness – not of disparagement or mockery, as is sometimes supposed. (Is the legend of the Wandering Jew, cursed never to rest after mocking Jesus on the way to crucifixion, a similar misinterpretation? I had always assumed it was simple anti-Semitism, but perhaps prejudice is never simple.) That was the other sense in which wine was a lubricant, of course: a balm and incentive to soldiers, as well as a gift to quieten the plebs. There is a theory, says Fabio, that most of Rome's many fires were due to ordinary people burning the record of the bread and wine they'd been given by the state, in order to reap more. And, certainly, they had a lot of fires; at the Crypta Balbi museum, with its layers of uncovered brick and pipes, there is clear evidence of scorched clay and lead. The theatre was erected by Balbus in 13 BC, and destroyed by fire shortly after Vesuvius erupted. It is only after we are most of the way round the slightly lacklustre museum that I realise why the name Balbus sounds familiar. This Roman benefactor was the nephew of Cornelius Lucius Balbus, Caesar's friend and banker from Cadiz. Truly, says C, all roads lead to Rome …

The vinegar tradition is a long one. 'My grandfather made wine and every year it was different,' says Fabio: 'sometimes, it did resemble vinegar.' This, presumably, would also have been what my own ancestors made and drank, ushering in the Sabbath and celebrating life's most important moments. The wine has changed more than the rituals. Eventually, progress trickles down, and so does the capacity to defy life's uncertainties and create wine that tastes just as it should, year after year, as long as you accept that how it should taste will never be all that good. Strip out uncertainty, in other words, and you are not left with much. Still, there are advantages. Nobody, unless they are destitute, need drink vinegar now, although there must be some millionaires, paying vast sums for rare pre-phylloxera wines, who have done so.

The rich may occasionally choose to drink badly; it is the poor who have historically drunk copiously. Roman youths, who once associated power with alcoholic capacity and wicked switchblade knives, would play dangerous drinking games. If you didn't have a knife you were not a man, says Fabio, telling me hair-raising stories of a 'king' of drinkers forcing others to drink, or teasing them into violence. 'We Romans have always had a very ferocious sense of humour.' There are old ballads of sons, one good, one bad, the father long dead, where the bad son ends up killing his beloved mother in a drunken rage. 'The wine of Castelli was cheap and good and so these stories are true,' he says.

These days, there are few such tragedies; as for Fabio and his friends, they are abstemious to a point that sounds, to me, dangerously close to teetotalism. But I suppose that is progress.

I'm ready for some cheap, good wine myself by this point, but there's no way I'm going back into the Underground. Rome is one of the few places where the past is on the surface and modernity is beneath, and anyway wandering, in this city of all places, seems like the right thing to do. So I walk north, until I can descend into the Circus Maximus, that gigantic depression that once seated 150,000 citizens, held rapt by the charioteers' skilled, frantic attempts to guide sweat-streaked horses around the huge circuit. From the centre, risking death by imaginary steed, I stop to gaze up at the rather creepy dark hollows in the giant, ruined brick structure on the Palatine Hill beyond. Here, they say, was the cave in which the she-wolf suckled Romulus and Remus, and as I walk I think about natives and foreigners: Romulus, the fratricide, welcoming all comers, then carrying off the Sabine women against their will (having first rendered their menfolk too drunk to protect them) to provide those settlers with mates. Rome founded on rape and murder, or the alternative founding myth in which Aeneas, the foreigner, comes in and creates the city from nothing, and Romulus and Remus, parentless though they be, are his direct descendants. In the *Aeneid*, our hero finds the place that will become Rome occupied already – but by other wanderers, exiles from Arcadia in the Greek Peloponnese. Look back far enough and almost all of us, grapes and humans, come from somewhere else. At what point, I wonder yet again, does the intruder claim the right to call that foreign soil home?

I walk along one side of the enormous terrain that houses the Forum, the Colosseum and countless other remnants of almost a thousand years of Roman occupation: different cities from different eras, all layered like strata of soil, just as they were in Ostia. Then I wind up the Capitoline Hill and come out, to my pleased surprise, on the Piazza del Campidoglio, a beautiful square, tiled in careening oval patterns and enclosed by painted, pillared palazzi. The space was designed by Michelangelo, who turned its focus 180 degrees, from ancient Rome to Holy Rome, although a replica of a bronze statue of the Palatine wolf suckling her twin human cubs offers a crude reminder that the Empire is not mocked. The original, once considered ancient but probably medieval, is in the Museo Capitolini, also on the square. But it's too late, the museums are closed, and I am working my way towards the delightfully named Via dei Serpenti: like Eve, I am open to vinous suggestion. I pull up a seat at the bar of Al Vino al Vino, order a glass of decent and inexpensive Barbera, and pull out my book. 'I tried to read that but didn't get anywhere with it,' says a voice in my left ear; a young man, clearly a tourist, with the kind of generic American accent that places him as someone whose English is learned rather than native, but gives no more clues. I am surprised: the book is Josephus's *The Jewish Wars*, written 2,000 years ago by the controversial Joseph ben Matthias, or Flavius Josephus, another Jew with two names, and the eyewitness who described for posterity the giant vine that wreathed the doors of the Temple in Jerusalem. He had been a member of

314

the Jerusalem priesthood, who fought in the wars of which he writes; he was enslaved and then freed by Titus, before becoming a historian and apologist for the Romans. His is the only contemporary account we have, although his references to a Jewish rebel named Jesus, and his subsequent crucifixion, have been shown to be sly later additions. It is a ripping tale of murders and lies and destruction; still, it's not obvious reading matter for a twenty-something backpacker. But my new friend, it turns out, is an Israeli, looking to understand his country's distant past. We talk of the Jews' downfall, from privileged race, exempt from worship of the Emperor's cult, left to till their own fields, prune their own vines and worship their own god. There were a few untoward events – Pompey invading Jerusalem, enslaving the inhabitants and defiling the Temple's inner sanctum with his presence; the Emperor Caligula going one further, trying to set up a statue of himself in that same Holy of Holies – but on the whole, cordial relations were maintained until the deterioration, invasion and destruction of the 60s and 70s. How and why did this happen? Was it the lack of calculation of the Judeans, or the gaping maw of Rome that could not resist swallowing everything? C, the academic, argues convincingly against such reductive conclusions, but we have wine and common ground, and it is an enjoyable discussion unsullied, in large part, by prosaic considerations.

After the war, the Jews were subject to a special tax, the *fiscus iudaicus*, which was paid to the Temple of Jupiter in Rome; given that this was the money they had previously tithed to the Temple the worshippers of Jupiter had destroyed, this must have constituted insult to injury. The coins struck by Emperor Vespasian to celebrate his son Titus's victory baldly announced *Judea Capta*; they were still being minted 15 years later, under Vespasian's other son, the Emperor Domitian, whose grape-squeezing rulings would lead to his murder and the end of his imperial dynasty. Just and kindly wine, offering balm for insults, medicine for injuries – and occasionally, tangentially, revenge for desecration.

The Colosseum is a confusing place. On the one hand, it is magnificent: gargantuan, curved and tiered, undiminished by the depredations of time, trembling earth and thieves on its symmetry, the ticket touts in tacky costumes, and the cavities, resembling large bullet holes, pocking its walls. These last were made not by guns, but by enterprising commoners digging in for the bronze clamps they knew would be holding the stones together – because building methods had not changed in the intervening centuries. When I walk out of the bar on to the Via dei Serpenti, look down the street and see that extraordinary shape rising at the end, it thrills me. This is one of the finest symbols of Roman power – that same power, fuelled in part by wine, that is still spreading vineyards across the world, into Patagonia or the far south of Western Australia, and still defining, for many, the borders of civilisation.

On the other hand, this is also the original theatre of cruelty: a stage for gladiatorial combat, for murders and martyrdoms. The Flavian Amphitheatre took its modern name from a 100ft-statue of himself that Nero had erected nearby. (It was later altered, tactfully, to depict Apollo.) The Colosseum has survived partly through luck and partly because, as the place where so many early Christians died for their beliefs, it became holy ground for a religion that began, after all, with a martyr's agonies.

And then there is its genesis. The Colosseum was financed by booty from the Jewish Wars, including the sale of slaves, and was almost certainly built by those slaves. As much as the remaining fragments of the Temple in Jerusalem, now known as the Wailing Wall, this structure is a monument to disaster for the Jews. And yet I can't hate the Romans. They did not destroy the Jews. (And they were capable of it: Trajan's Column, an extraordinary stone frieze that still rears improbably on the Via dei Fori Imperiali, celebrates two wars against the Dacians that pretty much wiped those early Romanians from the face of the earth.) If Rome's victory became the starting point for 2,000 years of wandering, it is worth recalling that the Jewish Wars would not have happened without internecine fighting and generally impolitic behaviour by the Jews themselves; I'd rather call us fools than victims. And the Romans, after all, are to thank for what I drink.

I walk up the Via Sacra, the Sacred Way, to the Forum complex. Between the Forum, once Rome's marketplace and fulcrum, and the Colosseum, stands a different kind of monument. Here, in the so-called Eternal City, between the place of bread and the place of circuses, I find a piece of my past more solid than my dining table, and a light that has shone for 2,000 years. This is Titus's Arch, and on its inner curve are detailed carvings in age-greyed white stone of the great victory over the Judean Jews. The menorah which those stone figures carry is the only known representation of one of the treasures of the Jerusalem Temple, the destruction of which is part of this arch's boast. It is both sad and glorious – testament to the Jews' importance, as well as the Romans' power. And, like my grandpa's birth certificate, like wine, like memory, it both preserves and transforms the past.

On Titus's Arch, Roman triumph reigns eternal. Senate and people parade forever; above them, Titus himself is glorious, victorious – even deified, a god celebrating the downfall of monotheism. The vanquished are bound, humble, and above them, unmissable, the great menorah is held aloft, as if in mockery of the candlestick's original representation of Judaism as 'the light among the nations'.

I stand near the arch for a long time, trying to decipher more details. We believe the menorah to have been gold, but, as with Reims Cathedral, we have no idea of the other colours used, and so Rome for us has faded to shadowed white. It has faded in other ways, too. We do not follow their beliefs or, with very few exceptions, read their language. We don't know how that language was pronounced any more than we can truly taste the wine they drank. For all the senses except sight and touch, they are lost to us, and even those are softened and drab, corners worn away, limbs lost, colours vanished.

Other tourists ebb and flow around me. With very few exceptions, they recognise the menorah for a Jewish symbol. The rest of the frieze needs explaining – but not that. They may not have any idea what it is for, but so what? It is carried aloft, an emblem of vanquished power, but it signifies something else, too: endurance. I have two menorahs at home, one very old, silver, damaged – a family heirloom. As with so much else, I have no idea where it came from. The other was a present from C. His children are not Jewish, but I am teaching them to light those candles: a mystical gift, from my threadbare past to these living symbols of continuity. When they are older, we will try to pass on our love of wine, too. What they accept, which conversations they try to continue, will be up to them.

The arch, solidly grounded, reaches upwards, a proud statement of power and exceptionalism. It is at once humanity's most admirable and most detestable quality, that longing to exceed the reach of those before. It has built palaces and destroyed worlds.

We all look back as well as forward, reach down as well as up. You don't have to be Aeneas to seek to recover the past – every person who has paid an entry fee into this enclosure is doing it. And eventually, of course, downwards is where we are all headed. Perhaps it is that tension, between upward yearning and remorseless gravity, that pulls us towards wine. The vine, after all, has this balance just right. Rooted and reaching; transmuting sunlight, offering the nectar for worship and for friendship, but transforming soil, too, and never losing the memory of where it has come from, even when we who drink it have forgotten …

I look at C, busily photographing, imprinting and transforming the present, trying to create lasting beauty out of a stone monument that was itself built purely to defy future oblivion. C lowers his camera and smiles at me. There is a third direction: we must reach outwards, too, towards one another. The living take precedence.

On my last day, en route to the station, I take a little detour. Actually, I take two. The first is into a museum, Palazzo Massimo Terme, because I am passing: there will be Bacchic statues, I think, and so there are. A young copper Dionysus, long, slender thyrsus in hand, vine shoots adorning his diadem, and an older, bearded equivalent, in glowing marble, more prudently wreathed in a toga, are both Roman copies of more ancient Greek statues; a bronze railing from a Roman ship recovered under Mussolini has vertical bars topped with carved Bacchic heads, an astonishing extravagance. There's a fourth-century sarcophagus where the friezes are New Testament scenes hung with grapes; there are mosaics where Bacchus looks out, waiting to bring joy or madness. Everywhere, this testimony to the central importance of wine. How much poorer our lives are for having marginalised it! I think, as I climb to the last floor.

There I find something extraordinary: colour. In a room built to the exact proportions of the original, painted between 30 and 20 BC, the frescoes transported from Livia's underground room render me breathless. She was the wife of Augustus; this, most likely, was a room where she sheltered from the summer heat, with no windows but endless exhilarating testimony to the beneficial power of that pitiless sun. Against a background of misty blue, a garden riots, the grass a pelt of green where birds wander, the trees a festival of fertility, with spring and summer and autumn all represented at once. Laurels, myrtles, oleander and cypress; fruit trees (including vines, naturally) and flower bushes all call out Time, challenging its tyranny. (Perhaps the challenge was to Vertumnus: when not seducing Pomona with stories of vines, he was god of seasons and of change.) The room was buried and rediscovered in 1863, and its survival suggests that the painter's vainglorious taunt, like Titus's, has proved successful. Here are images that Livia and Augustus looked on. The resemblance is fragile: the colours are surely faded, the carefully muted electric light is nothing the Romans would have known, and we look on these still-vibrant frescoes knowing that we cannot get into the heads of those who saw them fresh-painted. But we are not here to replicate 2,000-year-old experience. I have been trying, throughout this journey, to use my senses to form a connection to the vanished past. And in this small room, unadvertised and almost deserted, soothing as a cold beverage on a blazing day, I look and look, and feel that, if I have not succeeded, here I can at least come close. I remember the guide at Reims Cathedral, angry about the historically inaccurate placement of colour, and I think again how wrong she was. It would be nice to know how things truly were, of course. But what we can do is to reach out, across the unbridgeable gulf. Just as Christians put stained-glass windows in churches – windows that altered and brightened and faded with the changing light – in acknowledgement of God the ultimate painter, we must fill the inevitable blanks in our lives with imagination. If we can't, we are left with a few old stones and a drink that was born yesterday.

Our very last detour is into Trimani, a bar with an adjoining wine shop round the corner from the station, for the final glass of the journey. Rome's oldest living wine bar (1821, apparently) lacks ambience – tile floors, square tables, bright lights that are particularly cruel after the gentle loveliness of Livia's walls – but a curl of fried mackerel with red cabbage is tasty compensation, and we drink smoky, slightly bitter Ester Greco di Tufo 2010, which slices nicely through the oily fish. Greco is the white grape which, when made near Tufo in Irpinia, becomes mineral and substantial in a way other Grecos aren't; the village may well be named for tufa, the volcanic rock the Romans so loved to build with. And Esterina Centrella, who makes this wine, is an Irpinian (sixth of seven siblings) who left for Belgium but then came back again. Esther was a biblical queen who saved the Jewish people from Haman, a proud and cruel minister who was eventually hanged on the gallows he had erected for his Jewish victims. Her victory is celebrated at Purim – a festival, like so many, that enjoins us to look back at the horrors of the past, then celebrate having escaped them. The past must neither crush us nor be crushed by us; it must have its rightful place. This, perhaps, is the thinking behind name changes like my grandpa's. It is certainly the reasoning behind the Purim injunction, so unusual for Judaism, to drink too much. The command is to imbibe until you no longer know the difference between 'Cursed be Haman' and 'Blessed be Mordecai' – Esther's cousin, and the hero of the story.

It is rather a bloodthirsty tale, it must be said – but let us consign that aspect to oblivion, and concentrate on survival: outwitting hatred, and drinking and rejoicing when you have done so. And in this spirit, we raise glasses of the golden yellow wine, glowing like a promise, and clink, and drink, and go home.

I am one of the lucky ones, free to travel where I will, with a table and a hearth awaiting my return. Nostalgia may define the longing for the irrecoverable, but there is another kind of nostalgia, that has less to do with pain than with pleasure, which is simply the memory of a place where one was truly welcome. The past isn't all agony and upheaval, any more than the future is simply oblivion. It is to this, the eternal hope and promise of the present, that I bow my head every time I dip my nose into a glass. Like Manuela, we must find our place, and rest there, but we can't grow too attached. Movement is not a curse but the life force; only the dead can avoid it – and perhaps even they cannot. 'In no fixed place the happy souls reside,' wrote Virgil: this is what leaves them free to meet us again, one way or another. They are fleeting, these encounters: a glimpse, a taste, a scent inhaled. A brief memory, individual or shared. But that is surely as it should be. Through sensual enjoyment and the remembrance of happiness we make the permanent transitory. That is the gift of the living to their dead. We hold them close, even as we turn to one another.

We must live our lives, and honour with wine and with every sense at our disposal the roots and stems from which we sprang, taking our encounters, with the living and the dead, as we find them. Nothing – not grapes nor shades nor stories – is entirely irrecoverable; everything has the potential to be twice-born. In my mind, my father raises a glass, shaped like an elongated tulip, half filled with ruby-coloured wine: perhaps a

Château Hautes Graves Beaulieu Pomerol 2001, one of the few wines of his that remain to me, or perhaps it is his 1996 Tim Adams Cabernet Sauvignon, from South Australia's Clare Valley, which C and I drank last year. His hair is still black, save the wings of silver at his temples. He smiles, and laughter lines concertina the outer edges of his twinkling blue eyes. He has already nosed and swirled and nosed again; now his glass chimes gently against mine. I'd love our fingers to brush but I know that is not possible, ever again. Still, the wine's perfume is reaching up to caress my nostrils and my tastebuds are prickling in anticipation. C is beside me, a breathing presence, impatient. And so I end back where I started, with a glass raised in the only possible toast to all that we lose and find: to life. *L'chaim!*

Farewell: the ancient port city of Ostia, outside Rome

Acknowledgements

No book gets written without the patient assistance of a lot of busy people with much better things to do than aid a monomaniac in her quest. I'd like to single out Sebastian Payne MW for loaning me a wonderful, out-of-print reference book and Carla Capalbo for putting me in touch with Manuela Piancastelli. The Authors' Foundation awarded me a grant which helped greatly with travel costs; others who facilitated the wanderings of this grateful vine include Françoise Peretti of the Champagne Bureau, Paco Gutiérrez of the Spanish Tourist Office, Angeline Bayly from Sherry Wines UK, Julia Trustram Eve of English Wine Producers, Sinead Hanna of Visit Kent, Alexandra Gerolami for Inter-Rhône, Valerie Lewis of Enotria & Coe and of course, the wonderful Gaetano Petrillo of the Wine Bus.

I haven't got space to thank all the winemakers, including several who did not make it into the final text, who shared their enthusiasm, their knowledge and their wines with me, but I am very grateful. My attempts to figure out what we do and don't know about Roman grapes were aided immeasurably by Jeremy Paterson on the geography and José Vouillamoz on the science, while Jane Anson shared her erudite and very readable articles. If, despite their kind assistance, there are factual mistakes, the fault is entirely mine. Thanks to Laura Barber for astute advice, Wendel Caplan for practical help and Marina O'Loughlin and her husband for lending us their lovely Sicilian house; if I could have written the whole book in that idyllic environment it would be a lot better than it is. Thanks to Helen Lewis at the *New Statesman* for offering me a column that has enabled me to explore different ways to write about wine, and to the lovely people at the Wine Society, whose encouragement has meant all the more to me from an institution my father held in such high regard. A particularly heartfelt thank you to Jamie Birkett, my editor at Bloomsbury, who came up with a perfectly sensible idea for a wine travel book and remained staunchly good-natured and supportive as I ran amuck with it; without his astute comments, constructive criticism and endless flexibility, and the assistance of the rest of the team at Bloomsbury, there would be no book at all. Lastly, love and gratitude to my stepchildren, Reuben, Ishbel, Beatrix and Nora Brierley-Moyes, who have been dragged to more vineyards and ruins than any child should have to put up with and whose responses have often broadened my mind more than the experience can have enriched theirs. As for their father – if it isn't clear in these pages how much he means to me, then I have failed in my allotted task. For the photographs he has taken, the constructive comments he has made and the stupid errors he has spotted, to say nothing of the cooking and the talking, the wines and the laughter, I thank Craig Moyes. To him, and to you, patient reader, I raise my glass.

Permissions

The following extracts are reproduced by kind permission of the copyright holders.

p. 13 Lines from Tacitus's *Agricola and Germany,* trans. Anthony Birley (Oxford: Oxford University Press, 1999). By permission of Oxford University Press.

pp. 98–9 Extract from Ovid's *Metamorphoses*, Book XIV: 'Vertumnus woos Pomona', trans. A. S. Kline, Copyright © 2000.

p. 187 Poem by Abd al-Rahman, trans. D. Fairchild Ruggles in *Gardens, Landscape and Vision in the Palaces of Islamic Spain* (University Park, PA: Pennsylvania State University Press, 2000), p. 42.

p. 232 Lines from *The Odyssey of Homer, a New Verse Translation*, trans. Allen Mandelbaum (New York: Bantam Classics, 1990).

p. 285 Lines from Virgil's *Aeneid,* Book VI, trans. Seamus Heaney (London: Faber & Faber, 2016). By permission of Faber & Faber.

Bibliography and Further Information

A full bibliography and list of featured winemakers and their importers are available at:

www.thewanderingvine.co.uk.

A Note on the Author

Nina Caplan is an arts, wine and travel journalist. She is the wine columnist of the *New Statesman* and also writes for *The Times, Decanter, Condé Nast Traveller* and others. She has been awarded the Louis Roederer International Food and Wine Writer of the Year, Louis Roederer International Columnist of the Year and Fortnum & Mason Drink Writer of the Year. *The Wandering Vine*, her first book, won the Louis Roederer International Wine Book of the Year award in 2018.

In the past, Nina has been employed by publications including the *Guardian* and *Time Out*, but these days she wanders too much to remain deskbound. She lives in London and Burgundy.

@ninacaplan

A Note on the Type

The text of this book is set in Bembo, which was first used in 1495 by the Venetian printer Aldus Manutius for Cardinal Bembo's *De Aetna*. The original types were cut for Manutius by Francesco Griffo. Bembo was one of the types used by Claude Garamond (1480–1561) as a model for his Romain de l'Université, and so it was a forerunner of what became the standard European type for the following two centuries. Its modern form follows the original types and was designed for Monotype in 1929.